SELLING OUT OR BUYING IN?

Debating Consumerism in Vancouver and Victoria, 1945–1985

In the late 1950s, residents of Vancouver and Victoria negotiated a shopping landscape that would be inconceivable to today's consumers: most stores were closed for at least half the day on Wednesdays, prevented from opening during the evenings, and banned from operating on Sundays. Since that time, however, British Columbians, and Canadians more generally, have made significant strides in gaining greater flexibility in shopping regulations.

Selling Out or Buying In? is the first work to detail the process by which consumers' access to goods and services was liberalized and deregulated in British Columbia in the latter half of the twentieth century. Dawson's in-depth exploration of the debates between politicians and everyday citizens regarding the pros and cons of expanding shopping opportunities challenges the sense of inevitability surrounding Canada's emergence as a consumer society. The expansion of store hours was a contingent and highly contested development that pitted employees, owners, and regulators against one another. Dawson's nuanced analysis of archival and newspaper sources reveals the strains that modern capitalism imposed on the established rhythms of daily life for British Columbians during the post–Second World War period.

MICHAEL DAWSON is professor of History and Associate Vice-President (Research) at St Thomas University.

Selling Out or Buying In?

Debating Consumerism in Vancouver and Victoria, 1945–1985

MICHAEL DAWSON

UNIVERSITY OF TORONTO PRESS
Toronto Buffalo London

© University of Toronto Press 2018
Toronto Buffalo London
utorontopress.com
Printed in Canada

ISBN 978-1-4875-0220-1 (cloth)   ISBN 978-1-4875-2186-8 (paper)

♾ Printed on acid-free, 100% post-consumer recycled paper with
vegetable-based inks.

Library and Archives Canada Cataloguing in Publication

Dawson, Michael, 1971–, author
Selling out or buying in? : debating consumerism in Vancouver
and Victoria, 1945–1985 / Michael Dawson.

Includes bibliographical references and index.
ISBN 978-1-4875-0220-1 (cloth)   ISBN 978-1-4875-2186-8 (paper)

1. Consumption (Economics) – British Columbia – Vancouver –
History – 20th century. 2. Consumption (Economics) – British
Columbia – Victoria – History – 20th century. 3. Consumer
behavior – British Columbia – Vancouver – History – 20th century.
4. Consumer behavior – British Columbia – Victoria – History – 20th century.
I. Title.

HC79.C6D39 2018   339.4'70971128   C2017-907098-3

This book has been published with the help of a grant from the Federation
for the Humanities and Social Sciences, through the Awards to Scholarly
Publication Program, using funds provided by the Social Sciences and
Humanities Research Council of Canada.

University of Toronto Press acknowledges the financial assistance to its
publishing program of the Canada Council for the Arts and the Ontario
Arts Council, an agency of the Government of Ontario.

Canada Council
for the Arts
Conseil des Arts
du Canada

ONTARIO ARTS COUNCIL
CONSEIL DES ARTS DE L'ONTARIO
an Ontario government agency
un organisme du gouvernement de l'Ontario

Funded by the
Government
of Canada
Financé par le
gouvernement
du Canada

Canadä

Contents

Illustrations

Preface

I once spent the better part of a day trying to purchase an apple in Charlottetown, Prince Edward Island. It was a bitterly cold Sunday in March 2002. Having travelled across the country the night before, I was convinced that maintaining a healthy diet would help me adjust to the four-hour time change. So I set off in search of fruit. To my chagrin almost every store I encountered was closed up tight. And the leads the locals offered me were not inspiring. One well-meaning fellow encouraged me to visit the local gas station, which, he was pretty sure, sold fruit. After considerable hesitation I took his advice, but to no avail. My luck improved, somewhat, an hour or so later when I came across a merchant with a not entirely unappealing, though minimal, selection of shrink-wrapped apples and oranges. I cursed Sunday shopping laws something fierce that day. And I've vented my frustration at government store-hour regulations that have restricted my access to goods and services on many occasions since. The city of Fredericton, New Brunswick, where I live, maintained a strict ban on Sunday morning shopping until 2013.

However, I have also been on the other side of the counter, so to speak. I helped pay my way through my undergraduate studies by working as a bank teller during the summers. I invariably ended up with a Tuesday to Saturday schedule which meant that, come the weekend, I was entirely out of sync with my friends. Their workweeks finished at 5 p.m. on Fridays, and when we gathered together – as we almost always did on Friday nights – at one of their houses, or plotted – much less often – to travel to downtown Vancouver for a concert or some other form of entertainment, I did so with the knowledge that I would have to wake up early the next morning to go to work. The problem was not that I arrived at work hung over (that only happened once or twice, and you'd be surprised how many of my co-workers were similarly cursing the echo in the vault on those days). No, my issue with this work pattern was that because I was a responsible employee, and knew that I'd have to get up early on Saturday morning, I limited my Friday night leisure time. Why couldn't banks just stick to a Monday to Friday schedule like the other businesses that employed my friends, I wondered.

As a consumer of retail goods and services I have oftentimes been frustrated with regulations that hinder my access to what I (think I) need, when I (think I) need it. Yet I also possess enough empathy and self-awareness to know there are bigger issues at play here – other people's quality of life, for instance. I am thus very much conflicted on the specific issue of regulating consumer access to goods and services. And I have found myself increasingly interested in examining the relationship between consumption, work and, leisure. My very fortunate position as a fully employed historian in academe has allowed me to pursue this interest.

This project began under the auspices of a SSHRC postdoctoral fellowship at the University of British Columbia. Bob McDonald generously agreed to supervise the fellowship and some ten years later helped me bring the project to a close by providing valuable feedback on (what was supposed to be) the penultimate draft of the manuscript. Additional funding from St Thomas University's Senate Research Committee and in the form of a Wallace and Margaret McCain Course Release Award also played a crucial role in helping me complete this project. Kat Davidson's work as a research assistant was exemplary – thank you so much for saving me from further time in front of the microfilm screens!

Thanks also to UBC Press and *Urban History Review* for allowing me to reprint some previously published material. Parts of chapter 6 appeared in a similar form in "Leisure, Consumption, and the Public Sphere: Postwar Debates over Shopping Regulations in Vancouver and Victoria during the Cold War." They are reprinted with the permission of the publisher from *Creating Postwar Canada*, edited by Magda Fahrni and Robert Rutherdale © University of British Columbia Press, 2007. All rights reserved by the Publisher. Parts of chapter 2 appeared in a somewhat different form in "Victoria Debates Its Postindustrial Reality: Tourism, Deindustrialization, and Store-Hour Regulations, 1900–1958," *Urban History Review* 35(2) (Spring 2007): 14–24, and are reprinted here with the permission of that journal.

My long-time colleagues in the History Department at STU are a fabulous bunch of people: intelligent, generous, ambitious, and just mischievous enough to make sure that ours is often an academic workplace to be envied. My new colleagues in STU's Office of Research Services possess a similar set of characteristics – who knew university administration could be such fun?

Since moving to Fredericton, "from away," in 2004 my family has developed close friendships with a fantastic group of people who include Michael Boudreau and Bonnie Huskins, Kimi and Frank Sauvé, Lisa Todd and Jacob Sweezey, Fran Lipsett, Darrow and Clare MacIntyre, and Elisabeth Hans and Mattijs Verhorst. Thank you for inviting us into your homes (and lives) and for filling our dining room and backyard deck with howls of laughter and words of encouragement (and almost always knowing when to employ the latter rather than the former). And, of course, many thanks to my parents and my in-laws for their never-ending support. They've now (mostly) mastered the art of knowing when to ask how "the book" is coming along and when to quickly move the conversation on to something else.

Len Husband enthusiastically championed this project from the moment I pitched it to University of Toronto Press. He has been an absolute pleasure to work with – which is no surprise, of course, because that's what everybody has been telling me for years now! My thanks as well to Frances Mundy and the rest of the UTP staff for their assistance throughout the production process. The external assessors offered forthright and valuable suggestions and I've done my best to incorporate as many of their insights as possible. Thank you for your very constructive feedback. Catherine Gidney, as always, pushed me to rethink and refine my arguments. Thank you for again showing me that I only need one introduction – not three!

This book explores the tension between work and leisure – a tension that very clearly shapes my own life and the lives of many other academics. I began this project in 2003. Its origins thus predate the birth of my eldest daughter, Alexandra, who has just celebrated her thirteenth birthday. Her sister, Emma, was born in 2011. I've thus spent many hours sitting in front of a computer screen working on this project instead of doing the kinds of things that we enjoy together: playing board games, preparing "fancy" dinner parties, reading "Chirp" magazines, or, yes, going shopping. I'm not sure what they thought I was up to when I "disappeared" downstairs to my office for long periods of time. At some point, when they're older, I'll probably try to explain why I was so committed to working on this book – and on the many other writing projects that have come to occupy my time. For now, I hope it's enough to simply tell them that I've poured my heart and soul into this book for over a decade and that because of this I'm dedicating it to them. I'm guessing that it will probably see less use than many of the other gifts that they've received over the years. But that's okay. I'm keen to pull some of that stuff off of the shelf too so that we can spend more time together.

SELLING OUT OR BUYING IN?

Debating Consumerism in Vancouver
and Victoria, 1945–1985

Santa's Lament

In December 1949, with Christmas Eve just days away, the residents of British Columbia's two largest cities faced the daunting prospect of relaying some unsettling news to their children. "Santa Claus worked under tension," the *Victoria Daily Colonist* reported on 22 December. Indeed, the newspaper explained, "he was open to arrest" as police officers stormed a Hudson's Bay department store in Vancouver the previous afternoon. "Santa, the old gent who symbolizes benevolence and goodwill," the newspaper revealed, "was in the toyland of one of the 100 stores that opened today in defiance of a Wednesday-closing by-law." Bewildered children could find faint hope in the reporter's observation that while "Santa could be prosecuted under the Shops' Act ... police didn't list his name in the record of employees."[1]

The *Colonist*'s readers may well have been taken aback by the threat facing Saint Nicholas, but news that there was a conflict over local store hours could hardly have come as a surprise. Since the turn of the twentieth century, merchants in Vancouver and Victoria had been expressing their concern that inflexible and poorly constructed laws were forcing them to keep their stores closed on what would otherwise have been some of the busiest shopping days of the year. These laws were part of a regulatory regime – designed to ensure that store clerks and merchants secured acceptable amounts of leisure time – that included mid-week closing, prohibitions on evening sales, and the well-known ban on Sunday shopping.

By 1949 the Wednesday-closing situation, in particular, had reached a boiling point. A local bylaw required Vancouver merchants to close their stores on Wednesday mornings, and provincial legislation forced them to remain closed on Wednesday afternoons. This situation was in effect throughout the year but was particularly frustrating for many store owners during the busy Christmas shopping season.[2] Hence, as Wednesday, 21 December, approached, word spread that most Vancouver stores would follow the lead of the Bay and break the law. The Bay insisted that it was planning to open for just the one Wednesday and that it had no intention of flouting the bylaw once the Christmas rush was over. The penalty for breaking the provincial law was $10 for a first offence, while the maximum fine for breaking the city bylaw was $100. Several observers noted that these fines did little to dissuade illegal store openings.[3]

Tellingly, the Bay and its followers faced resistance from other chain department stores. One Eaton's executive explained that without question stores must obey the law and remain closed; another reiterated this point: "It's illegal ...We don't plan anything controversial." An official from Woodward's, a local chain department store, indicated that it would not be defying the law. The Army and Navy store was more ambivalent, stating that it would not open if the other large stores remained closed as well.[4] It was, in fact, the city's smaller stores that provided the critical mass to turn the Bay's actions into a growing movement for change.[5]

Police court officials publicly reminded merchants that they risked fines for disobeying the law; meanwhile, Mayor Charles Thompson issued an unequivocal statement regarding the city's intention to prosecute offenders: "When the law is broken, the duty of the police is to prosecute."[6] With hundreds of stores now planning to open on Wednesday the 21st, Chief Constable Walter Mulligan publicly stated that the only option for the police was to serve these establishments with summonses.[7] A showdown was on the horizon.

Unmoved by such warnings, the city's smaller stores convinced the Retail Merchants Association (RMA) to support this "Wednesday opening" campaign. Although reluctant to become involved, the RMA now offered to temporarily pay the court fines for members who opened on 21 December. It also arranged for merchants to hand over summonses to its counsel. With hope for a compromise solution fading, two trade unions, the Retail Clerks' Union, Local 1518, and the Amalgamated Meat Cutters, Local 212, both AFL-TLC affiliates, planned to picket the Bay on the Wednesday in question. Neither union had members working in the store, but they vowed that their representatives would carry placards telling customers that the store was breaking the law.[8] As the day of reckoning approached, Assistant City Prosecutor Stewart

McMorran turned his attention to employees, warning them that they too could be prosecuted and fined up to $100.[9]

As events unfolded on Wednesday the 21st, it became clear that this showdown would produce a fair number of sparks, but not much fire. Media reports initially suggested that roughly one hundred retail stores had defied the Wednesday bylaw – though later estimates put that number closer to two hundred. Yet despite Police Chief Mulligan's warning of impending prosecutions, authorities took no immediate action against the stores and no action at all against employees.[10] Thousands of shoppers descended on the Bay and other city stores. In downtown Vancouver, plainclothes police officers recorded the names of the stores, clerks, and customers involved; uniformed officers did the same in suburban areas.

Downtown stores reported steady business while sales remained slow in the suburbs. Hundreds of customers had been waiting for the doors to open at the Bay and were admitted a few minutes before 9 a.m. Once inside they stood in the aisles listening to the store choir singing carols. When they turned their attention to shopping, they encountered special deals on turkeys and hosiery. The city's Granville Street merchants reported that their business was down 10 to 15 per cent in the morning but picked up around noon. One tailor described business as "terrible"; a shoe store proprietor and a jeweller pronounced sales "excellent"; and a women's clothing store was enjoying "good" but not unusual patronage.[11] The *Vancouver Sun* informed its readers that most downtown retailers had reported a rush of business on Wednesday afternoon after a slow start. The Bay gleefully reported that "the store was filled all day."[12] Sales results, then, were mixed.

Also decidedly "mixed" and muted were the positions taken by the principals involved. In the end no union protesters were on hand for the Bay's opening. George Johnston, spokesperson for the Retail Clerks' Union, revealed that his members would not be "picketing" but emphasized that public opinion was "most resentful" of the Bay's actions.[13] Moreover, despite its support for these maverick Christmas openings, the RMA in fact publicly expressed its desire to strengthen the existing law so that police could immediately padlock stores that opened on Wednesdays.[14] While the RMA wished to maximize opportunities for Christmas sales, it championed a more rigorous approach to store-hour regulation enforcement more generally.[15]

And what of the city officials who had spoken so forcefully about their determination to hold lawbreakers accountable? A week after the showdown, Mayor Thompson announced that the city would delay the issue of business licences to stores that had opened illegally. This was a weak punishment as even Thompson acknowledged that this did not mean that stores without licences would be forced to close in the new year. The city frequently gave operators until 1 March to renew their licences.[16] At best, Thompson could maintain that the stores that had opened illegally would not get licences until they promised to obey the law in the future.[17] In the end, the *Vancouver Sun* reported, two hundred Vancouver stores were fined $10 each for opening illegally on Wednesday, 21 December.[18]

In March 1950, with the explicit aim of avoiding similar disputes in the future, the provincial government passed a bill suspending the Shops Regulations and Weekly Holiday Act for the seven days prior to Christmas.[19] Throughout the 1950s and early 1960s the city councils in Vancouver and Victoria joined with provincial governments in liberalizing the rules and regulations surrounding shopping hours in the lead-up to 25 December. If the fines and licence suspensions suggested that the merchants had *technically* lost this specific battle, by the mid-1960s there could be little doubt that those arguing for decreased store-hour regulations, and more expansive shopping opportunities, had won the war.

The December 1949 showdown in Vancouver between local merchants and City Hall is hardly the stuff of Heritage Minutes, historical monuments, or documentary films. No streetcars were overturned; no protesters were jailed; no great political speeches were delivered; and it is not even clear that those determined to snap up Christmas goodies at the Bay that Wednesday morning were much distracted from their efforts by the intense debate raging in the newspapers. While shoppers at the Bay expressed their enthusiasm regarding the maverick Wednesday opening, a reportedly glum Santa dutifully carrying out his public relations duties at the Bay lamented his fate: "Frankly, there were a lot of things I had to do today."[20]

Santa's errands, like those of many store employees and merchants throughout the city, had been postponed in light of this temporary and illegal expansion of shopping hours. His leisure time, and theirs, was sacrificed in order to ensure that others could secure timely access to consumer goods and services. The tensions inherent in this development structured long-running local debates from the 1940s to the

1980s that focused on mid-week store closures, evening shopping, the move to "wide open" store hours, and, eventually, Sunday shopping. These debates often dealt with very specific local questions, but they addressed broader North American trends that would play a central role in the development of modern consumerism, such as an increasingly mobile citizenry and growing numbers of women in the paid workforce. They highlighted and incorporated social and cultural tensions that reflected concerns with securing civic prosperity, the influence of external capital on local communities, the moral benefits and costs of consumer convenience, the desirability and feasibility of state-sponsored economic regulations, political and philosophical models of governance, and the place of religion in public life. In short, the disputes over what time the corner store ought to open or whether drugstores ought to be permitted to sell "hardware" were part of a broader conversation and debate about how people increasingly enmeshed in a consumer society ought to prioritize and shape the relationship between work, economic development, leisure, and consumption. "Profit," "income," "jobs," and "convenience" were all part of this conversation. But so was "time" – and a desire to protect established rhythms of daily life amidst the increasing pace of modern commerce.

The Christmas Shopping Showdown of December 1949, it is true, was about as prosaic, awkward, and complex a historical moment as they come. Some stores wanted to open; others did not. City officials felt obliged to enforce existing laws but did so somewhat feebly and to little effect. Unionized workers threatened a public protest but changed their minds. The leading merchants' organization, the RMA, steadfastly supported stores that willingly broke the law *this* time but demanded harsher punishment for stores doing so in the future. There is no indication that the showdown was a turning point in local, regional, national, or international history. Yet in the roughly two hundred pages of print that follow I hope to demonstrate that we can, indeed, learn important lessons from incidents such as this – about the historical development of consumerism in Canada and about Canadian society more generally.

In Canada, as in the United States, a consumer society emerged "when the ancient dual economy of mass subsistence and elite luxury gave way to an economy capable of delivering vast and diverse stores of goods to the general population."[21] In addition to securing, and becoming reliant upon, increasing numbers of mass-produced necessities, people used these commodities "to establish new personal identities and to break with old ones." Consumer goods, historian Gary Cross explains, "became a language, defining, redefining, and easing relationships between friends, family members, lovers, and strangers." The dominance of consumerism, which Cross usefully defines as the belief that "goods give meaning to individuals and their roles in society," has convinced many observers that its spread was preordained.[22]

In fact, like all elements of human existence, the context in which consumers shopped for goods and services over the course of the twentieth century was the product of experiment, conflict, and negotiation. For example, an increased capacity to produce alcohol was met with strict limits on its sale and consumption;[23] innovations in consumer credit that facilitated and encouraged immediate gratification spawned counselling agencies to assist those who had overindulged; unsafe foods, vehicles, and other products encouraged advances in consumer protection legislation; increasingly powerful advertising techniques convinced government regulators to limit commercial access to children. And, most pertinently for this study, those championing expanded opportunities to conduct commercial transactions faced resistance from others who were keen to ensure that consumerism did not fully colonize their available leisure time.[24]

If, as Donica Belisle argues, mass merchandising played a key role in transforming Canada into a modern nation between the 1880s and the 1940s, the period from the 1940s to the 1980s witnessed a consolidation of Canada's consumer society.[25] In part this was simply the product of economic expansion between 1945 and the early 1970s. Real per capita income more than doubled during this period. Automobile ownership increased dramatically, as did Canadians' access to home appliances.[26] With more disposable income in their pockets than ever before, many Canadians enjoyed the fruits of consumerism. As Doug Owram explains, consumerism pervaded the suburban baby boomer experience in Canada in the 1950s and 1960s. Television, a consumer item that served as a commercial medium, was a key element in this regard, for it beamed commercials into living rooms across the nation – commercials that intersected effectively with a peer culture that frequently evaluated identity and belonging based on one's ability to secure the latest fashion item or toy. But the boomers' parents also played an important role. Many of them had "grown up in the hard times of the 1930s and the spartan times of the Second World War" and seemed determined to ensure "that their children should have the things and comforts they had not known."[27] By the postwar era, then, shopping had become not just a means of self-fulfilment and status acquisition, but in many cases also a means by which family members negotiated their relationships and – in the case of outings to a local department store, for example – shared common leisure time.

But it was not simply a desire for toys or luxury items that signalled the centrality of consumerism in Canadian life. As Bettina Liverant notes, the Great Depression highlighted "the extent to which Canadians had come to *depend on buying* their food, clothing and shelter." Hence, from the 1930s on, "adequate consumption ... was discussed as a marker of democratic citizenship."[28] Throughout North America a political consensus emerged insisting that "spending, rather than reduced work time and increased leisure" was the key to economic prosperity. Governments openly encouraged consumption while labour unions increasingly prioritized a "living wage" over earlier calls to protect or enhance workers' time away from the factory.[29] After the Second World War such sentiments reflected the fact that while tangible class differences continued to determine people's access to consumer goods and services, the vast majority of Canadians – particularly those in urban centres – had incorporated shopping, in its various forms, into their weekly routines. Food and clothing likely topped the list of Canadians' needs on their regular trips to the growing number of corner stores, department stores, supermarkets, and shopping malls, but other "necessities," such as home repair items, also fuelled a desire to secure (or sell) goods in a timely manner.

As the scope of consumption changed after the Second World War, so too did the experience of shopping. The rapid development of shopping centres in the 1950s and 1960s brought stores to within easy reach of growing suburban populations and provided comfortable weatherproof settings that enhanced shopping's reputation as a recreational rather than strictly utilitarian pursuit. The expansion of credit cards in the 1960s made it easier for shoppers to buy now and pay later. Advances in transportation efficiency dramatically expanded the range of products available. And computer technology, especially the invention of the bar code, improved the ability of companies to meet consumer demand while greatly enhancing their capacity to track consumer behaviour.

Economic growth is, of course, always uneven, and while many Canadians enjoyed newfound spending power, many others faced lives of poverty and destitution. Indeed, as Kenneth Norrie and Doug Owram point out, "the very prosperity" of this period "made poverty all the more stark by contrast."[30] In cities across the country, Canadians debated the merits of unemployment insurance, taxation initiatives, and government spending priorities – all issues that helped determine who benefited from the country's burgeoning consumer culture and who did not.[31]

In much the same vein – though with much less attention from historians – Canadians debated when and how they should have access to consumer goods, for the authorities' decisions on such matters directly affected the lives of shoppers, merchants, and retail clerks alike. The economic exchanges that propelled Canada's economic expansion required physical meetings between shoppers, on the one hand, and merchants and clerks on the other. Determining when it was appropriate to facilitate such exchanges proved highly controversial even – and perhaps especially – in this era of intensifying consumer activity. For despite such significant economic growth and the transformation of the shopping landscape, one thing remained consistent: the necessity of securing time for the consumer and the sales clerk to meet face to face to complete a transaction. In an era before television shopping channels and Internet purchases, and with due acknowledgment of department store catalogues, consumerism in Canada was predicated largely on customers walking into stores to purchase goods and services.

But when should this occur? From one perspective, it seemed, the more opportunities for consumption, the better – after all, more sales meant more profits, greater economic growth, and happier customers. But from another perspective, extending opportunities for consumer purchases meant hardship – for employees who had little say over their work schedules, for example, or for merchants who worried that extending their hours of operation would increase their costs without guaranteeing a concomitant increase in consumer patronage. In short, while some people forcefully argued for expanded shopping hours, others sought to limit those hours in order to protect their economic bottom line or their way of life. For this latter group, extending store hours was less about "buying in" to Canada's consumer society than it was about "selling out" an older lifestyle that offered a welcome balance between work and leisure.

This book explores the consolidation of Canada's consumer society by focusing on how people in two BC cities responded to, and debated, initiatives designed to dramatically increase consumers' access to goods and services. As Bruce Mallen and Ronald Rotenberg note, "retailing and shopping hours affect almost every man, woman and child in this country."[32] They are thus a key component of daily life in a modern consumer society. Whether you have worked behind the counter at a clothing outlet in the mall or have had a hankering for a cheeseburger at 2 a.m., rules surrounding the hours of retail sales have affected you on some level. Critical scholarship, however, has not been much focused on this issue. In *The Overworked American* (1991), Juliet Schor warned that since the late 1960s many Americans had been facing a longer workweek, and she lamented that while the tension between work time and leisure time was a fundamental concern for many people, it had garnered little attention from "government, academia, or civic organizations."[33] If this particular development has not secured the attention it deserves from scholars, we can at least take heart that the study of consumerism is now firmly entrenched as an acceptable and worthy pursuit. The Canadian literature alone boasts insightful histories of advertising, department stores, gendered consumption patterns, and that most "Canadian" of commodities, the donut.[34]

This book takes up Mary Louise Roberts's call to demonstrate "that there was nothing natural or inevitable about the development of modern consumption practices."[35] Indeed, the debates over proposals to expand shopping hours illuminate the contested and contingent nature of consumerism. In tracing developments from the 1940s to the 1980s, the chapters that follow make it clear that while we now have greater access to goods and services than ever before, this development was fraught with tension and controversy. Population growth and suburban expansion did much to shape debates – and the development of consumerism more generally – but they did not, as some scholars have suggested, determine how those debates ended.[36] As suburbs expanded, so too did consumers' access to goods and services. But this expansion accounts for neither the extended duration of the debates nor their passionate nature. The store-hour debates in Victoria and Vancouver were prolonged and divisive ordeals that sent most politicians running for cover. In offering their views on seemingly mundane issues such as where frozen food should be sold on a Friday evening, Victorians and Vancouverites found themselves actively debating the merits and drawbacks of the consumer society that their purchases (and their labour) were putting in place.

Moreover, while we now know a great deal about both the capitalist apparatus that encouraged Canadians to consume in the second half of the twentieth century and the ways in which individual consumers negotiated their relationships with specific goods and services, the voices that dominate the following pages offer us something quite different: a sense of the ways in which Canadians *debated* consumerism.[37] These voices also highlight the complex nature of the public sphere – the arena in which merchants, clerks, consumers, and politicians expressed their views. As Gary Cross notes in his survey of consumerism in the twentieth-century United States, "the Victorian notion that some time and place should be free from commerce took decades to die; it had promised a 'peaceful refuge' from the market, forcing Americans to defer desire and, most important, pledge themselves to a family life beyond the consuming self."[38] The debates explored in this book focus specifically on this process: the manner in which shopping hours expanded and how and why some people championed this development while others challenged it with all their might. This was a battle that employed but also belied rhetorical flourishes that declared the interests of clerks and merchants, and independent and chain stores, to be fundamentally incompatible. It was also a conflict in which pro- and anti-regulation forces consistently sought to appropriate Cold War ideology for their own purposes.

Overall, the historical significance of store-hour deregulation lies not so much in the fact *that* it happened, but in *how* it happened and, in particular, how the people of the time understood what was at stake in the decisions undertaken by their civic leaders. For in debating the merits of mid-week closing, evening shopping, "wide open" shopping, and, later, Sunday shopping, these people were part of a historical development that should not (and cannot) be reduced to the comforting assumption that the insatiable demand of consumers and the entrepreneurial initiative of retailers rendered the result straightforward and inevitable.

Themes, Sources, and Chapters

I have chosen a thematic approach to the chapters because I am convinced that the salient details of social, cultural, and economic life that were embedded in the intense arguments over something as seemingly prosaic and quotidian as the closing time of the local Safeway would be too easily lost in any attempt to construct a comprehensive narrative that aimed to keep all of the issues before the reader at once. There are, of course, drawbacks to such an approach. Thematic, rather than chronological, chapters do not lend themselves terribly well to documenting change over time, and concentrating on a particular theme for an extended period is perhaps not the best way to showcase the complexity of people's lived reality – gender, for example, permeates all aspects of our (shopping) lives even though I discuss it primarily in chapter 4. But given that my core aim here is to analyse rather than comprehensively reconstruct these disputes, I hope the reader will appreciate the two main benefits of this organizational structure: it allows us to burrow deeply into crucial aspects of these debates that offer counter-intuitive evidence about the development of consumerism in Canada; and it allows us to remain focused on these individual aspects long enough to appreciate the diversity of views on offer.

The focus on Vancouver and Victoria stems from the existence of a productive cache of primary materials; my own familiarity with their histories; a desire to maintain a manageable scope; and the opportunity the cities' stories provide to contribute to both the regional history of BC and the broader study of North American consumerism. Choosing two urban centres rather than just one allowed for a comparative perspective that highlighted both common and divergent policies and viewpoints. The limited data available indicate that people in large cities and suburbs elsewhere in the country engaged in similar disputes. I hope this study will encourage other scholars to delve deeply into local records elsewhere in search of further insights that will establish national trends or regional differences.

While I have drawn from archival records where relevant, I have relied mainly on newspapers for my sources – more than 2,100 articles from the cities' four major dailies. Reliance on these sources proved fruitful on a number of levels. First, they provided consistent coverage of these disputes over the course of the twentieth century – something that neither archival nor legal records could yield. Indeed, use of these sources proved to be the only viable, if painstaking, way to piece together the lost histories of the two cities' store-hour restrictions and debates. Second, they offered both reportage *and* editorial opinion that both described and interrogated municipal and provincial government decisions concerning store-hour regulations. And third, they provided multiple and competing viewpoints and reports that I could compare for the purposes of verifying accuracy. But, of course, newspapers do not provide an unvarnished or comprehensive view of the past. As commercial and political enterprises they make explicit and strategic decisions about what they report and how they report it. As mainstream newspapers intent on maintaining and expanding their circulation, they almost certainly prioritized some constituencies over others, thus underrepresenting the views of the urban poor and racialized minorities, for example. Moreover, my focus on two urban centres means that rural voices are largely absent from this study. It is important to note, as well, that the newspapers were less likely to solicit the opinions of those with little interest in shopping, or in shopping policies. Reading against the grain and delving into relevant archival sources could occasionally fill these gaps, but overall, I have reconciled myself to these (and other) shortcomings by recalling that my aim here has not been to produce a comprehensive history of store-hour regulations, but rather to explore specific aspects of consumerism's consolidation in the decades following the Second World War.

Chapter 1 provides a narrative overview of the *conflict*. It examines the origins and growth of local store-hour restrictions and places them in the broader context of the early-closing movement in Britain and elsewhere. It also documents the gradual elimination of the restrictions and the advent of our present seven-day shopping week. It concludes by examining the complex relationship between merchants and clerks. At times these two groups found themselves on opposite sides of the store-hour debates, but on many occasions they found common cause, either promoting or challenging store-hour restrictions *together*. Indeed, the lack of consistent divisions among the key participants in the debates undoubtedly accounts for the longevity of the disputes. Recognizing the duration of the store-hours conflict, and the multiple subject-positions involved in the debates, underscores the contested and contingent nature of consumerism's development.

Chapter 2 explores the tensions inherent in decisions about local store-hour restrictions in Victoria and Vancouver as the two cities endeavoured to secure their status as prosperous and business-friendly urban centres. Securing this status required civic leaders to cater to outsiders, especially tourists, and their emphasis on a quantitative evaluation of outsiders' contributions to the local community conflicted with a more qualitative assessment of the community's needs. While the pro-tourism lobby argued for reduced store-hour restrictions – especially the elimination of a mid-week holiday – proponents of store-hour regulations highlighted the important role that Wednesday closing played in preserving an acceptable quality of life for retail clerks and for the community more broadly. Competing conceptions of *community* interests, then, were on display from the moment that store-hour regulations were established early in the twentieth century. These conceptions highlighted tensions between work, entrepreneurial endeavours, leisure, and consumption. This chapter demonstrates that the expansion of consumerism in Canada did not necessarily abolish established notions of community. Instead, citizens continued to adhere to multiple and competing identities – and drew upon these to debate the very impact of consumerism itself.

Chapter 3 examines the role of the much-derided chain store in the development of Canada's culture of consumption. It compares the anti-chain-store rhetoric that infused the public battles over local shopping regulations with the reality of the situation – a reality in which chain stores themselves were divided regarding issues such as Wednesday closing and evening shopping. A powerful, and populist, critique levelled damning accusations at chains and suggested that corporate greed was carrying out a coordinated assault on the quality of life and standards of living for the cities' merchants and clerks. Some chains, such as Safeway, were determined – and at times cynical – advocates of store-hour expansion. But the battle lines over store-hour restrictions were not clearly drawn between large and small stores, between locally and externally controlled companies, or between independent operators and multinational corporations. Instead, each individual business attempted to *leverage* its own particular strengths in order to put forward a coherent and convincing case to civic leaders as to whether store-hour restrictions should be retained or abolished. Chain stores played an important role in the dramatic expansion of shopping as an economic and cultural activity in the second half of the twentieth century, but so too did independent operators as businesses of all sizes jockeyed for position in an increasingly competitive marketplace.

Chapter 4 delves into the gendered dynamics of the store-hour debates, examining the extent to which arguments about prioritizing leisure, work, and consumption reflected broader concerns about *morality*. It also highlights the manner in which moral concerns influenced the debates. It does so by focusing on popular stereotypes concerning female shop clerks and female shoppers and examines the ways these influenced the store-hour debates. The chapter explores competing conceptions of consumer convenience and highlights the varied ways in which participants understood issues such as family leisure time and the increasingly complex situation facing wage-earning wives and mothers. Gender informed all aspects of these debates, just as it permeated the broader experience of consumerism, but it was particularly prevalent when citizens attempted to assess the moral implications of expanded shopping opportunities.

Chapter 5 addresses the actual impact and enforcement of store-hour restrictions. Local authorities faced a number of difficulties when trying to encourage adherence to store-hour regulations. Beyond the obvious problem of how to deal with recalcitrant merchants determined to transgress bylaws in order to secure additional sales, city councils and the provincial government faced the unenviable prospect of producing coherent guidelines and rules that would maintain the efficacy of the regulations. Confronted with the arduous task of classifying stores and defining and differentiating their wares, the authorities consistently found their efforts undermined by ingenious merchants keen to profit from unforeseen loopholes. As campaigns to enforce the *regulation* of store hours grew increasingly complex, many municipal councils simply threw up their hands and either turned a blind eye to illegal activities or openly called for an end to restrictions on Wednesday or evening shopping. Today's seven-day shopping week is, in part, a product of this frustration. This chapter thus documents how the expansion of consumer culture was in many ways the product of a series of very specific regulatory decisions.

Chapter 6 examines the nature of the store-hour debates themselves by evaluating the extent to which the participants employed political *ideology*. Before the Second World War, participants in the debates drew selectively and partially upon liberalism to justify their positions. With the onset of the Cold War, however, they made much greater use of political ideology, as the many references to free enterprise, citizenship, and democracy attest. In our darker moments it might be tempting to assume that consumerism's expansion witnessed, and even facilitated, the demise of robust debate. But even amidst the politically restrictive culture of the Cold War, local citizens offered relatively informed assessments of their situation by drawing, sometimes quite creatively, upon the dominant ideologies of the time. By surveying the nature of the debate itself, this chapter offers a portrait of a public sphere that was perhaps more dynamic and complex than we might assume, while challenging some historical assumptions about Canadians' Cold War experience.

The final chapter, chapter 7, revisits the store-hour debates in Vancouver and Victoria in light of the Sunday shopping controversy of the 1970s and early 1980s. Even as the two cities abandoned the mid-week holiday, expanded their evening hours, and considered the merits of "wide open" shopping, the notion that Sunday should remain a largely commercial-free day of rest went largely unchallenged until the mid-1970s. Attempts by two mayors, Peter Pollen in Victoria and Jack Volrich in Vancouver, to reinforce provisions against Sunday retail activity proved highly controversial and, in the end, unsuccessful. This chapter documents the greater role that *religion* played in this more recent store-hour dispute but also highlights the extent to which the themes discussed in the previous chapters continued to serve as central factors in the Sunday shopping debates. Pro-Christian and secular forces were certainly visible participants in the cities' Sunday shopping debates, but the tone, scope, and end result of the debates were determined largely by factors that had structured earlier store-hour disputes. Despite much rhetoric to the contrary, Sunday shopping did not mark a victory for consumerism over Christianity. Many shoppers in the 1970s and 1980s easily reconciled their devotion to worldly goods with religious observance. This chapter thus explores the complex relationship between religion and consumption by demonstrating the ways in which these pursuits were, and were not, in conflict.

As a whole, the chapters take the reader back to a shopping context that, for some, will be difficult to imagine given our present 24/7, online shopping universe. It was a world in which government regulations closed stores for a mid-week holiday, banned evening shopping, and rendered almost all Sunday retail operations illegal. This regulatory regime, the product of late-nineteenth- and early-twentieth-century political culture, was abandoned amidst great controversy in the decades after the Second World War, and this led to what now, for most of us, seems to be a normal shopping environment. Yet there is nothing "normal" about our present consumer society. Its emergence was highly contingent and contested.

In September 1958, in an editorial calling for the elimination of store-hour restrictions, the *Victoria Times* argued that "simple economics" would eventually bring about the "Christmas-season full-week business schedule."[39] The reality was far more complex. Attempts to liberalize store hours were hotly contested in complicated and sometimes contradictory ways. That these debates often focused on seemingly routine and mundane matters makes this journey into the past equally familiar, unsettling, frustrating, and predictable – much like life itself. But such journeys are worth taking, for they allow us to recognize that the widespread contemporary reality of nearly unlimited shopping opportunities is a historically contingent product of human activities, choices, and debates. They also allow us to examine and assess the manner in which consumerism has come to occupy such a central place in our lives.

Chapter One

Conflict: Restricting and Liberalizing Store Hours

When I was very young in municipal government I was told that three things – dogs, garbage, and store hours – would occupy more time than anything.

Saanich Reeve Hugh Curtis, 1966[1]

During the 1950s and 1960s the issue of shopping hours provoked heated disputes in cities across Canada. Stores in St John's, Newfoundland, for example, challenged the legality of that city's "Saturday closing law." Retailers in Toronto demanded the repeal of all store-hour regulations, while their counterparts in Montreal insisted that late evening closing be switched from Saturday to a weekday. Some storekeepers in Saskatchewan campaigned for restricted hours despite a general trend in western Canada that saw the elimination of all-day or half-day closing and the arrival of six-day and evening shopping.[2] The issue of evening shopping was particularly prevalent as lobby groups squared off against each other in Ottawa, Toronto, Hamilton, Montreal, Halifax, Winnipeg, Regina, Edmonton, and Calgary. Battles over all-day or half-day closing persisted in St John's, Halifax, Saskatoon, Winnipeg, and Edmonton.[3]

Two key tensions shaped these debates, Bruce Mallen and Ronald Rotenberg argue. One involved the competing aims and interests of small, independent retailers and "larger shopping centres and discounters." The other reflected a conflict between consumers' changing shopping patterns and the desire of many merchants and employees to preserve their traditional working hours.[4] The general response of provincial governments across the country was to pass the issue on to municipalities and to empower local authorities to seek local solutions.[5]

Surging populations and a critical mass of retailers willing to expand their hours of operation in search of a competitive advantage ensured that these battles were fought first and foremost in the nation's largest urban centres and their surrounding suburbs.

By the 1970s and 1980s the store-hour issue in Canada had come to focus on Sunday shopping. Here the Supreme Court weighed in with two key rulings. The first, in 1985, declared the federal government's Lord's Day Act (adopted in 1907 to restrict trading on the Christian Sabbath) to be unconstitutional. The second, in 1986, declared that the provinces were free to enact laws forcing stores to close on Sundays and that their doing so would not contravene the country's Charter of Rights and Freedoms so long as the rationale for it was not religious.[6] By 1987 every province but Alberta had legislation in place establishing "a general prohibition against retail store operations on holidays including Sundays."[7] Yet the 1980s and 1990s saw a relaxation of Sunday shopping restrictions in every Canadian province – a sign that the tension over store hour restrictions had not disappeared – and the result was a growing trend towards seven-day shopping.[8] At stake in all of these local controversies was the power to establish and codify priorities pertaining to leisure time, consumption, working conditions, and entrepreneurship. In short, these store-hour debates were occasions in which Canadians grappled with issues that were, and are, central to our social, cultural, and political life. But how did store-hour restrictions come to be?

The Early-Closing Movement

Retail hours have a history related to, but different from, the history of working patterns experienced by industrial workers. As Michael Quinlan and Miles Goodwin note, "the campaign to limit trading hours, often known as the early closing or half-holiday movement, constituted a significant social mobilization in the nineteenth and early twentieth centuries." "Prior to working time legislation," they explain, "limiting trading hours represented the only practical means of curbing the hours of retail workers."[9] Even during the 1920s and 1930s, Canadian merchants and their families faced extremely long hours. As Sylvie Taschereau explains, Saturday nights could be particularly gruelling for family-run businesses in Montreal. "On Saturday nights and during the holidays at the end of the year," she notes, "it was not uncommon to keep the entire staff, including the children, both the owner's children and those that he hired, well past the normal closing time of 11 p.m., sometimes until almost midnight and even later."[10] It is important to understand, then, how these long hours were established and the methods by which they were reduced. Nineteenth-century Britain provides the most useful starting point.

According to Simon Rottenberg, late closing in Britain "was concentrated among shops in the working class residential neighborhoods of the urban communities," with shops keeping these late hours in order to serve the working poor returning home from their places of employment.[11] These long hours were made possible by advances in artificial lighting that could keep streets and shops bright enough to facilitate commerce late into the evening. But, of course, what was considered a convenience by many shoppers was quickly deemed a hardship by many shop assistants. The first campaigns in support of retail store-hour restrictions came on the heels of the Ten Hours movement launched by factory workers in the 1830s. The first coherent campaign for such restrictions appears to have developed in 1842 when a small group of men met at a tavern in High Holborn, London, to discuss ways to encourage the early closing of stores. Their resulting organization, the Early Closing Association, initially pursued this aim through moral suasion: it encouraged shopkeepers to voluntarily close their stores early.[12]

By the 1880s, however, the Early Closing Association in Britain was losing patience with its voluntary campaign and had begun to champion legislated closing.[13] By 1891 there had emerged a National Union of Shop Assistants, Warehousemen, and Clerks to lobby the government.[14] Early results were mixed; more tangible progress came in stages throughout the twentieth century. During the First World War, the Defence of the Realm Act restricted the use of artificial light and required most stores to close at 8 p.m. during the week and at 9 p.m. on Saturdays. Legislation was revised repeatedly and consolidated in a 1950 act that instituted a weekly half-holiday by insisting that all shops close at 1 p.m. one weekday per week.[15]

Not surprisingly, Britain's white settler societies emulated these campaigns for early shop closing. In Australia and New Zealand, the late nineteenth century saw a flurry of laws limiting evening hours and instituting compulsory half-day holidays.[16] Such laws, Evan Roberts notes, effectively "limited working hours by controlling trading hours."[17] And it was not just the disparate elements of the British Empire that fit this pattern: the end of the nineteenth century saw Germany's first legislated interventions in store-hour regulation.[18] In the late nineteenth and early twentieth centuries, then, early closing movements secured important restrictions on store hours in a number of countries.[19]

In Canada, too, this period witnessed campaigns to reduce store hours. In 1865, Bryan Palmer notes, "dry goods clerks in Ottawa" who were "engaged in early closing action ... outraged respectable society by 'daubing over with filth' the front of one mercantile store holding out against the attempt to have all retail outlets close by 7:00 p.m."[20] As Donica Belisle explains in her study of Canadian department stores, "the long hours store clerks worked was one of labour's earliest grievances against the big retailers." Some shop owners voluntarily embraced demands for early closing because this served their own interests and allowed them to cut costs.[21] But in Canada, too, the turn of the twentieth century witnessed significant instances of government store-hour regulation. In Ontario, for example, the Factories Act of 1884 served as the basis for early closing regulations, which were revised periodically into the 1930s. Such legislation focused on protecting the health and safety of employees in specific industries and paid particular attention to setting maximum working hours for women and young workers. That emphasis was superseded in the 1940s by legislation that aimed to encourage "job creation and equitable employment conditions"; this coincided with the arrival of the reasonably standard forty-hour week after the Second World War.[22] By the 1940s, then, government regulation of store hours was widespread.

A number of important factors explain the demise of these regulatory regimes in the decades following the Second World War. One was the dramatic increase in the number and percentage of women, particularly married women, in the paid labour force.[23] Women working outside the home found it increasingly difficult to carry out the shopping duties expected of them during the limited store hours available. The rise of the suburbs, supported by the "diffusion of car ownership," also played a key role, as did an increase in disposable income.[24] Together, these factors led to the development of shopping districts in new municipalities, which sought a competitive advantage by offering consumers expanded store hours. Moreover, once the forty-hour/five-day workweek became more prevalent (but not universal) in Canadian retailing after the Second World War, traditional arguments for early closing, which had focused to a large extent on employees' welfare, lost momentum.[25] Writing in 1969, for example, Bruce Mallen and Ronald Rotenberg confidently asserted that "sales clerks and employees of retail establishments would not object to more liberal hours, provided that they did not work more than forty hours per week and/or had the option of working overtime for higher rates."[26] Yet as the prolonged disputes across the country suggest, the expansion and deregulation of store hours was anything but straightforward and uncontested. In Canada, provincial governments endeavoured – quite successfully – to pass the awkward and controversial issue of store hours on to municipalities whenever possible. So in many ways it is at the local or civic level that historical analysis is best placed to explore the social and cultural significance of this issue.

Store-Hour Debates on Canada's West Coast

The debates I examine began in earnest in the first decade of the twentieth century when store clerks in Vancouver and Victoria, in keeping with international trends, petitioned for a common half-day, mid-week holiday.[27] Embraced by many merchants in both cities, the Wednesday half-holiday was enshrined in 1916 in provincial legislation that accorded retail clerks, otherwise unaffected by the province's hours-of-work legislation, a five-and-a-half-day week. The Lord's Day Act ensured that they did not work on Sunday, and the province's Half-Holiday Act guaranteed an additional half-day off each week. In the absence of any specific hours-of-work legislation affecting retail clerks, store hours and hours of work became, for many employees, one and the same. Despite growing opposition in the 1920s and 1930s from merchants and other commercial interests (especially those in tourism-related businesses), who saw the legislation as too restrictive, the provincial government retained the Half-Holiday Act, amending it as needed to promote its continued efficacy. The half-holiday in Vancouver and Victoria remained a controversial but workable compromise between consumers, merchants, employees, and larger commercial interests into the 1940s.

Many merchants in both cities adopted all-day mid-week closing on a voluntary basis during the Second World War, and the elimination or retention of this temporary war measure became a key issue for civic voters once the war was over.[28] In city-wide plebiscites, Victoria residents voted to return to half-day closing in 1946; Vancouver residents voted to retain full-day closing in 1947. But suburban expansion and the increased mobility of automobile-propelled consumers helped ensure that residents revisited the issue of store-hour regulations in an angry and divisive manner almost annually until the early 1980s.[29] As Table 1.1 confirms, the populations of suburban Victoria and

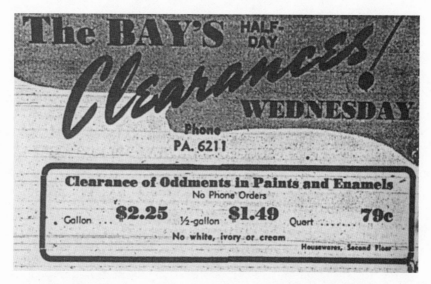

1.1 By the 1940s half-day closing on Wednesdays was such an established practice that it was incorporated into advertising campaigns. *Vancouver Daily Province*, 16 March 1943, 16. Reproduced with permission from the Hudson's Bay Company, HBC Corporate Collection.

Table 1.1 Population in BC's Southwestern Corner, 1881–1991

	Victoria City	Other Greater Victoria	Saanich Peninsula	New Westminster	Vancouver City	Other Greater Vancouver	Other Lower Fraser Valley
1931	39,082	9,166	12,968	17,524	246,593	52,405	57,480
1941	44,068	12,977	18,173	21,967	275,353	63,848	79,744
1951	51,331	22,113	30,550	28,639	344,833	123,828	139,157
1961	54,941	28,983	53,386	33,654	384,522	209,379	243,184
1971	61,761	31,348	78,645	42,835	426,256	286,421	385,660
1981	64,379	32,896	103,500	38,550	414,281	377,497	573,453
1991	71,228	34,007	130,687	43,585	471,844	448,585	820,844

Adapted from Jean Barman, *The West beyond the West: A History of British Columbia*, rev. ed. (Toronto: University of Toronto Press, 1996), 390.

Vancouver increased dramatically in the postwar era. Shopping centres like Park Royal in West Vancouver (1950), Oakridge in South Vancouver (1959), Brentwood Mall in Burnaby (1961), and Town & Country in Saanich (1961) emerged in rapid succession to cater to these consumers. They were both tangible products and symbolic representations of an increasingly competitive retail landscape.

Civic leaders aggressively courted new business while attempting at all costs to preserve their existing base of customers, even while reacting angrily when neighbouring municipalities did the same. Over the long haul, campaigns like these undermined support for initiatives such as Wednesday closing and restrictions on evening shopping; they also helped usher in "wide open" store hours. This development was part of a larger process of economic integration throughout North America, as communities that feared being left behind in an increasingly competitive marketplace sought to homogenize rules regarding consumers' access to goods and services.

City officials faced the difficult task of trying to prevent local people from being lured away to nearby towns and suburbs where the promise of easier and more convenient access to consumer goods and services awaited. They thus found themselves embroiled in a seemingly never-ending attempt to modify their local bylaws whenever nearby municipalities introduced more liberal regulations. This was a complex game of cat-and-mouse: neighbouring communities hoped to lure customers from nearby municipalities while preventing their own local customers from drifting away in search of goods and services. In the resulting atmosphere, many civic leaders issued dire warnings of future economic disaster should the cities' store-hour regulations continue to interfere with local stores' ability to maximize sales. Such arguments, however, did not go uncontested. Indeed, as the chapters that follow demonstrate, many people spoke out against the results of this intense competition, particularly as the end result came more clearly into focus: increasingly deregulated store hours.

That jurisdictions with liberal regulations could adversely affect neighbouring communities was clear to anyone who had lived through the Prohibition Era, when the goods in question were scotch or rum. Civic leaders in the United States, for example, had long been aware that wide variations in store-hour legislation between states created situations in which retailers in some states were left at a serious competitive disadvantage, even when the goods they were selling were more mundane.[30] The combination of shopping centre construction and

1.2 Increased automobile use played a key role in expanding shopping activity in suburban areas. As a result, downtown stores such as this one in Victoria faced increased competition from newly constructed shopping centres, which boasted more limited commutes for suburban shoppers as well as ample parking. Image I-01861 courtesy of the Royal BC Museum and Archives.

suburbanization had ushered in a destabilizing, ultra-competitive situation almost overnight.

From the mid-1940s to the late 1950s the debates focused primarily on the length of the shopping week. Many retail clerks and merchants fought to protect the five- or five-and-a-half-day shopping week. In this, they were opposed by *some* outside commercial interests, tourism-related businesses, and other retail clerks and merchants, who championed a six-day week as the most effective method of securing continued economic development. Quite often, initiatives to liberalize store hours

1.3 The Mayfair Shopping Centre, near the expanding suburb of Saanich, offered residents of Greater Victoria a convenient alternative to downtown shopping when it opened in 1963. Image I-03941 courtesy of the Royal BC Museum and Archives.

in Vancouver, Victoria, or one of the surrounding communities set off a chain reaction as one community after another tried to secure a level playing field for its merchants. Occasionally, local authorities launched predatory initiatives to (at least temporarily) provide local retailers with advantages over neighbouring stores that faced more stringent regulations.[31]

The proponents of six-day shopping eventually won out, but only after provincial laws and union contracts were in place to ensure that many store clerks would enjoy a five-day workweek. A turning point was a June 1954 plebiscite in Vancouver that narrowly supported ending mandatory Wednesday closing.[32] Three years later, Vancouver officially adopted a six-day shopping week; then in 1958, Victoria followed the lead of the neighbouring suburb of Saanich by rescinding its store-hour regulations, declaring city stores "wide open," and leaving merchants to set their own hours.[33] Such decisions at the municipal level were now possible because in 1958 the provincial government had finally divested itself of responsibility over store hours by revising its Municipal Act to transfer regulatory power over shopping hours to local authorities. But the debate over these regulations continued to rage.

In the early 1960s the focus shifted to evening shopping, and here again communities fought for an economic advantage by enticing consumers with first one and then two evening shopping opportunities during the week.[34] Expanded evening shopping arrived incrementally as municipalities rushed to respond to one another's initiatives. For more and more observers the logical outcome of this race for consumers was sure to be "wide open" store hours.[35] Throughout the 1940s, 1950s, and early 1960s, Vancouver and Victoria and their surrounding suburbs had desperately sought to secure the patronage of increasingly mobile consumers, and the result was a series of escalating beggar-thy-neighbour policies that contributed directly to the deregulation of store hours. Over loud resistance from those who worried about the end result, jittery city councils acted to stem the outflow of consumer spending.

By the mid-1960s the intensity of the debate had declined. By the end of that same decade, civic officials had abolished the half-day holiday almost everywhere in Greater Vancouver and Greater Victoria.[36] Shopping hours throughout Greater Vancouver were almost completely uniform, with stores generally closing at 6 p.m. throughout the week, 9 p.m. on Fridays, and 6 p.m. on Saturdays. Greater Victoria boasted completely "wide open" shopping with no local restrictions from Monday to Saturday.[37] Store hours in Vancouver and Victoria, then, had been dramatically liberalized, and the six-day shopping week had become a reality.

But despite BC's reputation as the most secular of Canada's provinces, stores remained closed, theoretically at least, on Sundays.[38] Indeed, until the mid-1970s the issue of "Sunday shopping" occupied but a minor role in the cities' local store-hour debates; a wide-ranging consensus recognized Sundays as "off limits" when it came to those disputes. Sundays were often employed rhetorically by opponents of store-hour deregulation, who argued that campaigns for six-day or evening shopping would inevitably lead to an assault on Sunday as a widely shared day of rest and religious contemplation.[39] From time to time, isolated complaints emerged about the limited availability of necessities, such as gasoline, on Sundays,[40] and media reports occasionally brought uneven enforcement of restrictions on Sunday sales to the attention of the public and city officials.[41] But except for a brief debate in Vancouver about the benefits and drawbacks of commercialized Sunday sport in the 1950s, Sundays rarely factored into ongoing disputes about finding the right balance between commerce, leisure, work, and consumption.[42]

On one level, local officials could more easily sidestep the issue of Sunday shopping. While they now had the authority to regulate evening shopping, regulating other Sunday activities would require the enforcement of a federal law, the Lord's Day Act, by the provincial attorney general.[43] In the mid-1970s, however, a growing perception that some retailers were selling wares on Sunday led civic officials in both Vancouver and Victoria to confront the situation head on. For the rest of the decade, civic authorities in both cities struggled to respond to growing disputes about Sunday shopping. Some bold retailers openly flouted Sunday closing rules, while newspaper columnists occasionally called into question the need for those rules. Some citizens feared commercialized Sundays and staunchly opposed them. City officials lacked the authority to prosecute retailers who transgressed the Lord's Day Act and urged the province to take action. Unwilling to become involved in local disputes, the province demurred until 1980, when it delegated control over Sunday shopping to municipalities through the Holiday Shopping Regulation Act. Municipal referendum results paved the way for expanded Sunday shopping in Greater Victoria and Greater Vancouver during the early 1980s. In 1989, when the BC Court of Appeal struck down sections of the act, "all remaining statutory restrictions on Sunday shopping" in the province "were eliminated."[44]

By the mid-1980s, then, consumers in Greater Victoria and Greater Vancouver enjoyed reasonably easy access to goods and services seven days a week. This development had been the product of a series of debates that began in the early twentieth century, intensified with a focus on Wednesday closing and evening hours in the 1950s and 1960s, and re-emerged in an equally contentious form in the mid-1970s and early 1980s to concentrate on Sunday shopping. This long-running conflict featured a multitude of competing voices that intervened in sometimes surprising and counter-intuitive ways. This was particularly the case for the merchants and clerks who were expected to provide consumers with goods and services.

Retailers and Clerks

One of the most interesting aspects of the store-hour debates is that while the issues always directly affected retailers and clerks, neither constituency held a consistent position. It is important to recognize the extent to which class structured the political battles over store hours. On many occasions employers and employees, despite class differences, found themselves in agreement. In their early-twentieth-century campaigns to secure common leisure time, retail clerks recognized both the importance and real possibility of securing merchants' support for restricted shopping hours. Retail clerks' solidarity may have been the driving force behind the cities' early closing movements, but support from a significant number of local merchants was crucial in making initiatives such as Wednesday closing a reality.[45]

At times a shared cultural and ethnic identity appears to have reinforced this bond. As historian David Monod explains, nativism could directly inform campaigns for early closing. "When the grocers' section of the RMA failed to get a proposed early-closing by-law passed in Vancouver in 1922," he notes, "it evoked the community-interloper image by blaming the failure on ... 'the invasion of Orientals and foreigners into our field.'"[46] At least twice, in 1919 and again in the 1930s, the Retail Clerks' Union in Vancouver similarly exploited anti-Oriental sentiment.[47] And during the Second World War, Patricia Roy notes, the Vancouver Barbers' Union demanded a "five-day work week lest Japanese 'again invade' the barbering trade and block improvements in working conditions."[48] Still, given BC's well-documented history of anti-Asian sentiment, concerns about competition from Asian Canadian merchants do not appear to have significantly influenced public debate on the issue.[49]

The shared allegiance among merchants and clerks with regard to the mid-week holiday continued after the Second World War and certainly contributed to the frustration endured by local and provincial politicians, who sought clear fault lines in the debate that might be exploited for a solution. Instead, politicians in a province renowned for its polarization between capital and labour found themselves confronted by a confusing litany of lobby groups and with no clear strategy to address the issue. In March 1958, BC's municipal affairs minister, Wesley Black, offered a succinct if exasperated summation of the situation: "We have the five-day week people come to us, the five-and-a-half-day week people, the six-day week people and even the clear blue sky people."[50]

Black's frustration was genuine. As the provincial minister ultimately responsible for resolving ongoing disputes over store hours in BC, he found himself overwhelmed by the multitude of perspectives on the issue. Indeed, a brief survey of the many organizations in Vancouver and Victoria involved in the debate speaks to the complex situation Black confronted. Postwar residents of Vancouver, for example, were constantly being encouraged to adopt the position of organizations such as the Continued All-Day Wednesday Closing Campaign, the Citizens' Committee Supporting the Six-Day Business Week, and the "Save-the-Wednesday" Committee, along with the Retail Merchants Association, the Vancouver Board of Trade, and the Vancouver Tourist Association. The situation in Victoria was perhaps even more confusing. In the 1940s and 1950s the local Retail Clerks' Union, the Retail Clerks Five-Day Action Committee, a Merchants' 5 1/2-Day Association, the Citizens Committee Against All-Day Closing, the Victoria Trades and Labor Council, the Retail Merchants Association, the Victoria Chamber of Commerce, the Victoria & Island Publicity Bureau, and the Six-Day Shopping Week Committee were among the various groups all campaigning for public sympathy and support.

This confusion was precipitated in large part by the fact that disputes only rarely pitted a sizeable block of employers against an influential and coordinated group of employees. To understand this lack of friction we must first consider the social identity of both merchants and retail clerks. In modern society, retail clerks are ubiquitous. But despite their central place in North America's economic development, clerks – and clerical workers more generally – are not easily categorized in terms of identity or class affiliation.[51] In the United States, clerks were originally viewed with a fair degree of suspicion. In the mid-nineteenth century, many Americans viewed clerking positions as an unfavourable alternative to the "productive toil" associated with manufacturing or farming.[52] Indeed, a popular perception portrayed clerks as "dependent," "subservient," and "enervated," but also acquisitive and self-absorbed. "Distinguished by an overly fastidious appearance and a carefully mannered speech," Michael Zakim explains, "the clerk nurtured a persona calibrated for personal advancement."[53] As Zakim reveals, clerks have not fit easily into our preconceptions of what workers do.[54] Instead of sharing a specific "craft identity," he notes, clerks possessed an "individualized sense of agency and opportunity" that focused on self-interest and advancement.[55]

Similarly, in his study of office and sales clerks in Philadelphia, Jerome Bjelopera convincingly argues that clerks emphasized "their position between the working class on the one hand and professionals and small-business owners on the other." In doing so, "clerical workers avoided connection with menial work and longed for full-fledged middle-class status." Indeed, even as tangible opportunities for advancement decreased over time, their dreams of upward mobility persisted. "Poignantly," Bjelopera notes, "in 1905 the Retail Clerks' International Protective Association (RCIPA), one of the few clerical unions, lamented that one-half of America's male sales clerks dreamed of becoming small-business owners."[56] The fact that many clerks in turn-of-the-century Vancouver "made the transition from retail clerk to store owner" underscores the fluid nature of these occupational categories.[57]

Sylvie Taschereau's examination of shopkeepers in Montreal suggests another way in which the class identities of merchants and clerks could overlap. While many families hoped for sustained success, social mobility, and a chance to pass their business on to their children, "the majority of these small businesses lasted for only a very short time." Hence, "until at least the middle of the twentieth century, proprietors often came from the working class, and their move into shopkeeping did not separate them far or for very long from their origins."[58] This connection to working-class culture may well have rendered them sympathetic to their employees' concerns.

Given these connecting threads between merchants and clerks, it is not surprising that campaigns for early closing sometimes boasted genuine cooperation between the two groups.[59] Andrew Neufeld notes that clerks' campaigns for shorter hours in Vancouver in the first decade of the twentieth century actually enjoyed a good deal of merchant support.[60] Canadian studies of more recent times caution against constructing too simplistic a model of labour opinion on the store-hour issue and encourage us to guard against the assumption that retail merchants invariably seek more selling opportunities. By 1969, Mallen and Rotenberg could conclude in their survey of the evening shopping issue in Canada that "labour unions take an interest in the topic, both because retail employees could be affected and because labour union members in general represent a significant portion of the consumer market" – a telling indication, perhaps, of the extent to which retail clerks' identity was complex and variable.[61] Mallen and Rotenberg found evidence that "retail sales clerks and organized labour do not seem to mind" evening shopping.[62] Also, merchants' actions often challenged generalizations about their motivations and interests. For example, a survey of Ottawa retailers in the early 1980s found "no strong support either for or against" a proposal to extend evening shopping opportunities in that city. And economist Stephen Ferris has differentiated retailers' attitudes towards store-hour deregulation on the basis of urban geography. Deregulation, he argues, "will be favoured by those with particular locational advantages who gain at the expense" of other retailers.[63]

Overall, a great many retail clerks did oppose expanded shopping hours, while many merchants in Victoria and Vancouver were frustrated by local store-hour restrictions and keen to challenge local bylaws. Yet on many occasions merchants and clerks collaborated to champion specific store-hour restrictions and even to campaign for store-hour deregulation. Early successful campaigns to secure store-hour regulations required cooperation between merchants and clerks, and for many merchants the notion that shopkeepers and their employees shared common interests remained a popular reference point into the postwar years.

For example, merchants often supported the continuation of Wednesday closing or opposed evening shopping, and when doing so, they highlighted the interests of their employees.[64] Thus in June 1947, when Vancouver residents voted to retain Wednesday full-day closing, the RMA's George Matthews celebrated the result and suggested that it was significant because it showed "the world what can be accomplished when employers and employees genuinely co-operate." Revealingly, the local Retail Clerks' Union (Local 279) echoed these sentiments and attributed the victory of the pro-Wednesday-closing campaign to the "co-ordinated effort of retail employees, 95 per cent of Vancouver merchants and to organized labor."[65]

Moreover, aided in part by increased provincial and municipal control over employees' maximum weekly hours, some retail clerks *actively campaigned* for six-day shopping.[66] Hence in the early 1950s Victoria's retail clerks found themselves embroiled in a bitter dispute between rival employee organizations. On one side was the Retail Clerks' Union and its representative, John Aubry, who favoured six-day shopping so long as his members could be assured of a five-day, forty-hour week. "We have no right to tell a storekeeper how to run his business," he explained. "Let them stay open as long as they see fit. Whatever is good economy for the employers will benefit the store workers also."[67] Charles Stewart, the business agent for the Vancouver Street Railwaymen's Union, concurred and announced that six-day shopping was "an issue on which labor and management can get together."[68] In contrast, Peter MacEwan chaired a Victoria-based employee organization, the

Five-Day Week Action Committee, which sought to preserve Wednesday closing in that city: "We want to co-operate with storekeepers," he explained. "If stores want to stagger our holiday by employing extra help it is all right with us. If they prefer to work with their present staffs and operate five days, that is all right, too."[69] Both campaigns boasted employer–employee alliances.

These examples illustrate the complex subject positions through which employers and employees participated in the ongoing debate about shopping regulations. Even as the status of many retail clerks evolved – from that of a quasi-apprentice who enjoyed a close working relationship with a store's proprietor, to that of one depersonalized employee among many in a shop or department store owned by a large corporation – the relationship between retail clerks and their employers did not fit easily into a binary opposition: of merchants versus employees, or of capital versus labour. This complicated relationship helped ensure that the conflict over store hours in two BC cities would be both extended and complicated.

⁓

Rooted in the early-closing movement, store-hour restrictions in Vancouver and Victoria comprised a complex regulatory regime governed by municipal, provincial, and federal laws. A consistent source of tension, this regime became the subject of increasingly heated debate in the 1950s and 1960s as suburban expansion and an increasingly articulate campaign to cater to consumer demand challenged restrictions on mid-week and evening store hours. Arguments in favour of serving the community interest by catering to consumer demand often focused on local shoppers and the hardships they faced because of store-hour restrictions.

As the following chapter demonstrates, however, the anti-regulation lobby also boasted strong representation from retailers keen to cater to the cities' growing number of tourists. These merchants fretted about missed opportunities that arose whenever visitors approached a storefront only to discover that the door was locked because of mandatory closing laws. Their demands for change often focused on community development and the idea that their own economic bottom lines were an accurate reflection of the cities' well-being. A pro-regulation lobby challenged their arguments and articulated a very different conception of community interests – one that championed the importance of protecting local leisure opportunities at the expense of tourists' convenience.

Chapter Two

Community: Tourism, Leisure, and the Quest for Civic Prosperity

It is crazy to suggest that a city which depends on tourist trade for survival should close down all day Wednesday.

Victoria Mayor Percy Scurrah, 1956[1]

We live in the city, not the tourists. We should have things the way we like.

Victoria furniture dealer Roy Denny, 1952[2]

"I always heard Victoria was dead, now I know it."[3] Such was the reaction of one visitor to British Columbia's capital city in 1927. Poised for a Wednesday shopping spree, she found herself denied that opportunity by the city's mid-week closing practice. She was not the only visitor to lament such restrictions. In 1949 the *Vancouver Sun* reported that a "group of 250 wealthy Los Angeles visitors was appalled to find no outlet for its good American dollars." "It has turned our trip upside down," lamented Earl V. Grover, president of the Los Angeles Chamber of Commerce.[4] The following year, another LA Chamber of Commerce official warned Vancouverites that two hundred Californians en route to the city would be "hopping mad" to discover the stores closed on Wednesdays. In light of such anecdotal evidence, the Vancouver Tourist Association embarked on a series of tourist surveys that suggested that over 80 per cent of visitors disliked mid-week closing.[5]

While some retail merchants in Vancouver and Victoria endorsed campaigns for shorter hours, many others maintained that such restrictions threatened their businesses as well as the economic viability of the larger community.[6] Shorter hours, they argued, meant fewer opportunities to sell goods. Supporters of store-hour restrictions countered with appeals to a very different bottom line – one that emphasized a more qualitative assessment of living standards and community priorities. Such counter-arguments were part of a broader transnational pattern that championed workers' access to communal leisure.[7] These tensions between commerce and leisure dominated debates over shopping hours in Victoria and Vancouver and ensured that the cities' adoption of expanded store hours was a highly controversial and contested process. In particular, as the cities came to embrace tourism as an economic strategy, local store-hour debates were increasingly structured by an oppositional tension pitting the leisure activities of local residents against the potential benefits derived from serving the leisure demands of tourists. The crucial question became: Whose leisure interests would these communities serve?

This battle took place as both cities struggled to establish themselves as viable economic entities. In this context, many civic leaders insisted on catering to the external gaze of potential visitors who might well be comparing Vancouver or Victoria with advanced cities elsewhere in North America. Easier access to consumption opportunities, they believed, served as a marker of progress and sophistication. Store-hour regulations designed to preserve an acceptable quality of life for shopkeepers and clerks, they argued, could not be effectively reconciled with the cities' determined efforts to attain what often proved to be a fleeting measure of economic security. As developing centres, both cities longed for external recognition, and many civic leaders emphasized the importance of securing a business-friendly reputation in order to encourage economic development.

In Victoria and Vancouver, civic leaders expended considerable effort luring tourists to town, first as potential settlers and investors and later on as a means to boost aggregate consumer demand.[8] The pro-tourism lobby argued that store-hour restrictions were incompatible with plans for civic development in that they proved an annoyance to visitors wishing to spend money in local shops and dissuaded entrepreneurs from bringing their skills and capital to southwestern BC. Proponents of store-hour regulations responded with their own understanding of community needs; this included a forceful defence of the regulations, which they believed played an important role in protecting local residents from a world in which capitalism dictated the rhythm of daily life.

The debates came to reflect a tension between the interests and actions of "outsiders" (tourists) and the needs of "insiders" (the residents of a particular community – or, more accurately, those local people who did not benefit directly from the tourist trade). The differing economic realities of Vancouver and Victoria shaped the two cities' approaches to securing and maintaining civic prosperity – in particular, the extent to which their economic development strategies relied on tourism promotion campaigns. With its more diversified economy and expanding role as the chief port city and service centre for a province heavily reliant on export commodities, Vancouver could view tourism as one economic pursuit among many. Victoria, by contrast, embraced tourism as a panacea for its increasingly vulnerable economic situation – first as a strategy for luring wealthy industrialists to the city and then as an alternative to industrial development.

Vancouver

For Vancouver, then, tourism was an important but not central component of the drive to reduce and eliminate store-hour regulations. The city's pro-tourism lobby vociferously opposed Wednesday closing on the grounds that it fostered among outsiders a negative perception of the city's business class and limited economic opportunities for local merchants. In May 1907, for example, Charles Woodward, founder and general manager of the local Woodward's department store chain, opposed the local clerks' campaign for a Wednesday half-holiday over the summer specifically on the grounds that it would harm the city's economic future. In doing so he directly addressed the issue of tourism. "First impressions," he argued, "are generally lasting and if the tourists or travelers visiting go away pleased we have made them friends and probably investors, and they become citizens."[9] Similarly, in February 1926 the retail merchants' bureau of the Vancouver Board of Trade endorsed abolishing the Wednesday half-holiday because it ostensibly limited tourism revenue.[10]

As the competition for tourism dollars intensified after the Second World War, so did the pro-tourism lobby's campaign against the Wednesday holiday in Vancouver, which had since been extended to full-day closing. In January 1947, one hundred Vancouver merchants made plans to organize a citizens' committee against compulsory closing. Leo Sweeney, a prominent tourism promoter and key figure in the Vancouver Tourist Association (VTA), chaired the group and argued that all-day closing did the tourism industry more harm than any other negative factor, including the city's notoriously wet weather.[11] In June

1949 the *Vancouver Sun* urged Vancouverites to reconsider their decision to "paralyze the community's commerce from Tuesday to Thursday." While insisting that it did not want to see a lengthening of the
employees' work week, the newspaper suggested that there was a
"growing belief that Vancouver should get back into step with other
large cities by combining a six-day service week with a five-day work
week." "It's done in every other major Coast city and most U.S. cities,"
the newspaper explained. In taking this position, the *Sun* placed the
VTA's concerns front and centre: "A group of 250 wealthy Los Angeles
visitors was appalled to find no outlet for its good American dollars
during a one-day stay in Vancouver on Wednesday." This incident, the
newspaper lamented, was part of a larger pattern: "People go away
with the impression that Vancouver is a hick town sleeping in its own
shade, inhabited by businessmen content to get by with a minimum of
personal effort and public service."[12]

Similarly, in a July 1952 letter to the *Vancouver Sun*, "DOWNTOWN
MERCHANT" lamented the missed opportunities to secure tourism
revenue. Mid-week closing, the author argued, was costing local merchants much-needed revenue and was giving tourists the impression
that the city was not interested in their business. "No other city of any
size on the continent has such compulsory one-day-a-week closing,"
the author complained, noting that a recent proposal to spend $100,000
on tourism promotion did not make sense if stores were mandated to
remain closed on Wednesdays.[13] That same year, the VTA attempted to
galvanize public support for its position by revealing that 86 per cent of
the visitors who called at its downtown office "found the Wednesday
all-day closing practice ... an inconvenience" that "curtail[ed] ... their
holiday of shopping activities."[14]

City restaurateurs found Wednesday closing particularly aggra-
vating. In 1947 the executive secretary of the Vancouver branch of
the Canadian Restaurant Association (CRA) expressed the organization's opposition to Wednesday closing and alluded to an organic, if
politically useful, conception of community: "Our suggestion is based
not simply on the fact that our industry is among those that would
be seriously affected by such closing; but on the wider grounds that
compulsory Wednesday closing would have an adverse effect on
the community of Vancouver as [a] whole."[15] Seven years later, R.C.
(Ross) Brown, president of the Vancouver Branch of the CRA, similarly
emphasized the deleterious effects that Wednesday closing had on the
city's tourism industry. "Visitors consider this closing an unnecessary

2.1 "Phelps ... what's this I hear about a 'Save the Monday, Tuesday, Wednesday, Thursday, Friday campaign you're busy organizing." Editorial cartoonist Len Norris wonders just how far the campaign to preserve common leisure time will go. *Vancouver Sun*, 4 June 1954. Image reproduced courtesy of Simon Fraser University Library, Special Collections and Rare Books.

and annoying inconvenience," he explained. "When reported back to their friends at home, Wednesday closing makes Vancouver a less attractive place to other tourists planning where they will go." The economic impact, he suggested, was alarming: "The loss ... of Wednesday retail business to rapidly expanding facilities bordering the City of Vancouver" would "have a serious effect on the general economic well-being of the whole City and hurt the pocketbook of every single Vancouver citizen."[16] These observers argued that the preservation of common leisure time for the local population came at a steep price – the city was unable to maximize its tourism revenue.

Not everyone was willing to accept pro-tourism arguments at face value. Evelyne M. Jackson, a Woodward's department store baker, was convinced that the focus on tourists' desires was a red herring designed to mask the greed of a small number of local merchants. "As far as our visitors are concerned," she wrote to Vancouver City Council in reference to American tourists, "they know they must be in Canada 48 hours before being allowed to take merchandise back across the line. Also visitors do not want to spend all their time in the stores and one day is just as good as another to them for shopping." "Don[']t try to pass the buck on to our visitors," she argued, "when it happens to be just a few of our local money grabbers who are trying to take this holiday away from us."[17] Thelma Pinkerton, a fellow Woodward's bakery employee, was similarly suspicious of claims that tourists demanded an end to Wednesday closing. In a 1950 letter to city council she drew upon her interaction with tourists to insist that visitors "are envious of our good working conditions and do not wish to spend their holidays in the stores." As a result, she explained, they "do not object to sightseeing on Wednesdays and shopping on other days."[18] At play here were competing notions concerning how best to serve the community's interests, with one side championing the idea that catering to tourists was necessary to ensure economic stability, and the other side determined to ensure that the immediate interests of local residents were not sacrificed to serve those of tourists and tourism-related businesses.

Victoria

Vancouver was keen to secure tourism expenditures, but it was not as dependent on tourism as Victoria. Today, Victoria's economy relies mainly on tourism, services, and the government sector. In the 1880s, however, civic leaders could be forgiven for believing that the city had a promising future as a manufacturing centre. During that decade, writes Peter Baskerville, the city's "gross value of manufacturing production increased 3.5 times," and "when ranked by per capita value of manufacturing production, Victoria stood fifth out of the twenty Canadian towns and cities with a population in excess of 10,000."[19] But the tide would soon turn. By the end of the 1880s, Vancouver had become the western terminus of the Canadian Pacific Railway and had supplanted Victoria as BC's leading port. Throughout the 1890s, Victoria's economy was outpaced by that of its mainland rival.[20] "By 1901," Baskerville notes, Victoria "had dropped from fifth to twentieth place in per capita value of manufacturing output."[21] "The prospects of Victoria becoming an important and diversified manufacturing center, so bright in the 1880s," he explains, "had been severely dashed by the turn of the century."[22] "Manufacturing and wholesale trade gradually took second place to tourism and government as the mainstays of the city's economy."[23] In Victoria, then, the stakes surrounding tourism and store hours were higher, and that, perhaps, accounts for its more contested evaluation of community goals and interests.

Victoria first began promoting tourism in the hope of attracting deep-pocketed visitors who would later return to reside in Victoria and con-tribute to the city's industrial development. Only later was tourism identified as an important generator of spending for the economy. Vic-toria's response to deindustrialization, then, focused firmly on catering to outsiders. Visitors to the city needed to be presented with a positive view of its possibilities. Early in the century this meant ensuring that potential investors and settlers saw Victoria as a vibrant and produc-tive centre offering attractive investment opportunities; later the key concern was to ensure that visitors keen to spend money in local shops were given ample opportunity to part with their cash. A central concern in both campaigns was the city's store-hour regulations.

By the opening decade of the twentieth century, proponents of tour-ism in Victoria had squared off against other members of the local com-munity on the issue of store-hour regulation, with each side claiming to represent the community's long-term interests. Opponents of store-hour regulations focused mainly on tourism's economic benefits. Sup-porters of these regulations – who took issue with the pro-tourism lobby – emphasized instead the social and cultural advantages of store-hour limitations. They championed the common half-day holiday that allowed community members to participate in shared leisure activities, and they insisted that store-hour regulations protected retail clerks from overwork and exhaustion.

As early as 1908, Alex Peden, president of the local Merchants' Pic-nic Association, signalled his opposition to a common mid-week half-holiday on the grounds that "it was not business-like," in that it forced merchants to lose trade and gave outsiders "a very bad impression of the energy and progressiveness of the city."[24] Arthur Lineham, a key proponent of the city's developing tourist trade, was more forceful in asserting his opposition to the half-holiday. In 1923 he explained that over the previous eighty years Victoria had been incapable of luring traditional industry. Drawing upon an understanding of tourism pro-motion that equated it with immigration literature, Lineham argued that tourism was the key to creating the right conditions to promote settlement and attract industry. He attacked the city's half-day holiday with vigour, arguing that "to close the town up tight any day in the week but Sunday is business suicide, and makes us the laughing stock of every stranger entering our gates. Every business man and patriotic citizen in Victoria will endorse me when I say that the time has come when we must wake up and use every means of securing additional population and money to meet our obligations."[25] In Lineham's view, proponents of the half-holiday were putting their own interests ahead of the community's well-being. The half-holiday, he explained, allowed "retail clerks and small storekeepers to have what they term a good time" without regard to "the majority in the community."[26] "There is no necessity," he argued, "to turn the town into a morgue one day in the middle of the week ... making us a subject of ridicule to all visitors and helping to ruin the retailers and responsible tax payers, who carry the burden of the day."[27]

Given Victoria's early understanding that tourism promotion was a means to attract industry and population, it is not surprising that tourism's proponents attacked store-hour restrictions on the grounds that they damaged the city's reputation – that is, its *desired* reputation – as a progressive and modern business centre that was eager to attract new customers and industry. Hence the Victoria Board of Trade's lament that "grandmotherly legislation" gave outsiders the impression that Victoria was "a village of lotus-eaters."[28] Economic growth, these observers argued, required investment capital, which would be increasingly difficult to attract if potential investors found themselves questioning the community's work ethic.

By the 1930s, however, tourism's proponents had begun to embrace a new rationale – one that recognized that Victoria would never be able to compete with Vancouver for traditional industry. As Victoria mayor David Leeming put it in 1934, the city's consistent failure to attract investment now meant that "the only hope of the City was to extend its tourist trade."[29] Recognizing that reversing the trend towards deindustrialization was no longer possible, and that a new approach to economic development was required, Leeming and his supporters increasingly championed tourism as an effective method of increasing demand for local retail goods. As Victoria came to rely on tourism for a direct infusion of expenditures rather than as a back-door route to settlement, secondary manufacturing, and agricultural development, many civic leaders argued that the city's prosperity was now more reliant on tourism than ever before. In making their case, opponents of store-hour regulations pointed both to tourists' complaints and to the concerns of a sizeable element of the local business community.

In this spirit the Victoria Chamber of Commerce's Tourist Trade Group (TTG) campaigned vigorously against a 1946 proposal to close Victoria's stores for a full day every Wednesday. The chamber's president, Major H.C. Holmes, wrote to Victoria mayor P.E. George to argue that any bylaw that forced businesses to close for two full days each week was "not in the best interests of the City."[30] For Victoria's tourism promoters, the city's retailers had an obligation to overcome their own self-interest in order to contribute to the greater good of the community. As George E. Macdonald explained in his brief to the chamber: "Victoria's [r]etail prosperity was due to [its] tourist business, shut this off, and millions of dollars will be lost to this City." Retailers, Macdonald warned, had "a responsibility to give service," without which tourists would be enraged and the city's economy as a whole would be threatened.[31]

Opponents of specific store-hour regulations, along with those who were leading a determined effort to eliminate those regulations entirely, could point to a good deal of direct and indirect evidence that tourists themselves found the half-day holiday, limited evening hours, and other restrictions to be frustrating. Indirect statements on behalf of tourists ranged from examples voiced by individual citizens to more general complaints levelled by the business community. In a May 1925 letter to the *Victoria Daily Colonist*, Victorian Dale Johnson argued against the city's Wednesday half-holiday by pointing out the inconvenience it posed for visiting tourists. When the *Kathleen* arrived in port the previous Wednesday from Seattle "with several hundred passengers all ready and eager to avail themselves of the opportunity of purchasing several different kinds of merchandise," he lamented, they "were disappointed to see all our stores closed."[32] More often, the tourists took their complaints directly to the local tourist office, which broadcast these laments within the local community while trying to prevent this sort of adverse publicity from reaching other potential visitors.[33] In 1956, local tourism promoter George Warren endorsed the idea of six-day shopping so that there would be no repeat of the recent Fourth of July scenario in which American visitors found themselves unable to spend money at local shops.[34] These claims were sometimes buttressed with statistical evidence purportedly demonstrating that tourists were now avoiding Victoria on Wednesdays.[35]

Not surprisingly, tourist-dependent businesses were among the most vocal participants in the debate over Wednesday closing. In 1951,

Alan Vizard of the Victoria Gift House accused supporters of the Wednesday half-day holiday of being short-sighted and of failing to recognize tourism's central place in the city's economy. "You would not get holiday centres like Banff and Jasper closing down in early afternoon during the tourist season," he wrote, "and the sooner Victoria realizes it is just a massive tourist resort and acts accordingly the better."[36]

Many civic leaders embraced Vizard's arguments. For Victoria mayor Percy Scurrah, it was "crazy" to argue that "a city which depends on tourist trade for survival should close down all day Wednesday." Victoria Chamber of Commerce president Stickney Harris Jr insisted that six-day shopping was a necessity in Victoria.[37] A fear that the city's tourism industry, like its manufacturing base, might be eclipsed by Vancouver's convinced many observers that outside competition, in the form of more relaxed store-hour regulations, might well prove the final nail in the city's economic coffin. Hence the TTG's claim in 1954 that the expansion of store hours was now an urgent necessity because both Vancouver and Seattle had six-day shopping.[38]

Central to the campaign to eliminate restrictions was the assertion that tourism brought economic prosperity to the city. In 1953, for example, A.E. Newberry pilloried the city council, and the citizens of Victoria more generally, for viewing antique shops with "a condescension almost bordering on superciliousness or disdain." In point of fact, Newberry asserted, such shops "attract more tourists, probably than anything else the city has to offer." As such they made an important if chronically unrecognized contribution to the local economy by bringing "new" money into the city. "The tourists do not come here to admire the beauty of the civic architecture or the excellence of the garbage trucks," Newberry maintained. "They may stand in awe for a few minutes to gaze at the Parliament Buildings and the Empress Hotel, but they have to pass these buildings anyway on their road uptown from the ferry boats." Tourists came to Victoria mainly to shop. Limiting their access to antique shops and the like, he argued, was a foolhardy and unfair move.[39] The TTG consistently worked to undermine the legitimacy of store-hour regulations by claiming that the entire community benefited from tourist expenditures.[40] Hotel owner James Neely summed up this position nicely in 1951 when he asserted that "what is good for the hotel association and the tourists is also good for Victoria."[41] Victoria store owner Jimmy Little took this argument one step further in 1958 when city authorities cracked down on stores transgressing Wednesday closing laws. Little draped a black wreath across his establishment's door

AFTER A CENTURY of PROGRESS

VICTORIA DIED TOL

Black Wreath Greets Store Closing

2.2 Victoria store owner Jimmy Little protests a crackdown on Wednesday openings in 1958. *Victoria Daily Colonist*, 18 September 1958, 9. Original photo by Jim Ryan. Image reproduced courtesy of the *Times-Colonist* newspaper.

and affixed a sign to its window that read: "AFTER A CENTURY of PROGRESS VICTORIA DIED TODAY" (see Figure 2.2).[42]

Just as the rationale behind tourism promotion changed during the 1930s, so too did the content of the tourism lobby's arguments. The economic dislocation of the Great Depression encouraged tourism promoters to embrace the "expenditure imperative" that viewed tourists primarily as a source of outside expenditure that boosted local aggregate consumer demand. From the tourism lobby's perspective, store-hour regulations remained anathema to tourism promotion, even though the tourism lobby's specific complaints changed over time. What remained consistent, however, was the notion that tourism had replaced traditional industry as the city's economic lifeblood. Faced with Victoria's failure to challenge Vancouver as an industrial centre, these proponents of tourism were anxious to ensure that the city was as tourist-friendly as possible. This informed their campaign to eliminate store-hour restrictions that irritated visitors. Like more recent tourism proponents who view tourism as a panacea for the complex social and economic problems that plague post-industrial communities, Victoria's pro-tourism lobby was anxious to protect its ability to lure outsiders to town.[43] But of course, not everyone in Victoria agreed that tourism was the best, or even an unproblematic, approach to securing the city's economic future.

Opponents of store-hour regulations came from a variety of subgroups, including employers, employees, consumers, and even some labour organizations. But each of these groups also boasted alternative voices that continued to embrace restrictions such as the Wednesday half or full-day holiday. Some supported store-hour regulations because they did not benefit directly from tourist expenditures and argued that expanding store hours would simply increase operating costs. Others pointed to the social costs that expanded store hours might bring and sought to preserve the retail clerks' mid-week respite and opportunities for common leisure time. Supporters of store-hour regulations often claimed to be championing the interests of the local community, which, they argued, was not necessarily well served by policies that focused on appealing to tourists.

Tourist-dependent operations such as hotels, restaurants, transportation companies, and souvenir stores railed against the injustice of restricted store hours; in particular, they came together in support of a six-day shopping week. But they were opposed by department and retail stores that did not benefit significantly from tourist expenditures. These latter operations pointed to the added costs that extended store hours generated.[44] Retailers whose clientele did not consist primarily of visitors contended that not everyone benefited from tourism and that the general interest of the community was being sacrificed to serve the interests of tourism-dependent businesses. In response to alderman Brent Murdoch's claim that the half-day closing was hindering the city's prosperity, Courtney Haddock, manager of the city's Woodward's department store, asserted that "the business you get on Wednesday is not worth the powder to blow it to hell."[45] Tom Denny, manager of Standard Furniture and a past president of the city's Chamber of Commerce, offered a more quantitative argument when he used provincial Department of Trade and Industry figures to assert that Wednesday afternoon shopping would put just $3 in the pockets of each of the city's merchants. After the additional operating costs of afternoon opening were factored in, abandoning the half-day closing was, in fact, unprofitable.[46] Denny's claim was clearly rather selective and somewhat facetious. Some store owners were certain to benefit more than others, and it was unlikely that tourist expenditures would be spread so widely across the city. But, of course, that was an important part of the story. Hence, Denny asserted, in a clever play on the usual pro-tourism rhetoric, that "what is good for the retail merchants is good for Victoria."[47] In defending supporters of the mid-week holiday, Denny bluntly asserted that "we are being no more anti-community minded than the real estate people and the banks who close all day Saturday."[48]

The divisions over tourism's impact were not based solely on careful calculations of where tourist dollars were going. During the 1920s and 1930s, some observers began to voice concerns that the city's single-minded determination to preserve its tourist business was placing the half-holiday in jeopardy and thereby threatening the community's social and cultural well-being. For A.J. Watson of the Bay department store, public debates about store hours in the mid-1920s boiled down to the question of whether tourists should be determining local bylaws.[49] In 1929, as the pro-tourism lobby pushed for expanded shopping hours, a spokesperson for local retail clerks reminded city council that longer hours came with a social cost for the clerks that could include "a discontented body" and the "break up [of] home life."[50] A 1936 letter to the *Times* from G.W. Robinson urged the city to place the clerks' welfare ahead of other concerns while challenging the Chamber of Commerce's perception that the half-day holiday threatened the city's tourist trade. Improved roads, he argued, held the key to expanding tourism, not longer store hours.[51]

Not surprisingly, as the pro-tourism lobby intensified its efforts in the 1940s and 1950s and embraced the expenditure imperative, the champions of local autonomy and the retail clerks' welfare responded in kind. In voicing his support for continued Wednesday closing, Reg Williams, president of the local Meat Retailers' Association, accepted that tourist expenditures were desirable but argued that the concerns and welfare of local residents must continue to be the city's first priority.[52] Furniture retailer Roy Denny concurred, though in a more forceful manner: "We live in the city, not the tourists. We should have things the way we like."[53] Peter MacEwen, leader of the local clerks' Five-Day Week Action Committee, which demanded the retention of Wednesday closing, offered a similar view by asking rhetorically, "What we would like to know is this – who is running the city – the tourist trade group or the city council?"[54]

During the 1940s and 1950s the *Colonist* newspaper asked similar questions in its editorials. Having acknowledged, in 1949, that "anything so firmly entrenched in the business life of the community as the weekly half-holiday cannot be disturbed without the strongest of reasons," the *Colonist* took its arguments a step further in 1951 by focusing directly on the welfare of the retail clerks. That clerks give up their weekly half-holiday, it argued, "would be a lot to ask of them merely for the convenience of tourists."[55] The following year the *Colonist* expressed frustration that no one had been able to reconcile the welfare of the local population with increased shopping opportunities for tourists. Recognizing that the city's store-hour regulations were undoubtedly hampering its tourism promotion efforts, the newspaper nevertheless insisted that the common half-holiday was worth preserving. The holiday, after all, provided a rare opportunity for communal recreation and allowed "one set afternoon" each week "so that friends may go places together" or "engage in organized sport and recreation." The welfare of retail clerks, the *Colonist* explained, was under threat, and the city as a whole had a moral duty to protect their interests. "These are the people who make up the 'we' who have to live in the city."[56]

Central to preserving the half-day holiday, then, was the defence of common leisure pursuits. In a reversal of Arthur Lineham's earlier arguments that a small number of clerks and merchants were putting their own needs ahead of the larger community, Harold Gray wrote to the *Daily Colonist* in 1953 castigating opponents of store-hour regulations for attempting to increase their profits by denying the city's retail clerks the opportunity "to enjoy together and with one another their weekly half-day holiday."[57] The abolition of the half-day holiday would mean that "groups would not be able to unite for sports or outings," argued retail clerk A.G. Kinnis. Rejecting a popular pro-tourist lobby proposal that retail clerks stagger their days off to suit the needs of their employers, Kinnis argued that "a staggered holiday system" would prevent workers from undertaking common recreational pursuits.[58] Fellow letter writer Alex McLeod Baird agreed, arguing that the Wednesday half-holiday had "grown to be a recognized day on which all store employees gather together and enjoy themselves collectively." Collective leisure, he argued, should not be allowed to fall victim to "the exploded wolf cry – 'Tourist.'"[59]

Like the pro-tourism lobby, those keen to defend store-hour restrictions were drawn from a wide range of backgrounds: employers, employees, civic officials, and consumers. They disputed claims that tourist dollars were spread evenly throughout the community and insisted that the social benefits – in particular common leisure time – that the community accrued through institutions such as the half-day

2.3 Like other shop employees, these members of the Spencer department store in Victoria required common leisure time in the 1920s in order to play cricket. Image F-05180 courtesy of the Royal BC Museum and Archives.

holiday should not be sacrificed to serve the interests of outsiders. Both sides were fully aware of Victoria's post-industrial reality, but both offered very different evaluations of tourism's role in addressing the city's economic challenges.

Moreover, both sides offered organic conceptions of community and put forward determined attempts to define community interests. The result sometimes pitted citizen against citizen and merchant against merchant depending on how one evaluated tourism's economic impact vis-à-vis the social and cultural influence of store-hour restrictions. Many factors led to the expansion of store hours in these two cities, but the concern to secure civic prosperity through tourism promotion was an important aspect of this development – albeit one that was more influential in Victoria than in Vancouver. In the end, the pro-tourism lobbies in both cities could be satisfied with the solutions

2.4 Other store clerks, such as those from the Dixi H. Ross Company grocery store, employed their limited common leisure time to pursue ... less wholesome activities at their staff picnics. Image F-06965 courtesy of the Royal BC Museum and Archives.

brokered in the 1950s, which eliminated Wednesday closing. But it is important to note the long-standing support for this institution and, in particular, the manner in which the local populations contested ideals of community welfare. Attempts to preserve desirable working conditions and opportunities for common leisure time consistently challenged increasingly dominant arguments regarding the need to protect the cities' economic well-being from the competition posed by other tourist destinations. As a result, the key dispute centred upon how best to reconcile the desires of tourists with those of the local inhabitants.

As the rhetoric employed by the pro-tourism lobbies suggests, many civic leaders in Victoria and Vancouver seemed to live in perpetual fear that outside competition would undermine and ultimately destroy the local economies for which they deemed themselves responsible. So they consistently argued that if the local community did not reduce or eliminate store-hour regulations, potential tourists would go elsewhere. In Vancouver, where tourism was an important but not central industry, such arguments often intersected with, and reinforced, broader concerns that store-hour restrictions were causing the city to lag behind North American trends. In June 1950, for example, a group of Vancouver retail merchants keen to eliminate the mid-week holiday openly emphasized the need to embrace a broader North American pattern. Vancouver, it argued, "is the only city of consequence on the North American Continent that is making a mid-week morgue of its business section by keeping its retail stores open only five days a week."[60] Four years later the group repeated its demands and, using much the same rhetoric, urged city council to allow the city to compete on a level playing field. City council, they hoped, would eliminate Wednesday closing and in doing so put Vancouver "in step with our neighbours, and in tune with our industrial progress."[61]

On the eve of Vancouver's June 1954 plebiscite on six-day shopping, the *Sun* published a front-page editorial titled "Let's Do Business Full-Time," in which it suggested that the upcoming vote would determine "whether we get rid of the old wartime custom of breaking the week into two parts separated by a dead day"; it hoped that voters would embrace this "chance to change over to modern merchandising practice." "This system works well in the other large cities on the continent," the *Sun* argued, explicitly connecting local bylaws to the notion that Vancouver deserved to be placed among the major cities of North America.[62]

The debate reached a crescendo on the eve of Vancouver's 1954 six-day shopping plebiscite. Explicit comparisons with trends elsewhere in North America were part of an ongoing debate in both cities about the extent to which local bylaws ought to conform to North American norms. Champions of store-hour deregulation consistently lamented that the two cities' restrictive closing rules hindered their ability to compete with, and be seen as, modern North American cities.[63] Conversely, supporters of the mid-week closing and other store-hour restrictions emphasized the drawbacks that other, less regulated cities faced or, less often, pointed to similar restrictions in other cities to suggest that BC's two largest centres were not all that unique.[64] This rhetorical battle evolved into a standoff, with opponents of local store-hour regulations reaching, whenever possible, for outside data to demonstrate the drawbacks of the local situation. The discussion remained at a rather abstract level, with supporters of local regulations dismissing the critics' data as irrelevant or at least incapable of substantiating a clear pattern that pointed the way to a happy balance between prosperity and social and cultural harmony. The extent to which Victoria and Vancouver "fit" into existing and emerging North American trends remained a consistent but not determining factor in the store-hour debates. Each city's "unique" situation could be a good thing or a bad thing depending on one's perspective on the store-hour issue. As the following chapter demonstrates, this debate over how best to enhance community prosperity while preserving community values also focused on the growing power of North American chain stores.

Chapter Three

Leverage: The Rhetoric and Reality of Chain-Store Dominance

Big department stores and chain stores are run by remote control by people who are merely investing their surplus money ... while the petitioners for these by-laws are men working in their own stores with their employees.

Victoria alderman Edward Williams, 1946[1]

Edward Williams was not alone in blaming chain stores for transforming his local community. In her 2004 study of shopping opportunities at English seaside resorts, Melanie Kay Smith lamented that the "arrival of ubiquitous chain stores" had "gradually resulted in the erosion of local character and distinctiveness, ironically, the very features that many destinations are so keen to promote."[2] In the American context, Gary Cross lays the blame for the decline of suburban leisure squarely at the feet of chain stores. While suburbs had initially offered escape from the hustle and bustle of American cities, he argues, they would eventually serve "less as lived-in spaces where kids roamed and adults traded tips on gardening and child care than as launching pads into the maze of freeway ramps, parking lots, and big box stores." Increased shopping hours, he emphasizes, played a key role in undermining "the ideal of the suburban weekend." "Chain discount stores and fast-food outlets," he notes, "used part-time employees to keep their facilities open during nights and weekends, times once jealously guarded for family and friends." And the impact on independent merchants was harsh: "self-employed storekeepers unwilling to forego their own social and family life became increasingly rare and thus less a force for limiting shop hours." Twenty-four-hour shopping, which followed on the heels of extended weekend store hours in the 1970s, marked, for

Cross, a poignant end to the long struggle to contain commerce and protect leisure time.[3]

This criticism of chains is not new. In the United States, anti-chain-store sentiment gained momentum after the First World War and crested during the late 1920s and early 1930s as independent merchants encouraged consumers to boycott "community-wrecking" chain stores and embarked on a "bitter legislative struggle" against the chains' growing influence through campaigns for state chain-tax laws. In 1928, in response to anti-chain-store organizations, which were created primarily in the southern and midwestern states, chain stores pooled their resources to create a National Chain Store Association, which attempted to deliver their side of the story in this public relations battle. As F.J. Harper explains, "the chains were widely accused, with varying degrees of justification, of paying low wages and working their employees excessive hours, maintaining inadequate deposits in local banks, refusing to support worthwhile civic projects and reducing opportunity by creating a 'nation of clerks.'" After the Second World War, "with the spirit of untrammeled free enterprise again in the ascendant, the militant independents finally abandoned the struggle," and anti-chain legislation was either repealed or increasingly ignored. To survive, independent merchants adopted some chain-store characteristics – for instance, pooling purchases and modernizing their stores – while striving to maintain what made them unique: "meeting local needs, *staying open at unsocial hours*, and providing the specialist service with which the centralized, uniform chains could not easily compete." Extending store hours, then, was one way that independent merchants attempted to ward off the chain stores in the United States.[4]

Canadian independent retailers faced a similar threat.[5] In Montreal, for example, small food retailers in the interwar period faced competition from "the new branches of large chains that had captured a substantial portion of the market during the 1920s." In response, Sylvie Taschereau explains, "associations of independent retailers urged their members as never before to spruce up their displays, to modernize their premises, and especially to streamline their management methods." To survive, these stores pursued a number of strategies, including maximizing the unpaid labour of family members, extending credit to preferred clients, delivering their products to customers' homes, "and remaining open well into the night."[6]

Not surprisingly, independent merchants resented the chains, especially department stores. As Donica Belisle notes, small shopkeepers proved "virulent critics ... who argued that department stores represented unfair competition. Labor leaders, meanwhile, condemned the stores' working conditions, and moralists decried the employment of women and the distribution of decadent advertising." In response, department stores turned to paternalism: "To combat critics' charges of employee exploitation, Eaton's, Simpson's, and the HBC offered among the best workplace benefits in the Dominion. By 1940 these included medical and retirement plans, life insurance, paid vacations, sports teams and facilities, summer camps, semiannual dinners and dances, and arts and leisure clubs." "Portraying stores' owners and executives as affectionate and fatherly overseers of employees, shoppers, and Canadians," Belisle concludes, helped these stores counter "charges of exploitation, greed, and materialism."[7]

Anti-chain-store activism declined in the United States during the 1950s and 1960s. Even so, chains remained central and controversial elements of postwar arguments about the nature of fair competition in the Canadian marketplace. Many observers viewed the battles over expanded store hours as contests between large chain stores and small, independent merchants.[8] For example, in the late 1960s the Retail Merchants' Association of Canada (RMA) contended that "small and medium-sized retailers and conventional outlets" favoured greater restrictions on store hours, while "discount" department and food stores favoured fewer restrictions. On this point the RMA encountered no argument from the National Retailers' Institute (NRI), a body of "junior department stores and discount department stores" that was affiliated with "chain and variety stores." The NRI, whose members included Woolworth, Kmart, and Zellers, opposed store-hour regulation while emphasizing that its "primary objective is to generate and maintain the maximum of shopping convenience for the consumer."[9]

Bruce Mallen and Ronald Rotenberg write that it was during the 1950s and 1960s that "the inherent issues between the small independent retailer and the larger shopping centers, department stores, and so on, came to a head."[10] As evidence, they point to a wide range of examples: the 1958 campaign by the Bay in Edmonton to abolish Wednesday afternoon closing and thereby secure a six-day shopping week and extended evening shopping; a 1959 campaign by small merchants and the local RMA in Saskatoon to secure greater store-hour restrictions in the face of a joint Chamber of Commerce and Urban Municipalities Association campaign to usher in evening shopping; the 1961 efforts by the Manitoba RMA to maintain existing closing legislation in the face of the growing influence of "discount department stores"; and the court challenge by the Rite-Way discount store in Peterborough, Ontario, that aimed to secure evening shopping.[11] Indeed, Mallen and Rotenberg note that in the early 1960s "a number of court battles across the country involved large department and discount stores which favoured unrestricted shopping hours and small retail merchants who wanted tighter control."[12]

The debates over store hours in Vancouver and Victoria took place amidst the rapid expansion of chain and department stores in Canada – a threatening development for many independent operators and one they vociferously protested. Local merchants throughout North America responded to the growing power of chain stores with public attacks on practices such as price-cutting and other forms of unfair competition.[13] To respond to charges like these, chain stores did their best to sell local communities on their positive qualities. In 1953, for example, B. & K. Economy Stores Ltd, a BC chain with twenty-three stores throughout the province, announced plans for a $400,000 expansion program for Greater Victoria and the community of Duncan to the north. Its general manager emphasized that "local labor and suppliers" would be used whenever possible and trumpeted the benefits that modern chain stores provided the shopping public. These chain-store "perks," the *Victoria Daily Colonist* reported, included large window areas for bright interiors, carrier service to cars in large parking lots, automatic turnstiles with "high-speed cash registers," and up-to-date refrigeration systems capable of consistently spraying "the produce with chilled water at regulated temperature."[14] On the occasion of grocery chain store Super-Valu's eighth anniversary in 1958, by which time it operated seventy-nine stores throughout BC, store representative Russell Norman celebrated the ascendency of chain stores. Chains delivered "greater efficiency for people to live better than ever before," he claimed. While the "old-style grocer had to have a high mark-up," chain stores offered discounted prices. Chain stores had also contributed to better food packaging that "lowered distribution costs." Moreover, he argued, through increased competition, food chain stores provided consumers with "a greater degree of cleanliness in the handling of all foodstuffs." Overall, he boasted, "the chain system" improved "quality control measures which benefit the consumer."[15]

As appealing as such a vision may have been for many local consumers, claims like these raised the ire of small independent store owners, many of whom viewed chain stores as a powerful and nefarious force determined to leverage any advantage they could – including expanded store hours – from their greater economies of scale. Indeed, for many proponents of store-hour regulations, chain stores were *the* chief villains in this dispute. They portrayed chains as the powerful lobby group most responsible for store-hour deregulation and denounced them as impersonal institutions largely controlled by outsiders who cared little for the welfare of local communities.

The rhetoric surrounding chain stores did not always reflect reality. Chain-store representatives participated in these debates, but not as consistently or as forcefully as these observers suggested. Moreover, in an increasingly competitive atmosphere, independent merchants pursued their economic self-interest as best they could – including, at times, by campaigning for expanded store hours. An examination of the ways in which critics characterized chain and department stores in these debates and of the more complicated manner in which they were actually involved in the process of store-hour deregulation can tell us a great deal about the nature of postwar capitalism and political culture. Chains sought to leverage their economies of scale and made much of their modern merchandising capacity; meanwhile, smaller independent retailers offered an equally selective self-portrait – one that was deeply populist and that emphasized the small shopkeepers' roots in the local community.

The Rhetoric

Chains were not always the prime targets of the pro-regulation lobby in the store-hour dispute. During the interwar period and the Second World War, chain stores encountered very few complaints.[16] However, as debates over store-hour regulations increased in scope after the Second World War, the spectre of chain stores became a popular reference point in both Vancouver and Victoria. The Eaton's takeover of local Spencer's department stores in 1948, and the construction of shopping centres featuring national chains in suburban areas, undoubtedly accounted for a good deal of this angst.

Some critics contended that chains were the leading force behind campaigns to eliminate local store-hour bylaws. Often these critics contrasted their own "insider" status with the external influence of "outsider" chains. Central to this rhetoric was a populist ideal that was both regionalist and nationalist in its outlook and that identified chains with eastern Canada and the United States. The result was a powerful chorus of voices in both cities that understood chain and department stores as having been central players in the postwar deregulation of store hours.

For Victoria alderman Edward Williams, for example, municipal bylaws were necessary to protect local interests from externally controlled chain stores that were intent on doing away with store-hour restrictions. In 1946, Williams railed against large chain and department stores, whose owners were not performing any of the actual sales work and were not local residents: "They are now out playing golf or they are in San Francisco or Timbuctoo [sic]."[17] He championed instead "our local man, who has invested his money, time and work here and who works in his own store."[18] These people, Williams claimed, supported store-hour restrictions: "We are dealing today with the big man squeezing out the little man."[19] The following year, George Johnston of Vancouver's Retail Merchant Employees' Union similarly accused large "outside" chains of working in opposition to local shops:[20] "They are owned by people who live outside the province and are not interested in the health and welfare of their employees."[21]

Often, such rhetoric blamed externally controlled chain stores for the ongoing campaigns to eliminate Wednesday closing and promote six-day shopping. Such claims were particularly widespread in Vancouver.[22] Bert Price, an outspoken local Social Credit MLA, had no doubts as to who would benefit from a six-day shopping week: "large eastern and American chains who are bent on eliminating their smaller competitors" and that cared little for local retail clerks.[23] Price's evaluation of six-day shopping supporters fit well with Social Credit populism.[24] Independent store owner Alex Warner concurred by focusing his anger on "eastern-owned department stores" in Vancouver that sought to "force the whole city to open six days a week."[25] Not surprisingly, Vancouver's self-proclaimed "Save the Wednesday" committee was equally blunt: "the big Eastern and American chain interests want a longer six-day shopping week to break down and demoralize any form of business and work hours."[26]

Similar arguments accused chain stores of leading the campaigns for expanded evening shopping, and, later on, of promoting wide-open store hours. In 1952, for example, as Vancouver moved towards Friday evening sales, men's clothier A.J. Warner objected to the growing influence of Safeway.[27] In a 1953 letter to the *Victoria Colonist*, Alex MacLeod Baird similarly argued that the "opening on Friday evenings of big chain stores is simply the narrow wedge which would gradually do away with our privileges, were it not for our government law."[28] When

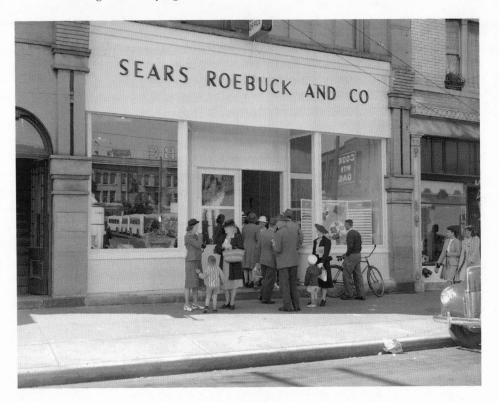

North Vancouver City Council approved "around the clock" meat sales in 1956, it faced opposition from a group of independent butchers, who accused chain stores of influencing the council and aiming to put them out of business.[29] In 1957, Bert Price spoke out again, arguing that "chain stores and outside capital" were the only merchandising interests pushing for wide-open shopping hours.[30]

In December 1964 the *Province* reported that the Vancouver branch of the RMA was now convinced that the growing momentum towards wide-open hours could soon lead to the Lower Mainland becoming a "shoddy duplicate of Eastern Canadian and American style Arab bazaars" and "retail jungles" such as Toronto and Chicago.[31] In a strongly worded letter opposing wide-open store hours in Vancouver, some local retailers demanded that "before city council listen [*sic*] to paid voices of certain prominent retail chains," it should "make some

3.1 and 3.2 (opposite and above) Line-ups outside the Sears, Roebuck and Company store on Pandora Street (1947), and the crowded floor inside the Bay store on Douglas Street (ca. 1936) sent shivers down the spines of many independent merchants in Victoria. Image I-01744 (Sears) courtesy of the Royal BC Museum and Archives. Image M07647 (the Bay) courtesy of the City of Victoria Archives.

attempt to listen to the people concerned[,] for after all the shouting dies down ... we are the people who live here and we do vote."[32]

Even observers who did not employ such blunt anti-chain rhetoric concluded that the actions of chain stores had at least indirectly led to the elimination of local bylaws. In 1956, when a new Vancouver bylaw permitted expanded evening shopping, clothier Fred Asher summed up the general feeling of small retailers: "If the big stores open, we probably all will. It's the big ones that will bring the traffic downtown. If the traffic's here, we'll all be open to get our share."[33] A year earlier, when rumour had it that Simpsons-Sears was considering opening a store in Saanich, just north of Victoria, members of the Victoria Chamber of Commerce retail merchants' group admitted that such a development could well force Victoria merchants to rethink their own store hours.[34] Retail Clerks Union leader John Aubry noted this concern when he argued that the six-day issue had arisen in response to the Sears announcement: "Victoria owners don't want a six-day week. But they are frightened because this new store will be open for six days a week and until 9 p.m. every day."[35] As Victoria and Vancouver relaxed shopping restrictions and embraced wide-open Monday-to-Saturday shopping, many critics placed the blame squarely at the feet of chain stores.[36]

Looking back on the long-running saga in 1968, Victoria's city clerk, F.M. Waller, recalled that "there were two factions, the department and other large stores wished wide-open hours and the smaller stores wished them closed in the evenings and one afternoon a week."[37] This understanding of the dispute fit well with the populist rhetoric that contrasted the identity and interests of local independent merchants with those of chain stores and found the latter guilty of leading the assault on store-hour restrictions. But was this an accurate understanding of the role of chain stores and external capital? Just how central were chain and department stores to the deregulation of store hours, and to what extent was the process of deregulation led by outsiders against the interests of local communities?

The Reality

Chain stores' activities and campaigns were certainly a factor in store-hour deregulation. But chains did not play the central role that some observers suggested. Sometimes large, externally controlled chains did push openly for store-hour deregulation. But more often chain stores took a measured approach to expanding store hours. On a number of occasions, in fact, chain stores were *not* the leading voice calling for an end to store-hour regulations. And chain stores could be seen at times lending their considerable muscle to campaigns aimed at *preserving* store-hour restrictions while small local independent stores took the lead in calling for expanded shopping hours. As Steven High has emphasized, the tendency to contrast capital with community can obscure as much as it reveals, and in the case of these debates over local store hours a more complex dynamic was at play.[38]

To be sure, there is tangible evidence that chain stores opposed a number of store-hour restrictions. Among the large chains, Safeway was the most forceful in its campaigns for expanded store hours, not only in Vancouver and Victoria but in smaller BC communities as well, like Vernon, Kamloops, and Chilliwack. The US-based grocer often launched court challenges that aimed to weaken or eliminate existing store-hour bylaws.[39] In September 1946, for example, Safeway successfully challenged the technical requirements of a petition by Victoria butchers for all-day closing, and in 1956 it played a leading role in Vancouver when grocery chains squared off against independent butchers on the issue of Friday evening meat sales.[40] These were concrete instances of an externally controlled chain seeking to expand local store hours.

Similarly, evidence of chain stores' support for six-day shopping is not hard to come by. In a March 1947 advertisement in the *Vancouver Daily Province*, the Bay noted that as an organization it favoured a five-day week for staff but a six-day shopping week "so that both customers and our staff may enjoy maximum benefits as to shopping and as to leisure hours."[41] In 1954 both the Bay and Eaton's in Vancouver endorsed the six-day business week,[42] with Eaton's placing an advertisement in the *Vancouver Sun* to stress the benefits of six-day shopping for customers, employees, and merchants.[43] Furthermore, when Wednesday opening became an option for specific classes of stores in Vancouver, the department store petition quickly amassed a 70 per cent majority downtown and a 60 per cent majority in the suburbs.[44] Simpsons-Sears also seems to have been at the centre of the campaign for six-day shopping in Burnaby.[45]

Not surprisingly, in some contexts chains eagerly and forcefully embraced expanded evening hours. In the aftermath of Vancouver's decision to allow certain classes of stores to remain open until 9 p.m. on Fridays, for example, four major grocery chains found themselves united against the butchers' union. The chains sought permission to sell meat on Friday nights, a move opposed by the Amalgamated Meat Cutters.[46] To support their campaign, Safeway and Super-Valu stores in Vancouver secured more than 21,000 names on a petition in favour of selling fresh meat on Friday nights.[47] Similarly, in April 1958 the manager of the Bay in Victoria saluted the merits of Friday evening shopping and boasted that Friday nights were his busiest time of the week.[48]

By the 1960s some large, externally controlled chain stores could be heard enthusiastically supporting wide-open store hours. In 1962,

G. Allan Burton of Toronto, vice-president and managing director of Simpsons-Sears, used his position on a panel at a Canadian Chamber of Commerce meeting in Vancouver to rail against antiquated store hours that prevented retailers from maximizing the use of their assets and demanded that stores be permitted to remain open as long as the customer wanted.[49] Both Eaton's and the Bay supported a 1967 proposal for wide-open hours in Vancouver.[50] In short, there is some truth to the argument that chain stores supported measures such as six-day shopping, evening shopping, and wide-open store hours.

But the position of chain stores also reflected some ambivalence. While these stores often boasted larger staffs than their independent competitors, the complexities and costs involved in revising work schedules to take advantage of additional shopping hours meant that abandoning store-hour restrictions had potential benefits *and* drawbacks.[51] In these situations some chain stores determined that they could maximize their profits by adhering to, and supporting, store-hour restrictions. Thus in July 1951 the Bay set a decidedly conservative tone in its first "definite statement" regarding Wednesday closing. Closing hours should be studied by a responsible group, it argued, in order to produce a policy to standardize hours throughout Greater Vancouver. This standardization "would be in the best interest of customers, employees and the businesses concerned."[52] In 1953, as residents of Victoria debated whether to continue with half-day closing, Allan Leith of Eaton's argued that the half-holiday was a fair compromise between traders and tourists and encouraged the city to stick to the current closing bylaw.[53] That same year Courtney Haddock of Woodward's reiterated his support for all-day Wednesday closing and urged large and small stores in Victoria to work out a common policy that acknowledged their different needs.[54] As late as 1966, while some chains eagerly embraced the "wide open" era, two of Victoria's three largest downtown merchandisers, Standard Furniture and the Bay, continued to support uniform hours for the area.[55]

Moreover, some chain stores viewed expanded store hours simply as an opportunity to create a level playing field. In September 1946, for example, representatives from David Spencer Ltd and the Bay in Victoria indicated that they wished to remain open Wednesday morning; however, if they were not permitted to do so they would accept that decision so long as all competing stores were also forced to close.[56] In 1960, Super-Valu championed wide-open hours on the grounds that it closed its doors on Monday afternoons in Esquimalt but many smaller stores did not.[57] Instead of spearheading a campaign to expand store hours, Super-Valu argued that it was simply playing "catch up" with small, local retailers.

Furthermore, chains did not necessarily rush to discard Wednesday closing. For instance, in July 1954, with six-day shopping now permitted in Vancouver, the Bay and Eaton's opted to open on Wednesdays as quickly as possible, while two smaller chains, Forst's and Wosk's, remained closed and Woodward's deferred its decision. According to Ed Forst, his stores would not switch until the six-day week was widespread, explaining that "it would not be fair ... for us to open all our departments while private stores selling similar goods were forced to stay closed."[58] In 1955 a number of chain outlets in Vancouver entered into a "gentleman's agreement" with independent stores to return to Wednesday closing. Barrington Clothing, Dick's Ltd, Dunn's Regent Tailors, Bill Smith Ltd, Tip Top Tailors, and Rogers Jewelers, all in the West Hastings area, agreed to close on Wednesdays, arguing that they were only doing five days' worth of business in a six-day week and that their arrangement would allow them to have a full complement of staff on hand during business hours.[59] Even as Victoria moved towards six-day shopping, the Woodward's on Douglas Street joined with five downtown furniture stores and a radio store in adopting all-day Wednesday closing.[60] Ed Forst's altruism may have informed such "gentlemen's agreements," but so did a desire to minimize operating costs and maximize profits.

Similarly, some chains hesitated to embrace extended evening hours. In 1953, when rumours circulated in Victoria that chain grocery stores had proposed opening until 9 p.m. on Tuesday and Friday evenings, one chain manager acknowledged that Friday evening opening was potentially beneficial but warned that an additional night would create "too big a staffing problem."[61] In 1958, as Victoria merchants scrambled to deal with the reality of wide-open hours, and some classes of shops met to agree on common closing times, even grocery chain stores had no immediate plans to expand their hours of operation.[62] A similar situation arose in Vancouver in 1956. When the city council passed a bylaw allowing stores to stay open until 9 p.m. Fridays and 6 p.m. (instead of the previous 5:30 p.m.) on other weekdays, the large chain stores did not immediately embrace these new selling opportunities. A spokesperson for the Bay noted that employees had family obligations that would be disrupted if the store stayed open until 6 p.m. In fact, it was a local chain, Forst's, rather than an externally controlled one, that took the lead and planned to immediately open all seven of its stores on Friday evenings.[63] In explaining that the Bay would consider late closing in the fall, a spokesperson noted that evening shopping in Calgary and Edmonton had proven very successful, but that did not guarantee similar success in Vancouver: "Every city is somewhat different. You have to experiment with it to find out what the people want."[64] As late as 1965, when councillors in Richmond, just south of Vancouver, approved a bylaw permitting wide-open shopping hours, Sam Redford, a spokesperson for the local Safeway store, objected, arguing that wide-open shopping hours were not economical and would not improve customer service or increase employment.[65] Hence chain stores showed considerable hesitation and exercised a good deal of caution when it came to capitalizing on store-hour deregulation.

Perhaps more important, large chain stores did not always lead campaigns to reduce or eliminate store-hour restrictions. In 1950, for example, when 207 Vancouver firms signed a petition endorsing the six-day shopping and five-day workweek as a solution to the city's ongoing dispute over Wednesday closing, none of Vancouver's three main department stores endorsed the campaign.[66] In 1954 two separate letters to the editor of the *Vancouver Sun* challenged the assumption that chain stores were leading the charge against Wednesday closing. N.H. Singer, claiming to represent two-thirds of downtown retailers, argued that it was not just easterners and Americans but a cross-section of retail businesses that sought expanded store hours.[67] The second letter, from "Independent Merchant," also argued that it was not easterners but a majority of downtown stores that supported six-day shopping.

"Independent Merchant" suggested that chain stores unanimously supported six-day shopping because of their experience in other cities; but this writer also argued that they were a small minority of supporters in Vancouver. As a store owner with thirty years' experience here and in the United States, "Independent Merchant" claimed to be losing money to competitors and noted that being allowed to open on Wednesdays would increase profits, which could result in "larger bonuses to our staff." "More business in the retail stores m[e]ans more money in circulation, more employment and greater prosperity for everyone."[68] In 1957 Burnaby's new early-closing bylaw was ignored by smaller stores and obeyed only by larger operations.[69] And of course, as we saw in chapter 2, independent merchants who depended on the tourist trade were particularly active in pressing for six-day shopping, if only for the summer months.[70] So while some chains were certainly hostile to store-hour restrictions, they were not alone. Independent merchants also found such regulation to be frustrating.

But perhaps most surprising is that on many occasions, chain stores openly *supported* store-hour restrictions. The Woodward's chain was particularly vociferous in its support for Wednesday closing. In 1946 employees from two Vancouver department store chains, Woodward's and David Spencer, organized a 25,000 name petition (at the time the largest ever presented in Vancouver) urging Vancouver City Council to preserve Wednesday closing.[71] The following year the *Vancouver Sun* reported that Woodward's was the strongest supporter of full-day closing. The company opposed as impractical – a "pipe dream" – the suggestion that staff holidays be staggered so that employees work five days out of a six-day shopping week. "We have 2000 employees at Woodward's," the store's general superintendent explained. "Under a staggered scheme 400 would be off each day; those in key positions could not be spared and when sickness, absenteeism and holidays are considered the whole scheme becomes absurd." Besides, he argued, working people had no difficulty spending all of their wages in the five days available at present.[72]

In 1953 both Woodward's and Forst's Ltd supported a petition signed by forty-five leading Vancouver retailers against allowing a plebiscite that could usher in six-day shopping.[73] Alex Forst, vice-chairman of the Save the Wednesday campaign, remained a staunch advocate of five-day shopping.[74] In the run-up to the city's plebiscite on six-day shopping in 1954, Woodward's placed an ad in the *Province* urging Vancouverites to vote against the proposal "because we believe in the 5-day week for our employees and guarantee it by staying closed one full day each week in all of our stores" (see Figure 3.3). It boasted that it practised Wednesday store closing at its stores in Vancouver, Edmonton, New Westminster, Port Alberni, and North Vancouver.[75] Similarly, an ad by Forst's, which it claimed was "inserted on behalf of thousands of the ordinary men and women who want to keep decent working conditions here," also called upon citizens to vote "no" in the plebiscite: "Vancouver is the only city on this continent where merchants voluntarily gave their employees a 5-day, 40-hour work week and guaranteed it with a 5-day business week. It has proven its worth in friendly relations between clerks and their employers and in lower retail prices to the public."[76]

As late as 1956 the Woodward's branch in Victoria continued to oppose the six-day week and was reported to be considering moving

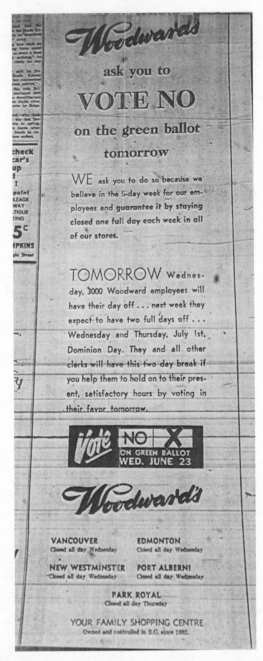

3.3 In the lead up to Vancouver's 1954 plebiscite on six-day shopping, Woodward's urged the public to reject six-day shopping. *Vancouver Daily Province*, 22 June 1954, 9.

towards a five-day week rather than the current five-and-a-half-day scenario.[77] The following year Woodward's opposed a proposal for extended evening shopping in Vancouver for the month of December on the grounds that it was bad for business and for its employees. Extended evening hours, it argued, made for less palatable working conditions and would "also curtail the family and social life of every retail employee in the city." In terms of the company's economic bottom line, extended evening hours would lead to higher prices as costs increased but "aggregate sales" did not.[78] Both paternalism and profit-seeking informed these decisions.

The Woodward's chain's consistent opposition to six-day shopping produced an intriguing backlash in 1969. When the company announced its opposition to wide-open shopping hours, one dissenting employee wrote directly to City Hall. "A Woodwards Employee" suggested that the store's employees "had practically no alternative but to sign the petition and telegram" that store management had organized ... Heres [sic] hoping we have extended hours, as it will mean more work for all of us, which would benefit everybody."[79] Here, perhaps, was the ultimate case of the little guy sticking up for store-hour deregulation against one of the region's most powerful chains. While some chains forcefully argued for the elimination of store-hour restrictions, others acted much more cautiously and even championed those same restrictions. Woodward's, it appears, had done the math and determined that regulators should restrict store hours. But from the employee's point of view, expanded shopping hours meant additional opportunities to earn wages.

While many observers saw the preservation of store-hour restrictions to be absolutely necessary for the survival of small, independent local merchants,[80] others argued that increased opening hours were necessary for them to survive. In 1950, as Victoria City Council prepared to repeal a section of the early closing bylaw that prevented small grocery stores from staying open beyond 6 p.m., alderman Waldo Skillings approved, noting that because smaller merchants were unable to purchase stocks in large quantities they should be allowed the opportunity to sell goods after 6 p.m.[81] Victoria's William Palmer, president of the Independent Merchants' Co-operative Association, offered a similar rationale: staying open in the evenings and on holidays was the only way to survive against competition from supermarkets.[82]

In a letter to the *Colonist*, Mrs Alice Colclough argued against store-hour restrictions on the grounds that they negatively affected small stores. Restrictions strike "against the livelihoods of family grocery owners who are such a help to their community," she asserted.[83] Victoria city lawyer Robert Harvey noted that department store managers at chains such as Woodward's received their salaries regardless of how long the store remained open or how much business was done. The "little man," conversely, depended on extended shopping hours and increasing business to earn a living.[84]

Victoria alderman Brent Murdoch pointed out that opposition to Wednesday opening came from some of the bigger stores: "They themselves do not want to stay open. But they don't want to see the smaller merchants getting any advantage at all."[85] In a revealing reversal of the usual pattern, Conway Parrott, chairman of the Victoria Chamber of Commerce's Tourist Trade Group, and a leading voice in favour of six-day shopping, argued that the opposition to the six-day week from the larger department store chains was the result of policies directed from head offices.[86] Store-hour restrictions, such arguments held, were hindering local independent entrepreneurs and negating one of the few advantages that small business could draw upon vis-à-vis larger corporations: a flexible approach to staff scheduling. Although their actions were not a central focus of the rhetorical flourishes that fanned the store-hour debates, a considerable number of small and independent merchants proved to be keen supporters of store-hour deregulation.

~

Faced with intensifying competition after the Second World War, small merchants and larger corporations responded as best they could. Aware of the importance of public relations, chain stores emphasized their modern accessories and the benefits of economies of scale. Independent operators publicized their "personal" service and their roots in the local community. It was not surprising, then, that many independent merchants and their supporters drew a direct link between chain-store expansion and the growing pressure for store-hour deregulation. But the reality of the situation was rather more complex than one might expect: chains did not always oppose store-hour restrictions, and small, independent operators did not necessarily yearn to protect those regulations. Instead, businesses (large and small, local and externally controlled) sought whatever leverage they could during a particular economic moment and appealed to politicians and the public with the argument that their economic interests and the general interests of local consumers and the community in general were one and the same.

The deregulation of store hours in Vancouver and Victoria was not simply the story of chain stores forcing longer hours on independent merchants. Not until the mid-1950s, when a broader shift in community perceptions on the issue occurred, did most chains formally oppose Wednesday closing and champion extended evening shopping. While it is tempting to ascribe to chains a pivotal role in determining the result of the store-hour debates, it is important to differentiate between the rhetoric and the reality. Chains that were determined to reduce or eliminate store-hour restrictions were important actors in this play, but they shared the stage with other, equally prominent allies, including independent merchants and even some retail employee organizations. And, just as important, their actions were resisted by a number of actors – including other chain stores. The business culture in Vancouver and Victoria was complex and fluid. Divisions could emerge between small and larger operators, but also (as we saw in chapter 2) between tourist and non–tourist-related operations, regardless of scale. That a powerful anti-chain-store rhetoric often overshadowed this complexity speaks to the significance of entrepreneurial populism in postwar political culture and the extent to which the binary opposition of insiders and outsiders consistently dominated evaluations of consumerism's impact.

Rhetorical flourishes often cited chain stores as the key force undermining store-hour restrictions. But the store-hour debates were comprised of a more complex reality in which businesses, big and small, local and external, attempted to leverage their particular characteristics as best they could in an increasingly competitive climate. As the following chapter demonstrates, the tendency to construct politically useful representations of chain stores was paralleled in the store-hour debates by a tendency to produce similarly selective representations of women – both as consumers and as store employees.

Chapter Four

Morality: Women, Families, and Consumer Convenience

Many mothers are employed part time in the stores and it has been proved by the recent city survey that juvenile delinquents come from homes where the mother works.

John Nicol, Retail Food and Drug Clerks' Union, 1966[1]

The family that shops together stays together.

Leslie Passmore, Saanich councillor, 1966[2]

John Nicol championed store-hour restrictions, and evening closing in particular, as a moral imperative that would help protect women from unpalatable working conditions and dissuade their children from wayward behaviour. Leslie Passmore, conversely, saw store-hour restrictions as an unnecessary regulatory burden that restricted parents' quality time with their children. Both men were appealing to their community's sense of duty to protect women and the institution of the family. Their statements highlight the fact that disagreements over the potential impact of extending shopping hours, while very much focused on the issue of consumer convenience, were not solely economic in nature; they were also infused with moral arguments.

The economic arguments examined in the preceding chapters on tourism and chain stores involved a moral dimension, just as moral concerns infused the disagreements over regulation, ideology, and religion that are examined in the chapters that follow. But participants in the store-hour debates dealt with a number of related issues explicitly as moral concerns. This chapter focuses primarily, but not exclusively, on the role of women: as retail clerks, guardians of the family, and consumers. References to morality certainly informed the arguments put forward regarding men who occupied similar roles. Complaints about the working conditions of male clerks, for example, or about the behaviour or motivations of male merchants, could sometimes call into question the moral righteousness of those involved. But the place of women in these debates was more highly politicized than that of men and centred on three issues: women's welfare, family well-being, and consumer convenience. While some observers keenly calculated the economic costs and benefits of providing consumers greater access to goods and services, others were equally determined to focus on the social and cultural costs of potential changes to shopping hours. As a result, these debates about the nature of consumerism focused intently on women's agency, family life, and competing conceptions of convenience.

That debates about working conditions and shopping were gendered is not surprising. Many historians have noted that changing ideals of masculinity and femininity have shaped popular perceptions of both labour and consumption.[3] William Leach notes, for example, that in the United States "as early as the 1840s and 1850s, especially in the urban centers, shopping had become a woman's job, reflecting the gender differentiation of roles that resulted from the separation of workplace and home and that was supported by the rise of wage and salaried male labor."[4]

Also, the task of serving consumers was falling increasingly to women.[5] At the beginning of the twentieth century in the United States, "women constituted a rapidly growing segment of the clerical realm." Indeed, the pace and scope of the transformation, or feminization, of clerical work in the United States is breathtaking. In 1870, of that country's 80,000 clerical workers, only 3 per cent were women; by 1920 the United States boasted around 3 million clerical workers, 45 per cent of whom were women.[6] The pattern in Canada was similar. In 1891, Donica Belisle notes, "only 10 percent of the sales and clerical workforce was female." By 1921 that number had increased to 33 per cent and by 1941 it had reached 41 per cent.[7] Women's participation in the paid labour force expanded dramatically in the 1950s and 1960s, a period that also witnessed an expansion in part-time employment – positions in the retail sector that helped facilitate expanded store hours.

Internationally, reform movements paid close attention to the situation facing female clerks. The plight of female shop assistants, or clerks, was a central concern for those involved in early closing movements.

Reflecting back on the history of Britain's Early Closing Association in 1931, an association secretary told a House of Commons committee of "its 'long and bitter struggle in educating the public against their bad habits of late shopping,' and of the organization of 'Women's Early Shopping Leagues' to arouse 'the conscience of women as to the gravity of endangering the health of their own sex, and especially that of the mothers of the future generation.'"[8] In the 1880s a Royal Commission in the Australian colony of Victoria "took considerable evidence from medical practitioners ... on the effects of long hours on the health of shop assistants." "Almost without exception," Michael Quinlan and Miles Goodwin explain, "these medical witnesses pointed to serious consequences, including exhaustion/fatigue, digestive disorders, neuralgia, minor glandular enlargements and the use of stimulants. Particular concern was expressed for the health of saleswomen and young workers, as well as the excessive use of gas lighting in shops." In its report, "the commission found the medical evidence alone provided a compelling case for restrictive legislation."[9] Women too could be centrally involved in campaigns for early closing. Australian female shop assistants, for example, played a key role in securing the Victorian Factories and Shops Act of 1896.[10]

In his comparative study of Minnesota and New Zealand, Evan Roberts notes that the campaign for shorter retail hours featured a tension between the interests of women as either consumers or workers as well as a tension between consuming either time or money.[11] Similar tensions emerged in British Columbia as public debate focused directly on the plight of female retail clerks and the female clients they served. Over the course of the store-hour debates in Victoria and Vancouver, the public's concern shifted from the plight of female store clerks to the needs of female shoppers. What remained consistent was the tendency for observers to construct women as victims of the status quo. Supporters of store-hour regulations emphasized the ameliorative effect of limited hours on overworked and downtrodden female retail employees. Opponents of store-hour restrictions argued that these unnecessary laws were causing no end of frustration and hardship for the cities' housewives. Both female clerks and female shoppers appeared in the press as damsels in distress requiring either more or less government regulation to improve their situation – a development that belied women's complex assessments of the benefits and costs of consumer convenience.

4.1 Supporters of store-hour restrictions lamented the plight of female clerks forced to endure long hours standing behind counters such as this one at Cunningham's Drug Store in Victoria. Image I-00915 courtesy of the Royal BC Museum and Archives.

Symbolic Women and Fragile Families

Early in the twentieth century, sympathy for female workers was a central component of the successful drive to secure the half-holiday in Victoria. Once it had been secured, the plight of female clerks retained a symbolic significance. Even the seemingly prosaic question of whether retail clerks should enjoy the half-holiday on a Saturday or a Wednesday was infused with gendered ideals about workplace stamina and social expectations. Among the most determined champions of Victoria's female clerks was Montana Rowlands, who wrote a lengthy and passionate submission to the *Victoria Daily Colonist* in 1916.[12] Wishing to "speak for the girls – especially those employed in the retail stores," Rowlands argued that female clerks did not just desire a half-holiday, they *needed* one. "If anyone doubts how much the girls need this holi-day," Rowlands taunted the newspaper's male readership, "let him try standing on his feet all day in some small space."[13] But it was not just the demands of the job that left female store clerks in need of the half-holiday; low wages combined with their six-day work week to deny them enough time to complete their domestic chores – tasks that Row-lands reminded readers were enmeshed in society's gendered expecta-tions regarding women's appearance and comportment. This situation was particularly galling for Rowlands, given that women lacked the vote: "I suppose I must make my appeal to the masculine mind alone," Rowlands lamented,

> since in British Columbia women have no voice in the things which greatly concerns [*sic*] them. Now, Mr. Masculine Person, how would you like to get up on your only day of rest and wash your hair (long hair takes a long time to shampoo, you know), do up your collars, cuffs, and blouses (for your employer expects you to appear spic and span always), sew on your buttons, mend your stockings, and, perhaps, make yourself a new blouse and corset cover, for, of course, you can't afford a dressmaker when you're getting only $7 a week. After doing all these things, and several more I don't remember just now, would you feel like going to church, or getting out for the air and sunshine you need? [14]

For Rowlands, this situation necessitated a Saturday half-holiday. This was preferable to the Wednesday alternative, she explained, because, combined with the full-day Sunday holiday, it allowed time for excur-sions out of town. Moreover, a Saturday half-holiday facilitated rec-reational activities because the retail clerks would be able to join up with employees in other fields of work who already enjoyed a Saturday afternoon off and devote this time to common recreation and sport. The half-day holiday, Rowlands argued, provided a workable solution to an unbearable situation in which female clerks found themselves increas-ingly exhausted. Rest and the opportunity for leisure, she explained, would revitalize retail clerks and allow them to better cope with the demands of their jobs.[15]

That same year a self-identified "Retail Clerk's Wife" wrote to the *Victoria Daily Times* expressing concerns about the low wages and dif-ficult working conditions faced by both male and female retail clerks. But she was primarily concerned about highlighting the negative effects that clerks' hours had on the male clerks' wives. "How about the wives of the married clerks?" she asked. "How do they manage to do their shopping, seeing that their husbands are working all the time the stores are open?" Sympathy, and practical solutions, must be extended "to the clerks' wives waiting at home in loneliness … until the early hours of Sunday morning for their husbands to arrive home, tired right out."[16]

While some female readers likely identified with her concerns, by no means did women address this issue with a united voice. The letter from "Retail Clerk's Wife" received a sharp rebuke from someone writing under the name "Workingman's Wife." Hoping to convince the newspaper's readers that a Wednesday half-holiday was a necessary alternative to closing stores on Saturdays, which were generally busier trading days, "Workingman's Wife" pulled no punches in her analysis. She admitted that she had not thought very much about lonely clerks' wives waiting home alone until the early hours of Sunday as a result of their husbands having to work a full day on Saturdays, simply because she had assumed that exhausted clerks "would be glad to go home and rest" immediately after work. Hence, she suggested, "it might be well for 'A Retail Clerk's Wife' to inquire where her husband spends his time between 9.30 p.m. Saturday and the early hours of Sunday morning. She may then get a better understanding as to the cause of his physical and mental exhaustion."[17]

Not content to question the ability of "A Retail Clerk's Wife" to keep track of her husband, "Workingman's Wife" attacked the husband's masculinity directly. Addressing his wife's lament that retail clerks were overworked, she countered mercilessly: "Unless your husband suffers from ricketts he will not receive any permanent injury from a working week of even 57 hours let alone 52 hours." Like other working-class participants in these debates, "Workingman's Wife" considered shopping itself to be a pleasurable activity, opportunities for which should not be curtailed without just cause: "If I thought that the pleasure and convenience we gain from Saturday's shopping worked a real hardship upon any man or woman I would be the first to stop it at any cost to myself."[18] Consumer convenience, in her mind, did not cause undue harm to the clerks and their families.

In 1918 Victoria opted for Wednesday, rather than Saturday, closing.[19] But the concern for female clerks' welfare remained prominent. In 1923 veteran retail clerk Caleb Hadland, then employed as a driver for the Acton Bros. grocery, urged his fellow Victorians not to be swayed by Chamber of Commerce rhetoric attributing the city's declining business fortunes to the half-day holiday. Declining consumer demand, rather than store-hour restrictions, Hadland argued, was to blame for the current recession. Half-holidays made it easier for clerks to stand for long periods of time, he continued: "Twelve years ago nearly all clerks in stores were men; now they are largely young women and growing girls who need the thoughtful consideration of employers, city councils and legislatures in order that we may have healthy future citizens and present contentment. We can't judge everything from the standpoint of the almighty dollar."[20] That women experienced challenging workplace conditions made the preservation of the half-holiday desirable. That women were responsible for the nation's reproductive future made it imperative.[21]

After the Second World War, interventions from women such as Rowlands, "Retail Clerk's Wife," and "Workingman's Wife" appeared less frequently in the press. More often it was men such as Hadland who spoke and wrote publicly about the plight of female clerks.[22] Moreover, in the postwar era, the reaction when female clerks showed the temerity to publicly express their views on such matters could be less than hospitable. In January 1947, for example, a group of twenty female clerks in Vancouver launched a petition against what they feared might become a six-day workweek and urged city council to preserve all-day Wednesday closing.[23] The following month they stepped up their campaign by standing in front of retail stores that were open on Wednesdays and collecting signatures for their petition. Mrs Anne Peterson, who organized the initiative, slyly responded to accusations that these women were picketing illegally by countering that the fifty to one hundred clerks were simply collecting signatures for their petition and were not officially organized. Organized or not, the campaign was not without incident: one "girl" was pushed off a sidewalk and into a gutter by an angry store proprietor.[24] A few months later, the *Sun* reported, the female clerks changed tactics: a delegation of local clerks visited City Hall and "made action against the all-day closing plan even more difficult for aldermen by lining up seven chic retail salesgirls, each wearing a fragrant gardenia corsage."[25] In this situation the female clerks' public campaign to draw support for their cause was reimagined by the apparently discomfited newspaper reporter as a more palatable sexual contest of wills.

Seemingly more acceptable were interventions by male merchants, who increasingly recognized female clerks' double-duty as employees and wives. Merchants increasingly incorporated into their explanations for opposing evening shopping the argument that the staffing challenges were too difficult to overcome. In 1956, for example, spokes-people for Vancouver's downtown department stores claimed that despite a new ruling that would allow their stores to remain open until 6 p.m., their businesses would retain the 5:30 p.m. closing time. According to one official this decision was based partly on the fact that the store employed so many female clerks, who, the store recognized, had domestic responsibilities that precluded evening employment.[26]

Concern for the plight of female clerks, then, was genuine and persistent – though it was more central to the debates early in the twentieth century than it was after the Second World War. Some observers championed store-hour restrictions as a tangible and effective way to improve working conditions for female employees. But the manner in which they made these arguments is revealing: most often, men spoke for these women in ways that objectified them as victims who needed to be saved or at least protected by local and provincial legislation.

Paralleling the long-standing call to protect female clerks from difficult working conditions was a contrasting campaign to liberate female shoppers from the constraints of regulated store hours. In 1917, for example, J.N. Harvey of both Vancouver and Victoria voiced his opposition to Saturday half-holidays because they would have dire effects on female consumers. Specifically, Harvey railed against a system that would force the "housewife" to anticipate her exact household requirements in advance of a Saturday half-holiday while drinkers and smokers had little trouble pursuing their vices on Saturday afternoons and evenings.[27] Voicing his opposition to the Saturday half-holiday that same year, Victoria resident John Cochrane similarly noted that it was unfair to expect the city's housewives to obtain the goods necessary for Sunday meals from the local market on Friday.[28] If some observers held up female clerks as the most symbolic and sympathetic victims of a world without store-hour restrictions, others presented female consumers – usually in the form of the idealized "housewife" – as the party most disadvantaged by such regulations.

When the store-hour debates were renewed in earnest following the Second World War, the trope of the vulnerable housewife-consumer remained a popular reference point. For example, in October 1946, Victoria alderman H.M. Diggon argued against Wednesday closings for fish retailers by claiming to speak "earnestly for the housewife who wants to buy fish on Wednesdays and has no refrigerator in which to keep it over from Tuesday to Wednesday."[29] Vancouver alderwoman Anna Sprott similarly argued that banning evening sales of meat and

4.2 "… try to bear up Miss Figby … it could have been SIX days a week …"
Cartoonist Len Norris acknowledges the strain that retail clerks faced amidst
debates about the ideal length of the shopping week. *Vancouver Sun*, 14 November 1953. Image reproduced courtesy of Simon Fraser University Library,
Special Collections and Rare Books.

fish would prove an unnecessary hardship for housewives and working women, thus adding a new twist to the argument by acknowledg-
ing the growing number of female consumers whose shopping time
was increasingly restricted by their own employment schedules.[30]

Tellingly, in 1957, when Victoria's forty-five-member Independent
Merchants' Co-operative Association launched a determined attempt
to challenge the regulations in the province's new Municipal Act that
would force its members to close in the evenings, its first step was to
circulate an open letter to the city's housewives seeking support. The
letter encouraged housewives to recognize their reliance on small merchants: "It is up to you to demand our services be maintained. It is the
little guy who gives you many services you are entitled to. He does not

hire help nor does he conflict with the principles of labor, but he sure pays plenty of taxes to our fair city's treasury department and is a fixture in your community you can depend on." To clinch their support, the association appealed to a familiar notion of idealized femininity – the mother as moral crusader: "If the liquor stores can stay open, why can't the small 'mom and pop' grocery also remain open to provide milk for the baby?"[31] Even as Victoria City Council was in the process of approving wide-open store hours for the city in 1958, store-hour regulation opponents, such as alderwoman Lily Wilson, continued to employ the trope of the dependent woman by suggesting that the city's housewives, who themselves worked a seven-day week, were anxious to see the stores open.[32]

Historian Evan Roberts notes that even in economic and legal contexts as different as the United States and New Zealand, public discourse assumed that women were natural shoppers and observers often worked from the assumption that women took a long time to shop, especially if they were "bargain hunters." But these women "were also often seen as 'housewives'":

Despite different personalities, tastes, and incomes, all shopped while their husbands worked. All housewives needed time to shop, and department stores argued they had to meet that need. In both Minnesota and New Zealand, department stores' service to housewives was strongly stated when stores felt opening hours might be limited. Facing a threat of Saturday closing in 1938, New Zealand retailers defended the shopping time of housewives. As in America, New Zealand retailers never called on any actual housewife to put her case to the Arbitration Court. The reality of married women outside of the paid work force in the mid-twentieth century is not in doubt, but the housewife who spoke on behalf of retailers was a *rhetorical construct* in service to their interests.[33]

Hence the campaign to maintain Saturday shopping could be buttressed with a claim that "for a housewife, Saturday was 'the only opportunity she has to get away to town and do the shopping.'" Retailers also emphasized the need to keep stores open to accommodate "unpredictable" female shoppers who did not plan ahead and were prone to "impulse buying." "Fictional housewives" were thus "effective advocates for department stores' wishes."[34] In Vancouver and Victoria, symbolic women served similar roles.

Family Values

Equally controversial – and contested – was the place of the family. Supporters of store-hour regulations argued that these restrictions protected the family from the deleterious effects of overwork. Those challenging the restrictions countered that they inhibited family development by limiting opportunities for quality family time.[35] Both sides' arguments highlight the extent to which citizens viewed the issue of store hours as one that affected community members not directly involved in retail shop labour; they also underscore the extent to which competing notions of idealized leisure time informed citizens' expectations.

Store-hour regulation proponents routinely emphasized their concern for family well-being. On the eve of a Vancouver plebiscite on six-day shopping in 1954, one woman offered a damning assessment of the likely impact of a "yes" vote. "As a wife and mother," she wrote to the *Vancouver Sun*, "I ask all voters to consider a 'No' on the Wednesday opening." Six-day shopping, she noted, would deny her family much-needed leisure time because it "may be the end of Wednesdays off for my husband to enjoy his garden or to take his son on picnics, hikes, to grandma's or even the ball games." The suggestion that work hours be staggered throughout the week conjured up unhappy memories of her own employment in a department store that seemed "like all work and no play" and proved drearily "monotonous." She also pointed to the deleterious effects on the province's youth, who "are certainly going to miss those days at the beaches, parks or on the mountains and getting to know our B.C. better."[36]

Several merchants offered similar arguments. In 1956 Alex Stevenson, spokesperson for Victoria's shoe repair stores, demanded a five-day shopping week so that employees could spend time with their families.[37] Faced with the prospect of wide-open hours, Vancouver shoe retailer E.S. Sheppard concurred: "We are in an age when the breakdown of the home is now suffering as never before. If a large segment of the population is now going to be subject to night work ... it is going to create a further serious problem in family relationships for the group."[38] In 1969 opponents of wide-open shopping took to the streets with placards denouncing the deleterious effects of extended store hours. Their forceful slogans included: "Kids ... Do You Know Where Your Parents Are Tonight?'" "Streets Unsafe ... For Women Workers At Night"; and "Want To Be A Big Brother? Be One For My Son. I'm Never

Picketers outside Vancouver city hall Wednesday night carry signs protesting any change in the hours city stores are open.
—Gordon Croucher photo

4.3 Protesters campaign against wide-open hours in Vancouver. (Original photo by Gordon Croucher.) *Vancouver Province*, 25 September 1969, 1. Image reproduced courtesy of Post Media.

Home. I'm Working!!" Those opposed to expanding shopping opportunities for the city's consumers were thus keen to highlight their commitment to protecting the welfare of the cities' families (see Figure 4.3).

Yet supporters of store-hour regulations did not monopolize the rhetorical uses of family togetherness. A number of observers antagonistic to store-hour restrictions managed to appropriate the issue of family welfare to support their claims that such regulations needed to be relaxed or eliminated. In 1952, for example, Edward Mallek, a member of the Victoria Chamber of Commerce retail merchants' group, and the head of a women's clothing operation, argued that one positive result of expanded evening shopping would be that it would encourage shopping as a family unit.[39] According to the *Colonist*, Mallek went so far as to suggest that greater opportunities for evening shopping might even reduce household arguments: "A woman tells her husband she is going to buy some article for the home at a certain price. But when she gets to the store she finds the article she went to buy is not to her liking, and she buys what does meet her approval, but pays a higher price. What happens? The husband will most likely object to the added expenditure. Argument, or some form of trouble[,] develops within the family."[40]

In the 1950s, media reports consistently trumpeted the connection between expanded shopping hours and family outings. Indeed, by 1956 some Vancouver aldermen keen to see all store-hour regulations eliminated suggested that the growing demand for evening shopping had a family dimension. The trend towards evening shopping, they argued, "is believed to be brought about largely by new trends in 'husband-and-wife shopping habits,' the difficulties of obtaining parking during the daylight hours and the overlapping of goods sold in various stores."[41] In voicing its support for "open shopping hours," in 1967, one Surrey department store boasted that wide-open hours in Surrey had resulted in "many compliments from happy Customers [sic] who can shop as a family in the evening." "Our experience has proven to us that many families prefer to shop in the evening," argued O.C. McKee, executive vice-president of Hamilton Harvey department stores.[42]

A similar situation emerged in Victoria. By April 1958 the *Victoria Daily Colonist* was reporting that Friday had become "a 'family' shopping night" as parents and children browsed local stores and couples embraced the opportunity to purchase large items together and thus benefit from discussing their purchases in advance. Friday evening shopping, the *Colonist* reported, also left the weekend open for other activities.[43] One shopping couple praised the convenience Friday evening shopping provided and even hinted at shopping's leisure component: "It is a very good idea. We are able to get out together and leave the baby with a sitter. We are usually busy on Saturdays and can't get downtown."[44] In December 1958, Hal Malone, the *Times* business editor, commented on the busy action of evening shoppers in the run-up to Christmas by boasting that "Victorians have taken to night shopping like Miklos Hargitay takes to Jayne Mansfield." "The main factor in increased nocturnal patronage," he explained, "is the family." "More and more, mother and dad are packing the brood into the family chariot for a night in the stores."[45]

By 1966 the *Times* was convinced that evening shopping was here to stay and suggested that women were the key constituency through

"I didn't hear you beefing when the liquor stores opened evenings . . ."

4.4 Province cartoonist Al Beaton wades into Vancouver's evening shopping debate with this 1956 editorial cartoon. Source: Al Beaton, *Laugh with Al Beaton: Cartoons from* The Province (Vancouver: *The Province*, 1956). Image reproduced courtesy of Kathleen Cameron.

which it had been secured. "EVERY HUSBAND WHO HAS been dragged off from some more pleasant pursuit to accompany his wife on a night-shopping trip will undoubtedly endorse the Victoria Labor Council's demand that stores be closed in the evening." But the newspaper was convinced that the popularity of evening shopping would ensure that any attempt to repeal it would be unsuccessful. "Admittedly many of the men wear a discontented look as they wheel baskets of groceries around the supermarket or take part in the ritual of buying shoes for the kiddies. But most of the women seem to enjoy this extra chance of family togetherness, this sharing of purchasing decisions with husband and family." If the public was so keen to have evening shopping, the newspaper concluded, they should get it.[46] That extended store hours could be championed as a key component of family leisure time would have struck many of the early campaigners for store-hour restrictions as both odd and alarming. But by the 1950s the notion that shopping time was leisure time had become a forceful argument against widespread store-hour restrictions.

The debates over six-day and evening shopping were directly connected to moral concerns about the place of women in society and about the best way to protect the institution of the family. As observers debated the merits of additional leisure and work time, both women and the family emerged as highly charged symbolic reference points. Supporters of store-hour restrictions sought to protect women and families from the negative impact of long hours and staggered shifts. Opponents charged that these very restrictions were particularly inconvenient for female shoppers and argued that they limited family recreational opportunities. Both sides positioned themselves as defenders of victimized interests, and what emerged was a debate framed as a zero sum game in which consumers' interests appeared irreconcilable with store-hour restrictions. In fact, consumer opinion was more complex than this polarizing debate would suggest.

Consumer Convenience

Central to the store-hour debates was the question of just what consumers wanted. Some participants in the debates spoke of consumer behaviour with a fair degree of reverence or awe and saw it as something that dictated business practices and, ideally, government regulations. Others embraced a more restricted notion of consumer sovereignty and suggested that through incentives and regulations, consumer behaviour could be modified to suit merchants', clerks', or community wishes.[47] But perhaps the most heated topic of debate was the nature of consumer demand itself.

From the very beginning, supporters of store-hour restrictions tended to argue that consumer demand was *finite*.[48] From this perspective it was logical to argue that additional evening shopping hours were unnecessary and that Wednesday closing simply resulted in deferred rather than lost sales.[49] For example, C.E. Herrett, a barbers' union representative in Vancouver, opposed the six-day week because "we know from experience it doesn't put any more money in the till, since the number of people who require haircuts isn't any greater in six days than five."[50] By contrast, some opponents of store-hour restrictions suggested that consumer demand was *infinite* and that any additional opportunities for shopping brought with them potential revenue.[51] Focused as it was on the temporary nature of tourist visits, the tourism lobby was particularly keen to emphasize that shorter operating hours meant less revenue, but other merchants also underscored the importance of minimizing the missed opportunities for securing consumer expenditure. For example, merchant Nate Singer, a firm opponent of Wednesday closing, argued against the idea that consumers would buy a limited number of goods regardless of extended hours of operation. In doing so he noted that much of the retail trade relied on "impulse buying. And there can't be impulse buying if stores are closed."[52]

By embracing this latter understanding of consumer behaviour, observers consistently presented consumers as ignored or victimized parties who deserved recognition and attention from the authorities.[53] Reginald Hayward, a former mayor of Victoria turned provincial politician, opposed all-day Wednesday closing in part by championing the notion of consumer sovereignty – and a gender-neutral understanding of consumer identity. Challenging the notion that only merchants should determine how store hours are set, Hayward argued that consumers deserved a say in the matter.[54] Rose Evoy, a North Vancouver dress shop proprietor, was even more blunt: the "public doesn't care whether merchants have time off. All they want is service and we should give [it] to them."[55] Opponents of Wednesday closing and strict limitations on evening shopping thus claimed to be championing the interests of consumers.

More surprisingly, champions of store-hour restrictions attempted to sell authorities on the idea that many consumers actually supported institutions such as the half-holiday. In 1952, for example, Harold Gray, a grocer in Victoria's Fairfield district, adamantly opposed any move away from the city's half-day Wednesday closing. He argued, primarily, that the interests of the city's three thousand retail clerks must be paramount while adding that independent small business operators must benefit from any change. But he also suggested that the city's shoppers should be consulted as well to determine whether or not they were actually inconvenienced by Wednesday afternoon closing. Gray went so far as to suggest, perhaps wishfully, that the buying public resented city council's attempts to modify "their habits" and would be very unhappy if their usual shopping patterns were disrupted to please "any minority pressure groups."[56]

Both opponents and supporters of store-hour restrictions, then, claimed to enjoy consumer support. But what of consumers themselves – and women in particular? Despite claims to the contrary from supporters and opponents of store-hour regulations, consumers' views were conflicting and complex.[57] To be sure, the media had no difficulty finding concrete evidence of consumers favouring store-hour deregulation. But reporters also uncovered a good deal of consumer support for store-hour restrictions and, it must be said, a fair amount of apathy as well.

Consumer support for six-day and evening shopping was widespread. A "census" of one Victoria store's customers in December 1952 found that almost every respondent favoured the city's stores remaining open at least one evening per week.[58] Six years later, opponents of Wednesday closing could point to the fact that more than six thousand Victoria shoppers had signed a petition calling for a six-day shopping week.[59] Interviews with individual consumers produced similar results. Mrs C.B. Storch emphasized the convenience factor when she celebrated the arrival of Friday evening shopping in downtown Vancouver: "I get home from work late on week nights and it's not easy to work in shopping on the weekend. Now I've got time to do all the shopping I want."[60] Louis Holker, an apartment house proprietor, emphasized his desire for the kind of convenience available to American shoppers: "In Portland, Ore., you can buy groceries from 6 a.m. to 10 p.m. Down there they usually go forward and we follow." Housewife Edna Lawler concurred and added a gendered understanding of the paternalistic relationship between male proprietor and female consumer: "I admire those gentlemen who will stay open for folks like myself who might run out of things. Another thing, we do feel under an obligation to the man who does stay open and help[s] us out."[61] For Mrs Walter Wong, convenience was paramount: "In my own case – a working housewife – Friday night is not adequate. Stores are crowded, parking difficult – surely two reasons that night shopping is popular."[62] Consumers themselves, then, could be counted on to champion consumer convenience.[63]

But some consumers were just as forceful in their support for store-hour restrictions. An April 1954 letter to the *Vancouver Sun* from "Contented Shopper" staunchly supported Wednesday closing and excoriated those who favoured six-day shopping. Consumers did not have the right to tell retailers when to open or close their stores, the writer explained. "It seems those in favor of Wednesday opening are a bunch of money-hungry car dealers, restaurant operators, real estate men, theatre operators, etc. ... I am a shopper who can do all my buying in one day each week." There was no need to expand shopping opportunities "when the majority of clerks and public are so contented with the present store hours."[64] That same year, supporters of Monday morning closing in the Vancouver suburb of Burnaby received strong support in a *Vancouver Sun* "sidewalk survey." The newspaper noted that "two North American customs – the big Sunday dinner and Monday washday – combined to make Monday morning opening unnecessary in the eyes of most shoppers." The female interviewees taking this view generally favoured all-day closing because "they always had plenty left Monday from the Sunday roast. Besides most of them were too busy doing the weekly wash to worry about food Monday morning."[65]

The conflicting nature of consumer opinion on the matter is clearly revealed in surveys conducted by the *Vancouver Daily Province* and the *Victoria Daily Colonist* in 1954 and 1958 respectively. On the eve of the June 1954 six-day shopping plebiscite in Vancouver, the *Daily Province* conducted "Man On The Street" interviews and found that, among consumers, apathy prevailed. Almost half the people questioned claimed not to care about the vote because it did not affect them.[66] Among the respondents willing to take a stand on the issue, opinion was clearly divided. Unabashed supporters of six-day shopping emphasized consumer convenience.[67] Mrs W.A. McCullogh, for example, suggested that Wednesday half-day closing was "hard on people with no refrigerators" because it meant that "they have to buy their perishables the day before."[68] Opponents of six-day shopping offered a variety of rationales for their views. Simon Tamminga of Vancouver supported the five-day shopping week because "stores are open enough for the money I've got to spend." Miss Mariam Mattila, a receptionist from Burnaby, also emphasized consumers' finite spending power in supporting five-day shopping: "I haven't enough money to spend [on] six days." Others explicitly identified the dilemma of having to choose between consumer convenience and workers' welfare and expressed their discomfort at having to do so. A Mrs McDowell, of Vancouver's West End, took a decidedly empathetic approach: "I don't know how the employees feel. It doesn't affect me. Let them do what they want. It's nice to feel the employees have some time off."[69] Consumer convenience was a popular rallying cry, but it was mediated by consumers' own calls to protect workers' welfare.[70]

And what of the notion that female shoppers were particularly keen to reduce or abolish store-hour restrictions? While opponents of

store-hour regulations often insisted that women were their key constituency, there is no evidence to suggest that women were necessarily more supportive of their endeavours to eliminate such regulations.
Indeed, a 1956 Market Research Associates opinion poll of Vancouver
citizens revealed that roughly two-thirds of respondents supported
evening shopping. Among men there was 68 per cent support, while
among women support was slightly lower, at 64 per cent.[71] Gender ideals clearly shaped how participants in these debates conveyed their
arguments. Both sides issued calls to protect women's interests and
family life. But female consumers were (and are) complex beings whose
opinions did not always fit neatly into the categories and stereotypes
that permeated the media.

Proponents and opponents of store-hour restrictions such as Wednesday closing or strict limitations on evening sales often viewed shopping
regulations as a moral issue. Their arguments demonstrated that consumer convenience rested uneasily with concerns about retail clerks'
and merchants' quality of life. But their arguments were also predicated on highly selective and profoundly gendered constructions of
retail clerks and their customers. As we saw with the public disputes
surrounding chain stores, this rhetoric did not reflect the more complex reality: consumers were divided over, and surprisingly ambiguous
about, the prospects of increased shopping opportunities.

Perhaps most interesting here is that consumers were not mind-
lessly seeking greater access to goods and services. Instead, they wrote
thoughtful letters to the local newspaper demanding that specific store-
hour restrictions be lifted or calmly suggested in interviews that the
authorities consider the employees' welfare and retain current regulations. The fact that they were active participants in the debates undoubtedly helped ensure that this controversial issue remained unresolved
for decades – even if street interviews eventually unearthed evidence
of consumer apathy. As much as retail store hours were an economic
issue, they were also a moral concern – a factor that greatly complicated civic leaders' prospects of reconciling the competing forces that
sustained these debates. As the following chapter demonstrates, their
frustrations, combined with some retailers' determination to evade
store-hour regulations, also played a significant role in undermining
support for restrictive store hours.

Chapter Five

Regulation: Evasion and Enforcement

Premier W.A.C. Bennett: There is no permanent solution to this problem of shopping hours – only trial and error.

Opposition politician: But mostly error.

An exchange in the British Columbia Legislature, 1958[1]

Decisions about what to regulate, and how regulations should be enforced, profoundly influenced the development of consumerism in Canada after the Second World War. In areas as diverse as monetary policy, taxation, welfare state programs, and trade agreements with other nations, the federal government intervened repeatedly to prioritize some interests over others. At the provincial level, financial regulations, taxation policies, and employment rules similarly shaped Canadians' postwar experience. Local regulations, too – in the form of zoning bylaws, for example – determined where Canadians could buy and sell goods and services. Store-hour regulations, then, were just one element in a vast network of rules that governed people's lives. But the controversy they provoked can tell us a great deal about the role of regulatory regimes in postwar Canada. In particular, it highlights the tensions between codified rules and everyday practice as well as the impact of what we might term "regulatory fatigue" – not just on consumers and merchants but on law enforcement officials and politicians as well.

From our present vantage point the modern reader can be forgiven for wondering how it was that citizens in Victoria and Vancouver managed to run their errands before seven-day shopping became a reality in the 1980s. The codified rules regarding Wednesday closing and evening shopping, for example, appear highly restrictive, and one is tempted to picture consumers being forced to commit to a tight schedule in order to shop efficiently. But as a brief spin on any major highway reminds us, posted regulations are rarely if ever universally or consistently enforced. And what is true of motor vehicle laws is certainly the case for other laws.[2]

Moreover, like factory legislation in Britain and store-hour regulations in Australia, store-hour laws in BC became "conventionalized." The small penalties imposed for transgressing local or provincial laws assumed "the status of minor technical or administrative offences."[3] In the Australian colony of Victoria in the 1870s, "errant shopkeepers could profitably defy the law," lamented Melbourne's chief inspector. "Several shopkeepers have openly stated that it pays them better to keep open and run the risk of being fined than to close their shops at seven o'clock." Lenient courts further limited the legislation's impact, while "provisions enabling local government to opt retailers in or out ... rendered the law an inspectoral nightmare." According to Michael Quinlan and Miles Goodwin, it was mainly problems with the legislation itself, rather than "retailer opposition," that undermined the overall effectiveness of laws.[4] As the other chapters in this book suggest, a great many factors contributed to the liberalization of store hours in Vancouver and Victoria, but the problems involved in creating and enforcing coherent regulations were an important part of the story.[5]

When it came to store-hour restrictions in Victoria and Vancouver, theory and practice could vary considerably. Periodic muckraking by local reporters highlighted the extent to which local bylaws were flouted. For example, in September 1958, as Victoria police chief John Blackstock proudly announced that observance of the Wednesday-closing laws was widespread and that no charges had been laid the previous week, a local reporter offered a very different view of the situation. In an article headlined "I Bought Forbidden Goods On Wednesday Afternoon," Piret Veldi listed the wide variety of goods available on Wednesdays, going so far as to boast that "I could even have bought a car." Some salespeople refused to take the risk, Veldi reported. Others temporarily embraced the possibilities of illicit commerce only to be overcome with fear and guilt: "A cautious grocer sold me a tin of tuna, handing it quickly across the counter. Five minutes later the breathless man caught up with me and gave me back 29 cents, the cost of the purchase." Many other clerks, Veldi noted, comfortably shared their

5.1 Caught in the act? The completion of a transaction such as the one pictured above could land a merchant or clerk in hot water – if it occurred outside of approved trading hours. Image courtesy of City of Vancouver Archives, CVA 1184-2116, photographer Jack Lindsay.

disdain for the current regulations while clandestinely completing illegal transactions.[6]

This chapter explores local authorities' efforts to enforce store-hour regulations and the determined and creative methods merchants and clerks employed to circumvent them. It focuses first on the reasons why merchants flouted the regulations and explores some of their evasion strategies. It then examines the penalties and surveillance methods city officials employed in attempting to enforce local bylaws. The complexity and confusion involved in attempting to police the regulations rendered enforcement uneven and ineffective. The growing realization

that the prospect of negotiating an efficient and fair system of regulations was unattainable played a key role in the demise of the old store-
hour regulations regime and the rise of our more recognizable "wide
open" system.

Transgressing the Law: Motivation and Strategy

That many merchants refused to abide by local store hours was apparent
to all concerned. Faced with a situation in which local merchants were
selling goods illegally in 1916, Victoria's city prosecutor, C.L. Harrison,
declared local store-hour regulations "unenforceable."[7] Throughout
the 1910s and 1920s a number of merchants found themselves in court
for contravening store-hour restrictions.[8] Often such cases stemmed
from visits by undercover police officers, whose purchases became evidence.[9] Witnesses in such cases in Vancouver often included the city
clerk, whose job it was to remind the court of the existing and often
arcane legislation.[10] In March 1936 the provincial government deemed
it necessary to intervene and introduce legislation aimed specifically at
merchants who sought to evade the spirit of the weekly half-holiday.
The new rules listed the specific goods that could be sold on the half-
holiday in an attempt to counter merchants' attempts to take advantage
of the confusion surrounding what was, and was not, a permissible
sale.[11] Almost from the moment store-hour restrictions were mandated,
creative merchants employed clever strategies in their efforts to evade
detection and frustrate the authorities.

After the Second World War, amidst the increasingly heated
exchanges concerning the legitimacy of store-hour regulations, more
and more evidence came to light indicating that store operators were
evading the law. A March 1947 survey of Vancouver retail merchants,
for example, found that almost three hundred stores remained open
Wednesday mornings in violation of the law.[12] A March 1953 investigation by the *Victoria Daily Colonist* resulted in the confident assertion
that Victoria was "only half closed on half-day Closing Wednesday
afternoons." "Anyone familiar with the city, or who walks up enough
streets," the *Colonist* observed, "can buy almost anything he wants
even though most stores are closed." "About the only item not for
sale somewhere in Victoria on Wednesday afternoons is furniture, and
even some of that might be bought at auction rooms," the newspaper charged. In fact, it declared, "the tourist who can't find something
to buy during the mid-week closing period just hasn't walked far

enough." It then listed the possibilities available despite the Wednesday-closing regulations:

> Liquor; any vegetable or fruit; meat, cooked or uncooked; magazines and books; china; cards; candy; anything in the "drug" line including a shaving kit; car parts; a cabinet radio; roller skates; tinned goods; hockey sticks; paint or wallpaper; and almost anything in the food line.
>
> He can buy clothing or shoes, or have a suit made up. And, if he wanted a really unusual souvenir, he could even buy a load of wood or coal although he might run into a little trouble later at the customs.[13]

Clearly a large number of stores were unwilling to play by the rules. But what was their motivation? And what strategies did they employ?

In December 1949, Vancouver retailers were breaking the law in pursuit of the fleeting promise of a brief increase in sales rather than from any consistent ideological opposition to the local Wednesday-closing bylaw. How else can one explain the fact that more than one hundred retail stores remained open on the Wednesday *before* Christmas in defiance of the bylaw despite stern warnings from city officials, yet willingly closed their doors the following Wednesday despite the city's decision to amend the bylaw to allow for Wednesday sales?[14] Other merchants systematically broke the rules because they believed that doing so was the only way they could survive.

Such consistent flouting of the rules required both courage and cunning. In 1954, as Vancouver City Council moved towards implementing a ban on selling frozen meats and fish after 5:30 p.m., the *Vancouver Sun* reported that many of the city's smaller grocers planned to defy the law because much of their business was conducted after the larger stores had closed for the day.[15] Earl W. Scott, proprietor of Scott's Grocery, was one merchant who suggested that most of these smaller grocers would sell anyway "and if anybody says anything you just tell them the customer bought the stuff the day before and is picking it up at night. They can't do anything about that." Scott's position was reinforced by Blanche Beaton, proprietor of Beaton's Grocery and Confectionary, who emphasized the importance of distinguishing between legitimate customers and plainclothes police officers. "If I knew a person, I would sell him frozen meat at night," she explained. Her store, like many others, required evening sales to stay in business. Moreover, having purchased a freezing unit the year before, she was relying on evening sales of frozen products to help pay off this purchase.[16] Alarmed that Victoria's corner stores were being forced to abide by Wednesday-closing restrictions while drugstores competing directly with these stores were not, William Palmer, president of Independent Merchants' Co-operative Association, bluntly told corner store operators in Victoria to disregard the Wednesday-closing restrictions. "Sell all your goods to customers, wheelbarrows full. We have enough customers to make a living. But be a little cautious and careful with strangers," he warned. "I have been pinched before for selling groceries on Wednesday. I have to, it's my livelihood."[17]

Some independent merchants broke the law because they knew others were doing so. In Vancouver, Norm Kwon, proprietor of the Delview Grocery, vowed to defy an evening closing bylaw so long as public demand made it worthwhile. "It is silly and ridiculous," he explained. "Other stores are ignoring the order and we will too."[18] Other merchants broke the law out of frustration with the slow process involved in facilitating the end of local store-hour regulations. In July 1954, on the city's first "open Wednesday" since 1942, some stores legally opened, but many others were still required to close at 1 p.m. because their line of business had not yet filed the necessary petition to obtain city approval for Wednesday afternoon openings. Hence, as licence inspectors and city police carried out a "day-long vigil to maintain the shopping bylaws," some merchants defied the law. Bert Robinson, operator of two meat markets, announced that both his shops would remain open even though the city's butchers had yet to receive approval from the city for six-day shopping, "unless I am forcibly lugged off to jail."[19] In all, more than two hundred illegal store openings were reported that day.[20] Clearly, merchants in Vancouver and Victoria were drawing upon a variety of motivations and employing a number of effective strategies for flouting store-hour restrictions.

Enforcement Initiatives

Faced with merchants unwilling to abide by store-hour restrictions, the authorities attempted to enforce store-hour regulations through direct surveillance and by imposing fines and business licence suspensions. This was no easy task, however. In fact, it would prove so complex and frustrating that some civic officials eventually threw their hands in the air and called into question the very possibility of regulating shopping hours. A number of factors informed these sentiments, but two key issues revolved around legal technicalities: the difficulty involved in accurately and consistently defining particular consumer goods, and the spectre of unforeseen legal loopholes.

Surveillance of local stores was an onerous task for local governments. In Vancouver the task belonged to the city's licensing office – an entity that could provide just a handful of officers to monitor the entire city. City officials were never entirely convinced that such an approach was sufficient, and they sometimes called for the police to assist in enforcing the local bylaws.[21] At times, the city took the lead and issued instructions to licence inspectors to prosecute store owners. In April 1951, for example, it ordered a crackdown on stores selling fresh vegetables on Wednesday afternoons, which was prohibited under the provincial Shops Regulation and Weekly Holiday Act.[22] Quite often, merchants themselves called for such crackdowns. In May 1958, for example, Ben Wosk of Wosk's Ltd, a downtown Vancouver appliance and furniture store, called upon city council to aggressively enforce store-hour restrictions on drugstores illegally selling items in the evening and on Sundays and holidays.[23] City officials often *announced* crackdowns in advance – very likely in the hope that store proprietors (and their customers) would police themselves. They deemed attempts to ensure total compliance with the vast array of regulations to be impractical and prohibitively expensive.

In August 1956, for example, after several years of lax enforcement, officials in the Vancouver suburb of Surrey announced in advance that an upcoming Wednesday would see an RCMP crackdown to enforce half-day closing.[24] In September 1957, surprise inspections in Saanich caught seven storekeepers breaking the suburb's Monday afternoon and evening closing bylaw when a licence inspector and plainclothes police officer inspected forty-seven stores.[25] Other communities employed similar tactics. In Victoria, police chief John Blackstock used the threat of crackdowns to try to keep local stores in line. In September 1958, speaking in the immediate aftermath of the Saanich decision to do away with store-hour regulation, Blackstock threatened to "crack down hard" on violators.[26] Victoria also occasionally resorted to employing plainclothes police constables, who posed as shoppers, in an effort to snare unsuspecting retailers.[27]

What sort of punishment awaited merchants who transgressed local shopping bylaws? Fines varied from community to community but generally ranged from $10 to $100 depending on whether the store in question was a repeat offender.[28] Such minimal punishments prompted one observer to note wryly that "at these bargain prices, it's well worth

5.2 "Mind you ... on Wednesdays it's going to be particularly noticeable ..."
Vancouver Sun cartoonist Len Norris addresses the authorities' attempts
to enforce Wednesday closing. *Vancouver Sun*, 12 May 1954. Image reproduced
courtesy of Simon Fraser University Library, Special Collections and
Rare Books.

testing the law," and indeed, merchants who favoured store-hour
regulations lamented the light penalties.[29] For the Vancouver branch
of the Retail Merchants' Association (RMA), frustration stemmed from
the fact that the city's method of enforcement allowed stores "to keep
operating for the rest of the day, even after getting a summons." The
RMA demanded, instead, a system that would permit authorities to
immediately padlock offending stores.[30] The RMA may well have been
pleased when, in late December 1955, three outlets of ABC Television
Sales & Service Ltd in Vancouver were forced to close following the
cancellation of the company's 1955 business licence. This drastic action
followed no less than six convictions for violating the Shops Early Closing Bylaw the previous year. But even this harsh penalty was surely

tempered by the fact that the licence was to be renewed on 1 January 1956 (albeit subject to cancellation again upon first violation).[31]

Clearly, the penalties for transgressing the law were hardly prohibitive for most store owners, and inconsistent enforcement undermined their legitimacy. Merchants complying with store-hour bylaws grew increasingly frustrated as their competitors' decisions to flout the regulations elicited little in the way of a response from the authorities.[32] Lax enforcement was the product of both limited resources and a lack of political will. Faced with a daunting task and limited funds, for example, Vancouver city licence inspector A.N. Moore admitted that his department would simply have to take the word of individual retailers regarding whether they were among hundreds of retailers who openly defied closing regulations on the Wednesday before Christmas in 1949.[33] In 1950, Victoria's city prosecutor Claude L. Harrison was so frustrated by a convoluted bylaw concerning the hours of operation for service stations that he went so far as to ask a local magistrate to dismiss a charge against the Dickson Bros. Service Stations because the law was "bad."[34] In 1954 a similarly disillusioned Vancouver alderman, George Cunningham, noted that enforcing "laws unacceptable to the public" was "an almost hopeless task."[35]

Faced with such sentiment, merchants who supported store-hour regulations occasionally took it upon themselves to enforce the local bylaws. So frustrated was the RMA with the lack of bylaw enforcement in Vancouver, for example, that it undertook a sting operation. On the afternoon of Wednesday, 28 June 1950, the RMA targeted twenty local stores about which complaints had recently been received. "Shoppers" were sent to these stores with orders to purchase five items: ketchup, olives, gherkins, vanilla extract, and a broom (or clothes pins if a broom was unavailable). The shoppers were able to obtain the items in all twenty stores. To make its case, the RMA presented its evidence in the form of a detailed chart to Alderman Showler and the members of the city's Licenses and Claims Committee and pleaded for the city to take the situation seriously.[36] In September 1957, merchants in Oak Bay near Victoria similarly decided to take matters into their own hands with a plan to enforce a new store-hour bylaw by policing their fellow merchants.[37]

In 1958 some frustrated Victoria city councillors even put forward a motion asking the city's police force to enforce Wednesday-closing regulations. While the motion was defeated, partly because it was considered unnecessary to ask the police to carry out their mandated tasks, it highlighted the fact that some observers remained unconvinced that the authorities were doing all they could to enforce such regulations.[38] The *Daily Colonist* was certainly not amused. While noting that city council was technically correct to conclude that a motion asking the police to enforce the law was redundant, it lamented that council was fully aware that the law was frequently broken, yet felt no great compulsion to enforce it. The result, the *Colonist* argued, was unfair to the merchants who obeyed the law.[39]

Definitions

What explains the hesitation on the part of local authorities to fully enforce their own bylaws? Enforcing local store-hour bylaws was an incredibly complex task. The technical details involved in attempting to regulate a wide variety of goods and shopping establishments produced a great deal of confusion and provided opportunities for merchants to avoid prosecution. Two key disputes highlight the difficulty that city governments faced in attempting to come up with concrete regulations for messy situations in which goods were often difficult to define. In Vancouver the city struggled to produce a comprehensive definition of "hardware." In Victoria, fittingly, local merchants, politicians, and the courts debated the meaning of the word "souvenir." Both debates highlight the extent to which the issue of store-hour regulations pitted merchants against one another and underscore that local authorities faced a nearly impossible task, especially when a store sold a variety of goods that were classified differently by local legislation.[40]

In the late 1940s a tense battle emerged between hardware and drug stores in Vancouver. The issue centred on the fact that while hardware stores were required to close on Wednesdays, drugstores, which were exempted from the closing law, were rumoured to be catering to consumers in need of materials traditionally sold in hardware stores.[41] The BC Retail Hardware Association targeted not only drugstores but also small grocers, which, it complained to city officials, continued to "sell mops, brooms, waxes and polishes" on Wednesdays and Sundays when hardware stores had to close. The city's response was less than welcoming. Alderman George Miller warned that strict enforcement of "hardware" sales would be "a hornet's nest" and noted that an attempt to do so a decade earlier had proven very difficult. Alderman Jack Cornett pointed out the difficult position of city officials and noted that drugstores and corner stores had sold such items "long before there were any hardware stores."[42]

Even less sympathetic was *Province* columnist D.A. McGregor, who dismissed the hardware stores' complaints as out of touch with the city's postwar economic reality: "I wonder if the hardware men and the other folk who are so insistent upon Wednesday closing ever think that the reason there is a sale for so-called contraband articles on Wednesday is that their customers – the great body of the public – want to buy them and that in closing up their places of business on a business day they are doing the public a disservice which the public more or less resents."[43] The city's prosecutor and police force were also reluctant to get involved in trying to define "hardware." As city prosecutor Gordon Scott noted, a judicial definition was required, and it would prove difficult to prosecute someone for selling hardware if such a definition was not clear.[44] Even more distressing for hardware retailers was Scott's assessment that the city licence department deemed the selling of items such as brooms and pails to be a legitimate business transaction for grocery stores.[45]

The matter rested there until July 1953, when the BC Hardware Association, acting on behalf of Vancouver hardware store operators, formally protested at City Hall the selling of hardware in drugstores and chain grocery stores. In doing so it demanded a firm definition of "hardware," again on the grounds that operators were seeking protection from competition when they were forced to close. Once again, the reaction of city officials was hardly encouraging. Announcing that he was neutral, licence inspector Art Moore proceeded to list a variety of products in hardware stores that infringed on other retailers' lines, including electrical appliances, paint supplies, floor coverings, clocks, china, and "even budgie birds and canaries." All were sold by hardware stores even though other merchants dealt with them exclusively and believed that no one else should handle them. Moore, along with Rhodes Elliot of the city solicitor's office, admitted that there was no clear definition of "hardware." Speaking on behalf of the hardware merchants, J.W. Stephens attempted to clarify their complaint: hardware merchants did not object to other retailers selling the same goods if they were licensed to do so, but they were opposed to other merchants selling those goods when hardware stores were legally obliged to close.[46]

The issue seems finally to have been resolved only when Vancouver abandoned Wednesday closing and hardware stores were permitted

5.3 The wide variety of goods on sale at hardware stores such as this one proved to be a major headache for competing merchants and city officials alike. Image M09455 (BC Coast Hardware, Victoria, ca. 1908) courtesy of the City of Victoria Archives.

to remain open and compete directly with the drugstores. But even after this decision, hardware stores continued to protest by focusing on evening shopping. In June 1958 the Vancouver division of the Canadian Retail Hardware Association joined the protests against drugstores being allowed to sell non-drug items (including electrical appliances, garden hoses, power mowers, and plastic utensils) on evenings and Sundays.[47] By September 1958, having interviewed various merchant groups in light of the battle between hardware and drug stores, Vancouver's city administration board reported to city council that twenty-four-hour shopping was the only logical way to prevent illegal selling and that it was simply not practical to restrict the types of goods that shops could sell; if stores were open they should be allowed to sell whatever was in stock. In the end, the report explained, it was simply not plausible to "allow a man to go to a corner grocery and buy a pound of cheese and some bacon, but not a tin of soup."[48] Such sentiments were increasingly widespread in the 1950s as civic leaders in southwestern BC halfheartedly maintained a complex patchwork of regulations but moved their communities increasingly towards wide open shopping.

In Victoria, a city increasingly dependent on tourism witnessed an ongoing division between tourism-dependent merchants and those whose trade centred on local consumers. At the centre was a long-standing dilemma over what should be considered a "souvenir." The city's fruitless quest to define a "souvenir" began in earnest in July 1949 when Victoria City Council's business and trade committee found itself considering a letter from the Victoria Jewelers' Association protesting the selling, after 6 p.m. and on Wednesday afternoons, of a variety of goods including watches, watch accessories, and chinaware at a hotel stand and two local stores. Such items, it argued, were usually associated with jewellery stores, and the selling of such goods amounted to unfair competition for the jewellery stores that were forced to remain closed. In its investigation, a committee of aldermen found that these articles were being sold as "souvenirs" – an activity that was legal under the current bylaw.[49] But this was only the beginning of a long-running saga.

In July 1952 two Victoria merchants, Earl Ward, manager of the Scotty Shop, and Hugh Morrison, manager of the London Shop, faced prosecution under a bylaw after police officers purchased items from their stores after 1 p.m. on a Wednesday. In Ward's case he faced charges after a police constable purchased two pairs of Scottish socks from his store. The defendants' lawyer, James J. Proudfoot, countered that the bylaw did not apply to these merchants because of the nature of the goods they were selling.[50] The key question in the trial, the *Times* reported, was whether "socks imported from Scotland [could] be classed as souvenirs," which Proudfoot had argued in court his clients were permitted under the bylaw to sell. Since the bylaw failed to explicitly define a souvenir, Proudfoot turned to *Webster's Dictionary*, which described a souvenir as "a keepsake or remembrance." City prosecutor Alan Bigelow responded with a contextual argument claiming that what a store sells *generally* should be taken into account.[51] City police court magistrate Hall was unsympathetic to the defence. Siding with Bigelow's argument and noting, for instance, that the Scotty Shop was a clothing and tailoring store, he rejected Proudfoot's "souvenir" argument even when the lawyer claimed that Ward possessed two trade licences – one for clothing and one for souvenirs.[52] In making his decision, Hall ruled that a sock is "an ordinary type of merchandise sold by the defendant."[53]

Earl Ward, however, was not one to keep his frustrations to himself. In February 1953, at a meeting of the Victoria Chamber of Commerce retail merchants group, he complained that drugstores and groceries were permitted to sell curios and souvenirs during hours in which a local bylaw forced souvenir stores to remain closed.[54] The difficulty involved in defining a souvenir was clear. The *Colonist* addressed the problem in an April 1953 editorial in which it expressed its frustration at competing interests that claimed to have clear support for their side in the store-hour issue. "There was no clear majority in favor of anything," it explained, while noting that instead of approaching a settlement, "the situation if anything is more confused than ever." It was "virtually impossible," the newspaper lamented, "to draft a civic bylaw to give an unmistakable definition of tourist business."[55]

Goods other than hardware and souvenirs were also subject to debate. In June 1953, for example, Vancouver opticians successfully argued that they were not retailers – as city licence inspector Arthur Moore had designated them – by noting that they restricted their Wednesday activities to filling out prescriptions (which was legal) rather than selling glasses (which was illegal).[56] The legal position of stores selling a *variety* of goods was even more complex. In the early 1950s such stores had to purchase separate licences for each distinct line of goods they sold. Hence, in 1954, when Vancouver City Council phased in six-day shopping and approved a bylaw allowing department stores and variety stores to open on Wednesdays, licence inspector Moore made sure to remind them that stores with more than one type of licence could only sell classes of goods approved for Wednesday selling.[57]

Because classes of shops had to petition for the right to remain open six days a week, and it took time to process and approve these applications, the result was confusion for shoppers everywhere. Some classes of shops were permitted to open on Wednesdays while others were not. In addition, stores selling more than one type of good were open for business but technically only permitted to sell some of their merchandise. For instance, the *Vancouver Province* warned that "you can go into a men's wear shop Wednesday and buy a suit or a sports coat" but "don't ask for a shirt to go with it. The law forbids the clothier to sell you one. He can't sell socks or ties, or other haberdashery either. But you can walk into a nearby department store and buy the suit, shirt and socks together." Moore acknowledged the situation and explained that it had arisen because according to the letter of the law, a clothier needed a separate licence to sell haberdashery as a sideline, and haberdashers had not filed a petition but men's wear stores had. Department stores, on the other hand, possessed a different type of licence and were thus permitted to sell all products.[58]

To be approved for Wednesday opening, a percentage of merchants in a class of business was required to sign a formal petition. Obtaining the necessary number of signatures on petitions was difficult and was further complicated, the *Sun* reported, because sidelines could be considered part of a class of business. Thus, jewellery stores were unable to meet the necessary percentage because a cigar store chain selling cheap watches refused to sign the petition, while "china shops learned that they must line up hardware stores that sell kitchen crockery." The answer, the newspaper argued, was to have each store licensed for the main line of merchandise and to grade fees upwards based on number of sidelines. Such as solution would allow the city to discontinue "the farcical pretense that a tobacconist who sells fountain pens is a stationary merchant."[59] Even smaller stores found themselves contending with inconvenient restrictions. Vancouver's musical instrument shops could not sell televisions or radios on Wednesdays because these items were classified as appliances.[60] As late as 1959, Vancouver still faced an awkward situation in which launderettes were permitted to remain open in the evening while laundries had to close.[61]

Such confusion and frustration appeared to weaken the resolve of many city officials in both cities. As they attempted to balance competing interests, the result often seemed to be regulations that were either too broad to address the complex nature of their local economies or too intricate to be clearly articulated to merchants and consumers. The lack of an obvious solution very likely combined with a desire to limit the political costs of taking a firm position on the store-hour issue to convince civic leaders to wash their hands of it once and for all. Not surprisingly, then, when in 1958 Victoria City Council passed a bylaw exempting sixty-seven classes of stores from the province's Municipal Act, and thus store-hour regulations, both "hardware" and "souvenir" stores were included on the list of stores no longer subject to store-hour restrictions.[62]

Loopholes

Given the technical detail involved, it is not surprising that enforcement initiatives were also undermined by a number of legal loopholes. In March 1950, for example, the provincial government felt obliged to amend the Shop Regulations and Weekly Holiday Act to prevent retailers from taking night orders on closing days and delivering the required item the next day. The amendment was aimed directly at a Vancouver department store's "'night owl' phone order service" as well as at preventing storekeepers from advertising that they would still take orders when officially closed.[63]

Members of the legal profession, acting on behalf of clients eager to circumvent store-hour restrictions, offered even more creative ways of evading the spirit of the regulations. The first charge laid under Vancouver's new evening bylaw in 1959 was against George Gromer, owner of the Import House on Robson Street, for selling an item (in this case a toaster) worth more than $10.[64] When the case went to court, Gromer's lawyer successfully argued that because the two plainclothes policewomen had no intention of actually purchasing the toaster, the transaction was never completed, and thus no law had been broken (see Figure 5.4).[65] In 1956, by defining a day as twenty-four hours, several grocery chain stores in Vancouver threatened to liberally interpret the local bylaw's reference to restricting stores to being open "six whole days in any one week" as allowing stores to remain open twenty-four hours a day, six days a week.[66] When Vancouver amended its city charter in 1957, a chastened city council made certain to include explicit wording that made reference to specific hours of operation rather than "whole days."[67]

The most egregious loophole, however, was a product of government ineptitude – or, in the minds of conspiracy theorists, a coy ploy to eliminate store-hour regulations altogether. When the provincial government introduced its new Municipal Act in 1957, a legislative error was set to leave the entire province without effective store-hour regulations.[68] In a memorandum to Premier W.A.C. Bennett, the Deputy Minister of Municipal Affairs, J. Everett Brown, explained that with such complicated legislation some mistakes were inevitable and in this case a key phrase had been accidentally omitted. The phrase itself seemed innocuous enough: "and remain closed continuously after the hour fixed for closing." But in a political climate in which store-hour regulation opponents sought any possible loophole, they seized

Bylaw charge quashed —sale not completed

The first charge laid under the city's new closing bylaw was dismissed by Magistrate Gordon Scott Saturday.

He ruled that George Gromer, owner of the Import House, 1058 Robson, had not completed the sale of a toaster in excess of $10 to two policewomen, as charged.

The bylaw prohibits the sale of electrical appliances valued at more than $10 after 6 p.m., unless they are for medical purposes or are classed as toilet articles.

The policewomen said, in evidence, they gave Gromer $20 for a toaster costing $15.71.

When they received their change, they identified themselves as policewomen and received their $20 back.

They then returned the change they had received from Mr. Gromer.

5.4 Dismissed on a technicality. The *Province* reports on the kind of court decision that helped undermine support for store-closing regulations. *Vancouver Daily Province*, 1 February 1960, 15. Image reproduced courtesy of Post Media.

upon the obvious: technically stores now had to close their doors at the appointed closing time; but they could reopen as soon as the closing time passed – at, say, 6:01 p.m.[69]

As soon as the problem was widely reported, city officials scrambled to obtain legal advice. According to the *Sun*, most municipalities would aim to implement bylaws that followed the intention of the Municipal Act. But not everyone was so forgiving, and some saw this as an opportunity to abandon store-hour regulation. "We don't care how long stores remain open at night," claimed Burnaby's municipal clerk, Charles Brown. "We wanted to see such regulations thrown out completely."[70] John E. Fitzwater, president of the Union of British Columbia

Municipalities, similarly welcomed this development.[71] The *Victoria Times* noted that given the mounting opposition to the new section of the act, "it was a handy discovery for the government."[72] Despite recognizing the problem, the provincial government explained that it could not be remedied until the next session of the legislature, which was several months away.[73]

The *Times* blamed the government for carelessly pushing forward with the amendment without allowing it to be reviewed by a legislative committee and went so far as to suggest that by publicly releasing the internal memorandum, Premier Bennett appeared to have been "inviting shop owners to ignore the intent of legislation rendered ineffective by faulty draughtsmanship."[74] The *Vancouver Sun* suggested that Bennett was "privately grateful for the mistake, because it gave him the chance to throw out the 'defective' law and stem a rising tide of indignation."[75] In an address to members of the Independent Merchants' Co-operative Association, Victoria alderman and Social Credit MLA J. Donald Smith went so far as to urge corner grocers to defy the closing clause of the new act; prosecutions, he explained, were unlikely.[76]

Vancouver, in revising its civic charter in light of the Municipal Act, picked up the key phrase and did not omit it.[77] Hence, the *Sun*'s blunt assessment may have been motivated by the fact that the end result of Vancouver's authorities having avoided the provincial government's mistake was that only Vancouver's merchants faced codified store-hour restrictions. Even nearby suburbs would now be free to lure shoppers away from downtown stores.[78] "Two years they worked on it," the *Sun* grumbled. The only answer when the provincial government met again on this issue, it argued, was for the government to hand over control of the issue to local municipalities – bodies that might possess the competence the provincial government so clearly seemed to lack.[79] Unimpressed with the provincial government's handling of the controversy, the *Times* bluntly asserted that the government had "pulled a boner" by rushing the Municipal Act through the legislature and pointed to the dangerous precedent of having government representatives encouraging people to break the law.[80]

According to the *Times*, Victoria's move towards wide-open store hours was simply a product of misguided attempts at enforcement. In saluting city council for siding with both the "buying public" and the "largest segment of city business," the *Times* opined that "strict enforcement of the law proved its inadequacy and its unpopularity." "The small-town atmosphere has disappeared in the tremendous growth that we have experienced since the war," but business practices had not kept pace.[81] The complexity of store-hour regulatory regimes did indeed play a key role in undermining their effectiveness. Some merchants flouted the restrictions. Merchants who did obey the law complained about uneven enforcement. City and provincial officials grew weary of an issue that seemed to offer no feasible political solution and an abundance of grief. The confusion over how one might define "hardware" or "souvenirs" underscored just how messy the situation was, while a series of loopholes highlighted both the determination of the system's opponents and the daunting resources that would be required to shore up the system's legal infrastructure. Together these factors went far to undermine the authorities' support for store-hour restrictions. Expanded shopping hours were thus the product not simply of consumer and business demands for change, but also of the very real difficulties involved in enforcing regulations. As the following chapter suggests, battles over the manner in which legal restrictions were decided upon and enforced came to be infused with ideologically polarizing but politically engaged rhetoric that attests to the vitality of the public debate in the two cities.

Chapter Six

Ideology: The Cold War and the Public Sphere

Is this a democratic country when the law makes you close up whether you want to or not on a Wednesday afternoon?

> Victoria novelty-shop proprietor Kelly Porter, 1949[1]

This group is just being dictatorial.

> Victoria merchant T.G. Denny laments the Victoria Chamber of Commerce's Tourist Trade Group decision to oppose Wednesday closing, 1951[2]

The postwar expansion of shopping opportunities occurred in very specific economic and geographic contexts – during a sustained period of economic expansion that combined with suburban population growth to place a significant strain on existing store-hour regulations. But it also occurred in a very specific political context – the Cold War – and at a time in British Columbia when provincial elections featured bitter contests between right- and left-wing parties.[3] Both geopolitics and disputes over provincial economic and social priorities offered daily reminders of the ideological battle between capitalism and socialism. Historians have begun to seek connections between the experience of the Cold War and the growing centrality of consumerism in Canadian life.[4] This chapter carries forward this research by documenting the complex ways in which Cold War rhetoric permeated debates regarding access to consumer goods and services.[5]

After the Second World War, merchants, employees, consumers, and local politicians in Vancouver and Victoria increasingly came to view the issue of store-hour regulation through the lens of the Cold War and expressed their views through rhetoric that drew on notions of free enterprise, political freedom, dictatorship, rights, and democracy.[6] In doing so, these different groups employed the same Cold War language in ways that suited their own interests. In short, they employed Cold War idiom as a useful but malleable rhetorical weapon. In examining this development, this chapter offers a window onto the public sphere and provides an opportunity to explore the connections between the Cold War and consumerism and to evaluate the extent to which Cold War concerns permeated Canadians' everyday lives.[7] The examples presented here suggest that Cold War symbolism pervaded Canadian society, but in unexpected and often contradictory ways.

From the beginning the debates in Victoria and Vancouver reflected the tensions inherent in liberal ideology, particularly tensions between individual and community interests.[8] But before the advent of the Cold War, these tensions were largely expressed without direct reference to explicit concepts of political philosophy.[9] The exception here was utilitarianism, which both supporters and opponents of store-hour restrictions employed as early as the First World War. For example, in a May 1916 letter to the *Victoria Daily Times*, "Storekeeper" took issue with merchants who favoured Saturday closing over Wednesday closing in the belief that such a closing pattern would have less impact on their own trade while negatively affecting others: "The adoption of a course which causes loss or misfortune to one's fellow-traders inevitably reacts upon the whole town."[10] Tellingly, a June 1916 advertisement urging Victorians to vote *for* a Saturday half-holiday employed a similar utilitarian logic: the opportunities for common leisure time, it argued, "will secure the maximum good for the largest number."[11] On the eve of Victoria's 1919 referendum on the issue, Mary Patton of Angus Campbell & Co., a women's clothing store, railed against merchants who were leading a well-funded campaign against Saturday closing. A strong proponent of the store clerks' desire for Saturday closing, Patton charged that "there will always be an unfortunate minority, but the greatest good for the greatest number is the rule which should be followed."[12]

Once the Wednesday mid-week closing had been established and become a prominent concern for those determined to decrease store-hour restrictions, tension persisted between individual and community interests. One of Victoria's most passionate early opponents of mid-week closing, Arthur Lineham, consistently argued that clerks and merchants who favoured the policy were putting their own interests ahead of the community.[13] Victoria's economic predicament, he argued in 1923, was caused by "the selfish narrow viewpoint taken by the majority of us." "Every move instigated by our local organizations," he charged, was accepted or rejected with reference to personal interests rather than its overall merits or demerits: "The viewpoint of the average individual is very often so narrow that he or she cannot possibly be made to see how indirectly they will get more benefit at some future date by sinking self for the moment and suffering some temporary loss or inconvenience thereby."[14] Victoria's W.M. Wilson concurred and wrote to the *Colonist* in 1924 urging civic government and business organizations to play a leading role in eliminating mid-week store closing. In doing so, Wilson too drew upon the rhetoric of utilitarianism: "I think it the principal duty if not the mainspring of the very existence of such institutions as the Chamber of Commerce and the City Council – to seek the introduction and promotion of such legislation as will be productive of the 'greatest amount of good to the greatest number of people.'"[15]

As the conflict over store hours receded from the late 1920s to the early 1940s, so did direct references to liberal notions of individual and community interests. But when the campaign to eliminate Wednesday closing was renewed after the Second World War, so too was the use of liberal rhetoric. In December 1946 the *Times* argued that the proposal for mid-week closing should be defeated "in the long-term interest of the whole community."[16] A similar rhetoric reappeared in Vancouver. A March 1951 letter to the *Vancouver Sun* directly questioned the fairness of closing bylaws: "No one questions the right of any group to organize for mutual benefit, but the principle of allowing such groups to legally control the actions of all persons engaged in that trade or occupation interferes with the freedom of the subject and is basically unsound."[17] The dilemmas involved in defining community interests without infringing on individual rights were an important factor in the debates over evening shopping in that city. Moreover, when the Vancouver Retail Merchants' Association campaigned to allow corner stores to remain open late hours without facing competition from supermarkets, it called for the authorities to begin "treating big and small operators on [a different but] equitable basis."[18]

Liberty, equality, and the difficulties involved in reconciling individual and community interests thus remained focal points of the store-hour debates well into the postwar era. But something about the debates changed dramatically with the advent of the Cold War. Earlier discussion had drawn only tangentially on notions of liberalism; now, the references to political ideology became much more explicit – and in some surprising ways. It is this development that I analyse here by focusing on three themes: differing notions of personal and political freedom, the growing connection between consumption and citizenship, and contrasting definitions of "democracy."

"A Half-Breed Monstrosity": Free Enterprise, Freedom, and Dictatorship

Postwar store-hour debates were rife with references to personal and political freedom. Opponents of store-hour regulation consistently denounced government legislation and civic bylaws for infringing on the economic freedom inherent in a free enterprise society. Logic dictated that supporters of store-hour restrictions were unable to make similar use of free enterprise rhetoric. They drew instead on the language of personal and political freedom and, much more frequently, on notions of dictatorship. The result was a series of heated exchanges, infused with Cold War rhetoric, in which the growing power of consumerism was alternately celebrated and challenged.

The call to defend "free enterprise" was a common one among corporations, business lobby groups, and small businesses in the postwar era. However, just what proponents meant by that term varied considerably. In fact, such pronouncements drew on two competing understandings of the relationship between business and government – understandings that were weighted differently depending on the situation. One strain drew a stark distinction between entrepreneurship and government activity; this understanding virulently opposed government intervention on the grounds that such activity was destructive. Large corporations like the Royal Bank of Canada and Hiram Walker gave voice to this strain in the 1940s when they embarked on advertising campaigns championing the free enterprise system in an effort to rein in plans for an expansive role for government in the postwar economy.[19] Business lobby groups also drew on this understanding when they submitted briefs to the Massey Commission expressing concern over competition from the state-run CBC and National Film Board.[20]

Such pronouncements were an attempt to create a political consensus that would ensure that government interference in business pursuits was kept to a minimum. As Reg Whitaker and Gary Marcuse observe, such a "consensus cutting across classes" and "defending 'our way of life' – crucially including free enterprise – against the philosophy of communism (and socialism) obviously appealed to businessmen contending with the demands of trade unions and fears of government intervention, nationalization, and regulation."[21] Expressed publicly, pronouncements like these offered a vision of free enterprise that vilified intrusive government regulation and that championed both entrepreneurial achievement and "consumer sovereignty" – the liberal economic notion that consumers were readily equipped to make rational purchasing decisions.[22]

There was, however, a second understanding of free enterprise – one that acknowledged that government played an important regulatory role in the economy. This understanding was perhaps best expressed by the BC Chamber of Commerce. In a 1955 policy statement, the chamber made the point implicitly. The "role of the government should be limited to the exercise of regulatory powers," it argued, because the "entrance of government into the field of production and distribution leads to socialism and dictatorship."[23] A decade later the chamber had honed its message to offer a bolder, more positive statement on the role of government. In its General Policy Statements for 1965, it explained that the "role of Governments is to create and maintain a favourable climate for enterprise." In doing so, the government would allow "competitive private enterprise" to "bring the greatest good to the greatest number of people of this province."[24] This strain of free enterprise rhetoric was more easily reconciled with postwar demands from entrepreneurs and business lobby groups for government regulation.

On this count, it is instructive to examine the selective approach to regulation adopted by BC tourism promoters after the Second World War. Even while protesting against what they considered unnecessary government regulations, such as mandatory BC automobile insurance for American visitors, civic tourism-promotion bodies endorsed a government act regulating tourist camps on the grounds that sanitary and enjoyable camping experiences would ensure repeat customers in the future. Camp operators themselves embraced these regulations in part because of the limitations they placed on the number of facilities and thus on competition.[25] In a similar vein, as the wartime housing shortage was exacerbated by the arrival of returning soldiers, Vancouver Tourist Association officials cooperated with the National Housing Registry to prevent local accommodation operators from charging exorbitant room rates.[26] Such actions and pronouncements illustrate the extent to which private enterprise embraced some forms of government regulation while eschewing others.

Businesses thus championed two variants of free enterprise ideology – one that emphasized freedom from government regulation, and another that recognized that government regulations helped create a positive entrepreneurial environment. They expressed the former, more selective, understanding most consistently during the postwar store-hour debates. Indeed, many merchants opposed to specific store-hour regulations worked from the assumption that any government regulation served to corrupt an otherwise perfect economic system. Faced with store-hour regulations that restricted their ability to sell goods, they argued that government intervention was both unnecessary and a threat to Canada's free enterprise system.

In 1954, for example, when Vancouver City Council considered appeasing local butchers by approving a ban on selling frozen meats and fish after 5:30 p.m., the frustration among small grocers was palpable. Earl W. Scott, proprietor of Scott's Grocery in the city's West End, vowed that he and other small grocers would find a way to continue selling meat and fish in the evening despite the new law. "It's getting so there's not much difference between the capitalist system and the communist system," he argued, before rationalizing that "this is supposed to be a free country, and if I want to operate 10 hours or 24 hours a day, that's my business."[27] Newspaper editorials and consumers expressed similar sentiments.[28] "I am inclined to think," retired Saanich resident Carl Fallas lamented, "that the bureaucrats are choking us to death. If a fellow wants to stay open, let him. If we are supposed to be living under capitalism, for God's sake let's have it and not a half-breed monstrosity such as we have now."[29]

Opponents of store-hour regulation forcefully expressed such concerns, but they did so by employing a highly selective understanding of free enterprise – one that failed to acknowledge, unlike the BC Chamber of Commerce, that state regulations often served the interests of entrepreneurs. For as Tom Traves explains, "freedom of enterprise in Canada does not mean 'laissez-faire'" but reflects a system in which the "coercive power of the state" played an important role in regulating and stabilizing the business environment in the postwar years.[30] These merchants, focused as they were on the specific issue of store-hour regulations, conveniently overlooked this more complex understanding of the relationship between state regulation and entrepreneurial freedom.

In doing so, they were echoing the pronouncements of businesses across the country that had seized on the free enterprise theme to challenge government intervention in the arts through briefs to the Massey

Commission and that were resisting an expanded welfare state through advertising campaigns. For Canadians not attuned to debates over arts funding or the intricacies of postwar reconstruction, the debates surrounding shopping regulations exposed them to Cold War rhetoric championing free enterprise ideology and warning Canadians about threats to their personal freedom. In this way, Cold War concerns informed not only debates about Canada's national destiny but more tangible local issues as well.

Closely related to warnings about threats to free enterprise were suggestions that store-hour regulations threatened personal and political freedom, and reeked of dictatorship – a spectre that could call forth threatening visions of both fascism and communism. As David Monod has demonstrated in his study of early-twentieth-century Canadian shopkeepers, retail merchants could be especially enthusiastic champions of regulation when it came to erecting barriers to new competition or preventing underselling through resale price maintenance.[31] In requesting regulations that restricted the business activities of their competitors, supporters of store-hour legislation were hardly resorting to free enterprise rhetoric. Nothing, however, prevented them from appropriating other aspects of Cold War ideology to serve their aims. Indeed, both opponents and supporters of store-hour regulations embraced rhetoric that championed personal and political freedom while raising the spectre of dictatorship.

Typical of the opponents' views was a 1951 letter to the *Vancouver Sun* arguing that coordinated attempts by store operators to have all stores in a given business class observe a common closing day were an assault on individual freedoms.[32] Seven years later the *Victoria Daily Times* echoed this sentiment by employing both the rhetoric of free enterprise and the theme of political freedom when it endorsed six-day shopping in Victoria: "Surely the whole debate comes down to ... the right of free citizens to carry on their businesses in a climate of freedom; to make money if they are efficient and hard-working, to lose it if they are inefficient or lazy."[33] The alternative to such a system, opponents of store-hour regulation charged, was totalitarianism or dictatorship – a point they incorporated effectively into their arguments. Thus the Victoria Chamber of Commerce's Tourist Trade Group included in its 1946 resolution objecting to compulsory all-day Wednesday closing the charge that such compulsion "is definitely opposed to all British ideas of freedom of the individual and is akin to [a] totalitarianism form of government."[34]

Not surprisingly, merchants were among the most likely to employ the spectre of totalitarian dictatorship. As part of its 1957 campaign to overturn new provincial regulations that would restrict corner stores to selling a limited range of goods after 6 p.m., for example, Victoria's Independent Merchants' Co-operative Association called on the city's housewives to lend their considerable political clout to the association's efforts.[35] In a letter mailed directly to citizens' homes, association president William Palmer did not mince words in his appeal to citizens to support small shopkeepers in their continuing battle for survival against increasingly powerful chain stores, which were coming to monopolize daytime sales. Evening operation, the association explained, was simply a matter of survival amidst this increasing competition, and the provincial government was only making matters worse by restricting evening sales. In encouraging the city's housewives to attend a public meeting on the issue, Palmer challenged their political allegiance directly: "It is up to you to support this meeting, or are we going to wear the hammer and sickle?"[36]

Victoria merchant Doris Ashdown was similarly keen to incorporate the spectre of Soviet dictatorship into her defence of her recently established "personal shopping service," which was threatened by the city's proposed all-day Wednesday-closing bylaw. With American visitors among her most important customers, Ashdown wrote to the *Daily Colonist* arguing that Wednesday closing would cost her dearly, given her client base. In doing so, she cast the proposed regulations as a threat to democracy, the British way of life, and even the beliefs of military veterans: "I wish to say that I am vitally opposed to compulsion as anything of the kind savors of dictatorship. I have lived during three wars in which the British Empire has given of her best and bravest to insure the democratic way of life. This is the way I believe in and that I desire to see continued, and I believe that is what the veterans – in the majority – who fought to insure it desires [sic] too."[37] Clearly, Cold War rhetoric that equated provincial and civic regulations with dictatorial powers, and that blended anti-fascist and anti-communist sentiments, was an appealing political tool for opponents of store-hour regulations.

Yet supporters of those same regulations also employed the rhetoric of personal and political freedom and the spectre of "dictatorship." In 1953, for example, Oak Bay resident Alex MacLeod Baird, a salesperson with Standard Furniture, spoke out in favour of preserving the Wednesday half-day holiday by demanding to know "what authority the city council have to interfere with private business and their employees."[38] In a similar vein, Victoria Chamber of Commerce member T.G. Denny argued that by ignoring a recent plebiscite in which the city's merchants had voted overwhelmingly to preserve the city's current store-hour regulations the chamber's Tourist Trade Group was "just being dictatorial."[39] Similarly, D.A. Gilbert, national president of the Retail Merchants Association (RMA), visited Victoria in April 1956 and called upon merchants to ensure that they were not "dictated to by the big chain stores."[40]

In taking this line of argument, the RMA and its supporters were in surprising company. During the Massey Commission proceedings, business interests eager to voice their opposition to government involvement in cultural pursuits "equated state-sponsored culture with the threat of communist totalitarianism." In response, Paul Litt explains, the "cultural lobby countered that it was powerful business interests ... that presented the real threat to individual freedom and opportunity."[41] Grocery store owners' complaints that they were being victimized by a chain-store "dictatorship" closely reflected the latter position, which illustrates the extent to which cultural elites and commercial interests could share a common language – one that drew on Cold War rhetoric in an effort to silence opponents.

Reg Whitaker and Gary Marcuse have suggested that "the very essence of the Cold War mentality" was "to demand absolute and unthinking fidelity to the 'right' side in the apocalyptic struggle between good and evil."[42] This mentality led to a binary logic that imposed clear limits regarding "the boundaries of legitimate dissent" and that closed off "certain options and possibilities as illegitimate, disloyal, or even treasonous."[43] The charge of "dictatorship" was a popular one in Cold War Canada. Even progressive teachers used it in their campaigns against their conservative opponents.[44] By employing this loaded term, both supporters and opponents of store-hour restrictions were seizing on and appropriating a potent Cold War symbol. The binary logic of the Cold War had thus permeated even local debates about what time the corner store should close. It had done so, however, at the behest of both sides. Unlike other documented instances, then, the use of this binary Cold War logic did not close down debate by silencing one side. If anything, it raised the temperature of the dispute as each side appropriated the symbolism to suit its own purposes. Cold War rhetoric in this context was a politically useful but malleable weapon that highlighted the dynamic nature of postwar debates over consumerism.

Consumption and Citizenship: The Right to Shop, the Right to Sell, and the Right to Leisure

Postwar debates about store-hour regulations also included numerous references to personal and political rights – a development that reflected the emergence of a culture of entitlement in Canada. The postwar era witnessed a blossoming of rights-based rhetoric. Throughout the 1930s and 1940s, advocates of the welfare state downplayed an earlier emphasis on "charity" to embrace a line of argument that centred on "entitlement." Support for direct relief, family allowances, and pensions, for example, was infused with a language of citizenship that championed Canadians' right to government support.[45] Immersed in this growing culture of entitlement, both supporters and opponents of store-hour regulations incorporated rights-based rhetoric into their public campaigns and pronouncements. In doing so, they added another level of sophistication to these exchanges in the public sphere.

Rights-based arguments in favour of decreasing or eliminating store-hour regulations took two complementary forms: the *right to shop* and the *right to sell*. Both featured prominently in a 1946 dispute over shopping opportunities in Victoria. In voicing its opposition to a proposal to legislate five-day shopping, for example, the *Daily Colonist* noted the possible deleterious effects that such a move might have on the city's tourism revenues before drawing its readers' attention to a more pressing issue: "The Canadian public is entitled to service upon an even basis" – something that would prove impossible if Victoria chose to restrict itself to a five-day shopping week and Vancouver did not.[46]

If the right to shop provided one element of the rights-based rhetoric employed by those opposed to overzealous regulations, the right (and responsibility) to sell provided the other. Hence merchant George MacDonald's blunt explanation of why he opposed Victoria's proposed five-day plan. "I'm not going to have any organization blackball me if I don't close my store on any particular day of the week," he argued. "This is not Germany, it is Canada."[47] The *Daily Colonist* brought both elements together when it argued "that many rights are involved. The public has a right to normal trading, having built its homes and businesses on that assumption ... Then there is the right of the proprietors who do not wish to close at midweek, but who value that trading day as much as any other trading day."[48] Such rhetoric championing both the right to shop and the right to sell reflected a growing link between consumption and citizenship. Indeed, opponents of store-hour regulations in Vancouver and Victoria shared this notion of "economic citizenship" with other Canadians, who during the 1940s framed their protests against rising meat prices and restrictions placed on the availability of margarine in terms of citizenship rights.[49] This conflation of consumption and citizenship, as Lizabeth Cohen notes in the American context, underscores the growing power of consumer culture at mid-century.[50]

Yet consumerism's growing power did not go unchallenged. While merchants and the public employed free enterprise rhetoric solely on the side of greater deregulation, the rhetoric regarding "rights," like that of freedom and dictatorship, was not nearly so one-sided. The champions of store-hour regulation developed their own rights-based arguments, which focused on one's *right to leisure*. Rights-based arguments in favour of early closing were certainly not unheard of before the Second World War – one secretary of Britain's Early Closing Association was reported to have insisted in 1928 that "no one has any right to want a kipper after eight o'clock at night" – but in the case of Vancouver and Victoria, it was the Cold War that infused the local debates with rights-based defences of leisure.[51]

For example, in 1953, Victoria store clerk H.A. Napper voiced his opposition to a proposal that would see clerks' hours staggered over a six-day week and the elimination of their common mid-week holiday by calling the public's attention to "the right of retail clerks to take part, if they wish to, in group activities, such as cricket, football, baseball, or any other game they may fancy." "It took our fathers a long time to win this right," he explained, "and some of us don't want to lose it."[52] More dramatic was Harold Gray's letter to the *Daily Colonist*, which railed against "shop owners" who sought to "take away from some nearly 6,000 retail clerks, the right and privilege ... to enjoy together ... their weekly half-day holiday." "Go to all the clerks for permission to change their holiday," he warned, "but let it never pass that we the public should take away a privilege from others that is not rightfully ours to take."[53] Here, then, were two eloquent champions of workers' "right" to common leisure.

Alex MacLeod Baird echoed their arguments and offered readers of the *Daily Times* a history lesson. "Following the history of our race if it were not for our laws – which preserve our rights – we would be wholly at the mercy of human greed," he argued. "Labor today represents a live potential section of the people – citizens who are taxpayers and represent a great proportion of the buying public, and are not a commodity as was thought years ago," Baird explained, tellingly equating workers' right to leisure with their role as consumers. It was this "right" that was now under threat and that required defending.[54]

Arguments in favour of retail clerks' right to leisure occurred in a context that was only just becoming familiar with such rhetoric. By the postwar era, Shirley Tillotson explains, leisure inhabited a secure place among the pantheon of "social rights" in Canada. The groundwork for this development had been laid in the 1930s when provincial governments across the country "put into law a new understanding of leisure as a universal citizen right" through legislation limiting hours of work and stipulating minimum annual holidays.[55] Government motivation during the Depression, however, was firmly focused on increasing employment. Hence, Tillotson explains, "the right to work, not the right to enjoy leisure, was the element of citizenship at issue."[56] Only in the 1940s and 1950s, she contends, was the right to leisure "explicitly asserted."[57] Such assertions coincided with a variety of conflicting pronouncements from social scientists and cultural critics, who argued about whether increased leisure time would improve or demoralize Canadians.[58]

The debates over store-hour regulations add an important dimension to these elite pronouncements: the voice of ordinary Canadians championing leisure not only as a positive element in their lives but also as an entitlement they were determined to retain and protect. As they had done with the rhetoric of freedom and dictatorship, both opponents and supporters of store-hour regulations enlisted rights-based arguments to champion their respective causes. The culture of entitlement that was firmly in place by the postwar period allowed participants in these debates to employ these pronouncements confident that their statements would reverberate powerfully among their fellow citizens. In expressing themselves in this manner, they were appropriating another element of Cold War rhetoric. Recognizing the presence of these voices in the public sphere highlights an important but as yet overlooked fact: postwar debates about mass culture and democracy were not the sole preserve of cultural elites. Ordinary Canadians were having their say as well.

Debating Democracy

Along with "freedom," "dictatorship," and "rights," "democracy" proved a popular buzzword during the early decades of the Cold War. Psychologists championed democratic approaches to childrearing, while cultural critics worried aloud that a vibrant democratic political culture was being replaced by a conformist mass culture.[59] Moreover, as Len Kuffert observes, there existed in Canada's "Cold War environment" a tendency to equate "the development of popular culture with political democracy and a kind of 'people's morality.'"[60] Many different interests thus claimed to be on the side of democracy.

Supporters and opponents of store-hour regulations were no different. Along with rights-based arguments and the rhetoric focusing on freedom and dictatorship, both sides of the debates embraced "democracy." Their use of democratic rhetoric, however, was more complex. While opponents of store-hour regulations deployed democracy in general arguments that asserted shopkeepers' right to open or close their stores, both sides in the debate invoked its spirit in detailed and intricate arguments over the method by which decisions about a community's store hours ought to be made. These debates focused on who was an acceptable participant in the decision-making process. Should the merchants determine store hours? Or should the public decide? The answers to these questions, not surprisingly, depended on the subject position from which one viewed the debates.

In their general arguments, critics of store-hour regulations consistently dismissed as undemocratic the civic bylaws and provincial statutes setting out the restrictions.[61] Often, these critics pointed to what they understood to be flagrant inconsistencies in store-hour regulations and questioned whether the system itself was democratic. In 1949, frustrated Victoria novelty shop proprietor Kelly Porter asked rhetorically, "Is this a democratic country when the law makes you close up whether you want to or not on a Wednesday afternoon?"[62] In 1954, voicing his support for a six-day shopping week in Vancouver, Vancouver Real Estate Board president Herbert R. Fullerton similarly equated democracy with free enterprise: "Under our democratic system of free enterprise, the individual is entitled to operate his business as he sees fit providing he does not injure the right of others by doing so."[63]

In employing the rhetoric of democracy to suggest a direct connection between democratic rights and their desire to be freed from unwelcome government-imposed restrictions, opponents of store-hour regulations drew on the binary mentality of the Cold War to cast themselves as defenders of democracy and their opponents as threats to their democratic rights. Ideally, such a manoeuvre would have succeeded in silencing the supporters of store-hour regulations. But when it came to determining the process by which regulations should be approved, rejected, or rescinded, both opponents and supporters of store-hour regulations embraced the rhetoric of democracy.

By far the most prevalent argument employing democracy in the campaign to reduce or eliminate store-hour regulations centred around the demand that the public, rather than the merchants themselves, decide the issue. This demand focused on two scenarios. One involved simply ensuring that civic officials solicited the public's opinion through referendums instead of relying on the input of lobbying groups. A second scenario witnessed opposition to the mechanisms of specific bylaws, many of which stipulated that classes of business could approve or repeal closing restrictions by obtaining the signatures of a certain number of business operators within a given class.

In demanding that civic government consult the wider public regarding store-hour regulations, these observers were motivated in part by the belief that the public, as consumers, would inevitably embrace wider store hours. Frequently, referendum results proved this optimism wrong, but the rhetoric itself remained consistent. Councillor H.M. Diggon led opposition in 1946 to Victoria's proposed bylaw on Wednesday closing by arguing that city council's decision was undemocratic because taxpayers had not had an opportunity to vote on the issue.[64] A meeting of Vancouver merchants in 1947 resulted in a similar call for a public referendum. While the majority of merchants at an RMA meeting favoured all-day Wednesday closing, dissenters calling for a referendum argued that it was "highly undemocratic for a small group of merchants to impose policy on the whole community."[65] R.H. Hiscocks, secretary of the local branch of the Native Sons of BC, went so far as to claim that Victoria's store closing bylaws were in "direct violation" of democracy and majority rule. Retail stores, he argued, must be subject to the will of the people.[66]

Former Victoria mayor and MLA Reginald Hayward went further in expressing his opposition to all-day Wednesday closing and his support for the city's decision to hold a referendum on the issue. Hayward equated consumption with citizens' decision-making power. In his understanding, merchants took on the role of politicians, while consumers voted with their pocketbooks. "Merchants have more than goods to sell: they have a service to perform," Hayward explained. "The public is the judge of the service it requires, not the merchants, and it is for the public to decide whether stores shall be compelled to

6.1 "To wit, did unlawfully remain open on Wednesday in response to some nonsense called the peoples' vote...." Cartoonist Al Beaton ridicules Vancouver's slow response to a referendum result endorsing six-day shopping. *Vancouver Province*, 23 July 1954, p. 6. Image reproduced courtesy of Kathleen Cameron.

close all day. The consumer, the customer, pays the bill." Consumers, he argued, "are the final judges of the service they require, or what they will buy or where."[67] Tellingly, Hayward thus incorporated a celebration of consumer sovereignty into his demand for a more democratic decision-making process.

Yet supporters of store-hour restrictions, and of Wednesday closing in particular, also embraced the rhetoric of democracy. But in their case, the "majority" that was expected to approve or rescind such policies was not the general public but those whose lives were most directly affected by the regulations: the merchants and clerks. Such was Victoria councillor Edward Williams's understanding in 1946 when he urged his fellow council members to "do what the majority of the merchants in any specific class want ... That is the most democratic way."[68] Reg Williams, president of the Victoria Meat Retailers' Association, pointed to the bylaws themselves as ensuring that the *real* majority had its say. In every case in which a bylaw regulating a particular class of business had been passed, at least 75 per cent of the licensed dealers in that class must have requested the action; therefore, he explained, the bylaw must be democratic.[69] For Vancouver appliance dealer A.M. Thomson Jr, a plebiscite on the issue of wide-open store hours was not "a democratic way to decide the issue." "It was by this means that unrestricted hours were forced upon merchants in some other areas," he noted. "To be fair a vote should be made only by the merchants and their sales staff."[70] "Let there be a vote by the thousands of retail employees on the issue and you know full well what the result would be. This would be the only way democratically to decide the issue."[71]

In arguing that the public had no right to determine store-hour regulations, some observers were keen to suggest that the public was not qualified to express its view on the issue. In a joint brief opposing a planned Victoria referendum on the six-day week, a coalition of organizations that championed the five-day alternative argued that "it is most illogical to expect the public to vote intelligently on a matter which merchants and their staffs find difficult to solve."[72] In Vancouver it was left to councillor Syd Bowman to bluntly express this view: "The public has no place in telling me how to run my business. This is an issue that the businessman should decide, because the public isn't aware of the problems to be faced."[73] Support for Bowman's assertion came from the Retail Merchants Association. H.C. Boulton, secretary-manager of the association's national body, argued that "even in a democracy, there must be *some* rules as to who is eligible and who is not, to express an opinion." Retailing, he argued, was a specialized field, and only those who were part of this field should have a say in determining retail hours.[74] A number of merchants, employees, and other supporters of store-hour regulations thus appraised the public's ability to contribute meaningfully to resolving the store-hour controversy and found it wanting. They expressed this view through Cold War rhetoric that championed democracy but set clear and self-interested limits on which members of the public should have the opportunity to determine the outcome.

On one level, then, democracy was just one more symbolic weapon employed in the store-hour battle. It was a useful way to suggest that an opponent's views were beyond the pale of Canadian political

culture. On another level, however, the exchanges regarding democracy serve to highlight a complex and rational debate in which participants evaluated the political decision-making processes that affected
their daily lives as retailers, workers, and consumers. Participants in
these exchanges argued not simply over the content of the regulations,
but also about the process by which such regulations should be determined. This was a debate about how democracy actually ought to work
and about the right of the majority to force its will on the minority. It
was also a debate about who rightly comprised the majority. Depending
on one's vantage point, the rightful majority ranged from all members
of the voting public, to members of the public who purchased goods, to
retailers and clerks employed in the retail trade.

"Public policy," Reg Whitaker and Gary Marcuse acknowledge, "is
usually debated in terms that mix expressions of self-interest with
assertions about the national or common interest." "The coming of
the Cold War to Canada," they explain, "was most often discussed in
lofty language and high rhetoric." Certainly, these postwar debates
over shopping opportunities fit this pattern. Opponents and supporters of store-hour regulations attempted to connect their own self-
interests with national concerns about Canada's future.[75] As a result,
the language of the Cold War permeated the everyday life of merchants, clerks, consumers, and local politicians in very tangible and
immediate ways. One lesson of this chapter, then, is that Cold War
concerns were not restricted to broad debates about the nature of postwar reconstruction, family life, or government institutions. Indeed, in
addition to these realms, Cold War rhetoric came to occupy a central
place in very specific and local debates about one's access to consumer
goods and services.

A second and related conclusion concerns the nature of public
debate during the postwar era. On one level, it is clear, as Whitaker
and Marcuse have argued, that Cold War politics stifled real debate on
a number of fronts.[76] However, as these store-hour debates illustrate,
citizens appropriated Cold War rhetoric to serve a number of different and often conflicting ends. Rather than closing down the debates
over store hours, Cold War rhetoric fanned the flames of conflict. Participants selectively employed notions of free enterprise, personal and
political freedom, dictatorship, rights, and democracy to serve their

own interests. Opposing interests embraced Cold War rhetoric as a useful and malleable tool. Postwar Canadian political culture was hardly a pluralist paradise in which all groups had an equal say, but the examples cited here indicate that the state and its allies did not monopolize Cold War symbolism. Canadians often appropriated it for their own uses.

A third conclusion directly concerns the nature of the consumer society that existed between the end of the Second World War and the mid-1960s. These debates over shopping opportunities were clearly informed by both a rights-based rhetoric that mirrored the sense of entitlement expressed regarding welfare-state initiatives and a more atomistic understanding of human activity that denigrated government interference in the economy and instead championed consumer sovereignty. In her study of twentieth-century American consumer culture, Lizabeth Cohen identifies these two strands of consumer identity as comprising the "citizen consumer" and the "purchaser consumer."

The former, Cohen explains, rose to prominence during the 1930s as Americans demanded that their government protect their interests as consumers through regulation. This understanding of consumer identity, she argues, was trumped in the postwar era by the latter category, which expected consumers to contribute to the common good in a more limited and self-interested fashion. Simply by purchasing goods when and where they pleased, this line of argument claimed, Americans would be voting with their pocketbooks. Rather than directly influencing economic policy through government departments and regulations, the consumer now wielded influence indirectly while allowing business to remain as free as possible from undue regulation.[77]

The debates over shopping regulations in Vancouver and Victoria suggest that the "citizen consumer" and "purchaser consumer" ideals coexisted well into the postwar era in Canada. Calls to retain store-hour regulations mirrored the former understanding of consumer citizenship, while demands that stores be given the right to set their hours according to consumer demand reflected the latter. These competing conceptions of the consumer's role in society highlight not only the stresses and strains that emerged as consumerism colonized leisure time in twentieth-century North America, but also the extent to which citizenship came to be equated with consumption.

Finally, by focusing on the format and nature of these debates, and in particular on what the participants had to say about "democracy," this chapter points to an underdeveloped but promising field of study for Canadian historians: the public sphere.[78] Future research may well reveal that the debates examined here were, alternatively, part of a final fleeting wave of thoughtful debate, symptomatic of an already decayed public sphere colonized by a culture of consumption, or part of a healthy public sphere that survived well into the twentieth century and perhaps beyond. At present, though, we should recognize that postwar debates over consumerism and leisure show the public sphere to have been more dynamic and vibrant than the existing literature on the Cold War period would suggest. As the following, and final, chapter demonstrates, the Sunday shopping disputes that emerged in Vancouver and Victoria in the 1970s and 1980s were also the product of a complex debate. They boasted not simply forceful arguments supporting religious and secular positions but also voices reflecting long-standing tensions that had informed previous store-hour disputes.

Chapter Seven

Religion: Sunday Shopping's Multiple Battlegrounds

The law on Sunday closing is ridiculous and most asinine.
>M.H. Fisher to Vancouver Mayor, Mike Harcourt, 1981[1]

If people cannot get their shopping done during the hours we now have which include Thursday and Friday evenings then it is about time we started teaching people how to organize their time.
>Chuck and Phyllis Craver to *Vancouver Sun* columnist Nicole Parton, 1979[2]

The dispute over Sunday shopping differed from earlier conflicts that focused on Wednesday closing or evening shopping in one important way: religion was a marked feature of the debates. In explaining the decline of Sunday observance in Canada, Paul Laverdure emphasizes three key factors: growing ethnic and religious diversity, the waning energy and influence of an aging "sabbatarian elite," and the decision by religious leaders to defer to governments on the issue of enforcement.[3] These three developments, which gained considerable momentum in the mid-twentieth century, marked a pronounced contextual shift in Canadian political culture. In many ways the advent of legally sanctioned Sunday shopping marked the declining influence of Anglo-British cultural conventions in British Columbia.

However, it is important not to overestimate the extent to which religion was a focal point in these campaigns and disputes. In fact, in many ways, the Sunday shopping debates in Victoria and Vancouver should be viewed as extensions of the earlier debates about store-hour restrictions and liberalization. Historical precedents and grievances weighed heavily upon participants in the cities' Sunday shopping battles.

This chapter briefly examines how Sunday shopping became a contested issue in Victoria and Vancouver. It then explores the religious dimension of these debates before highlighting the extent to which the five components of store-hour debates that have been examined throughout this book served to structure these more contemporary conflicts concerning consumption, leisure, and work.

Defending a Weekly Day of Rest

In the 1970s, Sunday shopping remained illegal under the federal Lord's Day Act. Illegality, of course, did not mean that all stores abided by the law.[4] By the mid-1970s a growing number of retailers in Victoria were flouting the Lord's Day Act and opening for business on Sundays. In 1975, as he neared the end of his term in office, Victoria mayor Peter Pollen decided to intervene directly, not on religious grounds but because Victoria's embrace of wide open Monday-to-Saturday hours appeared to be contributing to a growing momentum to challenge Sunday's status as a commercial-free day of rest. Pollen warned that unrestrained Sunday trade could result in Victoria becoming "another Los Angeles with Sunday commercial schlock."[5] Some viewed Pollen's campaign as a broader, and somewhat cranky, morality crusade, a perception reinforced by the creation of a committee of three aldermen to examine the "'possible proliferation' of Sunday retailing, bar-room strippers and pornographic movies" – three activities that Pollen warned were being "imperceptibly injected into the community."[6]

The *Colonist* explained the Sunday shopping situation to its readers in April 1975 by noting that "generally Sunday retailing has been confined to corner stores, restaurants and hotels, but the city has no legislation controlling retailing on that day."[7] This was the crux of the problem that Pollen and his supporters faced. Prosecutions under the Lord's Day Act required the approval of the provincial attorney general, and given provincial politicians' penchant for avoiding the issue of store-hour regulations, such approval was rarely forthcoming. By June 1978 the Retail Merchants Association had declared that Sunday shopping was "out of control" in Victoria, but the provincial government continued to withhold its essential support for prosecutions and announced only that it was studying the issue.[8]

Throughout the 1970s, then, an awkward stalemate existed: Victoria's municipal government officially opposed Sunday shopping but did little, if anything, to discourage merchants from opening their stores. Civic politicians could conveniently point to the attorney general's office as the key reason why the Lord's Day Act was not being enforced. The extent of Sunday openings in the city during the 1970s is difficult to determine, but it does not appear to have been great. However, it was certainly visible enough to ensure that the issue of Sunday opening remained a consistent and unresolved topic for debate on city council and in the city's two major newspapers.

Vancouver entered the 1970s with a slightly more restrictive store-hour regime than existed in Victoria, but it too boasted a business environment that offered considerable opportunity for consumers to secure goods and services. By 1969, Vancouver's retail establishments were permitted to operate six days a week and one evening until 9 p.m. while a number of nearby communities permitted shopping on one or two additional evenings.[9] Campaigns for wide-open store hours continued to face staunch opposition, but pressure for increased evening shopping resulted in the city permitting late closing. This change brought Vancouver into line with many surrounding municipalities.[10]

In Vancouver, too, the issue of Sunday shopping gained traction in the 1970s. The first rumblings came from the city's Gastown district, which, the *Sun* reported in 1970, was becoming "a popular spot for a Sunday stroll." As more and more local merchants opened up their shops to cater to these pedestrians, retailers in other neighbourhoods voiced their opposition.[11] Over the next few years, city officials reviewed and investigated the situation while continuing to contemplate the removal of all store-hour restrictions except the Lord's Day Act, which, of course, was beyond their purview.[12] After an intense public debate in 1974, city council voted to maintain its current store-hour regulations and level of enforcement – which, if media reports are any indication, was minimal. But the discussions and decisions did not focus on Sunday shopping.[13] That would change the following year.

In 1975, Alderman Jack Volrich turned his attention to the city's Sunday shopping situation.[14] He would play a leading role early in 1976 when the city began to consider a crackdown on Sunday retail openings – which would be hindered significantly by the fact that prosecutions for Sunday openings required the approval of the attorney general.[15] Volrich was keen to limit Sunday openings to drugstores and convenience stores; council, though, was also open to the possibility of making allowances for retailers in designated tourist districts such as Gastown.[16] To pursue this aim, the city asked the provincial government to amend the city's charter so that it could regulate Sunday

7.1 "Our women and children can rest easier in the knowledge that the forces of Law and Order are finally taking the offensive ..." Cartoonist Len Norris questions City Hall's priorities amidst the Sunday shopping debates. *Vancouver Sun*, 17 November 1970. Image reproduced courtesy of Simon Fraser University Library, Special Collections and Rare Books.

retail hours. To Volrich's growing anger, the province at first refused to respond to the request; eventually, however, it rejected the proposal on the grounds that any restrictions on Sunday shopping should be uniform across the province.[17] On being elected mayor in 1977, Volrich adopted a new tactic: he threatened to use the city's licensing power to force retailers to comply.[18] In August 1978, city council attempted to bring some order to the situation by decreeing that certain types of stores would be permitted to open on Sundays and holidays, including convenience stores, souvenir stores, lumber yards, and retailers in Gastown and Chinatown.[19]

This decision set the stage for a spectacular legal showdown with Harry Hammer's furniture warehouse, a retailer whose stores were not in a class that City Hall had permitted to operate on Sundays but that faced competition from furniture retailers in nearby Richmond, where municipal officials turned a blind eye to Sunday openings. Unable to prosecute Harry Hammer (as the store's promotion manager, Bernard Cobin, was known), Vancouver City Council attempted to rescind his business licence for what it termed "gross misconduct" – namely, disobeying City Hall.[20] Vancouver's *Sun* and *Province* lambasted city council for trying to punish the retailer through the back door because it lacked the legal authority to enforce Sunday closing.[21] Justice J.G. Gould of the BC Supreme Court was similarly unimpressed, and in January 1980 he rejected the city's "gross misconduct" charge. In doing so he voiced his disapproval of the "patchwork enforcement" of Sunday shopping, whereby the city permitted small operations to open while attempting to force larger retailers to close. He indicated that jurisdiction over Sunday shopping remained the responsibility of the provincial government. The province's new attorney general, Allan Williams, promised that new legislation was on its way.[22] But Volrich's bluff had been called. As keen as he and other members of city council were to crack down on Sunday shopping, they lacked the power to enforce their views. In Vancouver, as in Victoria, the issue of Sunday shopping generated a great deal of heated debate throughout the 1970s but little in the way of tangible or productive solutions.

Largely in response to the untenable situations in Victoria and Vancouver, the provincial government finally took action in 1980 by passing the Holiday Shopping Regulation Act. The act came into effect in August in response to a 1979 Union of BC Municipalities resolution calling on the provincial government to cede control over all store-closing hours to municipalities. The act codified existing practice, according to which some stores were permitted to remain open to provide specific "essential commodities." But more importantly, it allowed municipalities to exempt broad categories of stores from the act's stipulation that all stores remain closed on Sundays and holidays.[23] This was a legislative turning point that helped set the stage for court-driven, plebiscite-supported municipal moves towards Sunday shopping in the 1980s and 1990s. It is important, however, to recognize the social

7.2 In January 1981, concerned that the province's Holiday Shopping Regulation Act would prevent them from opening on Sundays, angry Gastown merchants descend on the governing Social Credit Party's headquarters in Richmond with a two-block long petition demanding Sunday shopping. Moments later they would wrap the petition around the building to make their point. Image reproduced courtesy of Post Media.

and cultural dimensions of this issue – specifically, the contested nature of store-hour liberalization and deregulation throughout the 1970s as the Sunday shopping issue came to the fore. To this we now turn.

Dear Mayor Volrich: Religion as Reference Point

A sense of the ways in which religion informed these debates about Sunday shopping can perhaps best be gleaned from Vancouver mayor Jack Volrich's mailbag. Some observers certainly equated his campaign to limit or eradicate Sunday store openings with a broader defence of Christianity. In 1978 a flurry of letters from angry and alarmed Christians arrived on the mayor's desk urging him to "speak against the upsurging withdrawals from Christian principals [*sic*]." Rex Werts, for example, reminded Volrich that "public leaders have a responsibility to see that God's guidance for the welfare of men is respected." "The Ten Commandments have not been annulled," he explained. "The commandment about the 7th day remains and, as Jesus said, that day was meant for people, not for business. In Canada, a quasi-Christian country, that day is Sunday." Mrs K. Charter was one of several writers keen to warn that Sunday shopping was further evidence that "we are getting so close to the civilizations of Sodom and Gomorrah," while H.W. Aitchison, secretary-general of the Association of the Covenant People, expressed similar concerns. "Sunday shopping," a Mr and Mrs Pridham lamented, "lowers the moral standards of the community." Albert Douch left no doubt as to his position on the issue in writing to Volrich: "I have been inspired by the HOLY GHOST TO WRITE TO YOU: to encourage you to please GOD: rather than man ... thousands, and thousands of CHRISTIAN people ... are standing behind you to have these stores closed on SUNDAY."[24] As historian Robert Burkinshaw notes, despite BC's secular character the province witnessed a flourishing of evangelical Protestantism throughout the twentieth century, especially from the 1960s to the early 1980s.[25] Such voices were well represented in the mayor's mailbag.

At times, letter writers broadened their references to religious worship to include more general demands for the protection of a weekly day of rest and relaxation. Hence, in a 1978 letter to Volrich, Mr and Mrs H.M. Brown of Vancouver pleaded for one day a week "for quiet & restful recreation and religious privileges."[26] Similarly, in 1979 a mini-convention of the Social Credit Party in Richmond lamented that "the people of British Columbia are gradually losing Sunday as a day of rest, renewal, relaxation and worship to increased pressures of labour, industry and business." "Almighty God," the convention reminded Mayor Volrich and others, had "graciously provided in the creation order a day of rest in every seven."[27] The BC Interfaith Citizenship Council, representing "Christians, Jews, Muslims, Hindus, Sikhs and many other faiths," insisted that the Lord's Day Act be retained "so that there is at least one day a week which is kept for rest, Worship and recreation."[28]

Of course, another series of letters embraced Sunday shopping and openly rejected the notion that religious concerns ought to play a role in restricting the city's store hours. Frank Holden of Vancouver, for example, pleaded with Volrich to "remember that we are not all Christians." Dr Art Hister was far more direct. "Your recent campaign to close stores on Sunday is absolutely ridiculous," he informed the mayor. "It is nothing but selective morality. When are religious Jews supposed to shop? When are working families with children supposed to shop together? Surely, in this cosmopolitan and growing city, the Lord's Day Act is an anachronism." Citizens "want Sunday shopping – those who don't can spend the day at home or at Stanley Park." A less restrained Burnaby resident, Paul Armass, suggested that Sunday shopping restrictions formed a bigoted and "stupid" system that had long outlived its usefulness. He implored the mayor to liberate Vancouverites from "the worn out fossils" who "dominate our way of living." Bill Edwards added a legal threat to his argument, reminding Volrich that he was the mayor of a cosmopolitan city "that embraces all colours and creeds." "If nothing is done to open all stores on Sundays," he threatened, "I will complain to the Human Rights Commission on Grounds of Religious discrimination."[29]

In the 1970s, then, Vancouver's mayor faced forceful arguments, infused with references to Christianity, that urged him to preserve Sunday as a day largely free of commercial activity. He received equally pointed and direct correspondence replete with the rhetoric of secularism demanding that he allow widespread retail activity on Sundays.[30] While explicitly religious or secular arguments appeared with greater frequency in letters to Mayor Volrich than in local newspapers in either Vancouver or Victoria, advocates of these positions were visible participants in this debate in both cities.[31] Indeed, the types of arguments put forward in support of, and against, a religious understanding of Sunday's cultural and social significance in both cities' newspapers were essentially the same.[32]

Religion, then, was an important reference point in the Sunday shopping debates in both cities throughout the 1970s. Mayor Peter Pollen, like Volrich, was attacked for "catering to a very vociferous religious minority."[33] And Pollen himself was fully convinced that despite the divergence of opinion on the issue, none of the city's aldermen "up for re-election" wanted "to appear as favoring a Godless Sunday."[34] But religion was just one factor in the debates. After all, even an outspoken opponent of Sunday shopping such as Pollen was keen to emphasize that "he had no religious or moral objections to Sunday business."[35] As the province moved to introduce its Sunday shopping legislation in

1980, a *Vancouver Province* telephone poll indicated that a "slim majority of Greater Vancouver residents" supported Sunday shopping.[36] Supporters overwhelmingly pointed to consumer convenience as the key factor in taking up this position; a small minority emphasized their belief that merchants should be permitted to set their own hours of operation. Many opponents of Sunday shopping informed the pollsters that they believed Sunday should be set aside as a "day for family activities." Twenty-one per cent indicated that their opposition arose from their belief that Sunday shopping "violates religious teaching." This was the same percentage that declared that the city was already plagued by too much commercialism. A slightly higher number, 26 per cent, indicated that Sunday shopping was unfair to those who would find themselves forced to work on Sundays.[37]

As the province moved forward with its legislation, it faced a brief and vociferous backlash from angry Christians. Amidst a spirited letter-writing campaign that urged the provincial government to abandon the bill, the *Vancouver Sun* could report that the "power of the pulpit is still a significant force in this province," for it seemed as though "the devout went home from their Sunday sermon about the evils of Sunday openings and dashed off a letter to their local MLA."[38] However, other reports should caution us against ascribing too much influence to Christian opponents of Sunday shopping. The *Province*, for example, reported that by June 1980 MLAs had received over 6,000 letters, and that while some had been sent by "Christian fundamentalists," many more objections came from "store employees and other workers worried that the traditional day of rest" would soon "be eliminated."[39] Similarly revealing is the fact that those who emerged to oppose the provincial legislation and then, more successfully, to mount the initial anti-Sunday-shopping campaigns during municipal referendums on the issue formed a broad-based coalition that included not only church groups but also labour organizations and "several large retailers."[40]

The Sunday shopping debates, then, featured both pro-Christian voices keen to protect the Sabbath and staunchly secular voices keen to expand consumers' access to goods and services on Sundays. But these voices shared the arena with many others. Indeed, a sustained examination of the dynamics of the Sunday shopping debate in Vancouver in the late 1970s and early 1980s highlights the continuities from times past between disputes over Wednesday half-holiday, evening, "wide-open," and Sunday shopping.

Community

As with earlier store-hour debates, those who advocated the continuation or expansion of regulatory regimes portrayed themselves as defenders of community against the homogenizing power of North American capitalism. Hence Pollen's dismissive response to supporters of increased Sunday shopping that they were advocates for "the Los Angeles approach"[41] while he championed his own campaign as an attempt to "de-emphasize the commercial bombardment of our citizens."[42] Saanich mayor Mel Couvelier echoed Pollen's sentiments in 1980 when he argued that "the people of Greater Victoria wish to preserve a way of life that is somewhat unique in North America. They do not want to follow the example of the United States where it is 'business as usual' almost every day of the year."[43] Many Vancouver residents similarly expressed their desire to defend a slower pace of life from commercialism's growing power.[44]

Yet the campaign to limit Sunday trade quickly raised the ire of the cities' tourism promoters. It did not take long, for instance, for Victoria's tourism officials to respond to Mayor Pollen's campaign to clamp down on Sunday openings. Terry Farmer, president of the Visitors Information Centre, was quick to point out that the city's tourism industry would be adversely affected if Victoria's stores were shut tight.[45] The *Victoria Times* denounced Pollen's plans as a "regressive step" and worried aloud about the negative impact on the city's tourism industry.[46]

In Vancouver as well, tourism was an important element in the Sunday shopping debates – but in a very specific way. In 1978, City Hall encouraged merchants in the city's Gastown neighbourhood to undertake costly renovations to preserve the area's historic character. In return, the city promised local merchants that they could sell their wares on Sundays to help recoup their costs. As one legal expert would later note, the city had "innocently misled" these merchants, for it was not in a position to offer such a guarantee. When the province succeeded in downloading responsibility for all store hours, including Sundays, onto municipalities, merchants in Gastown quickly reminded city officials of their promise and demanded that the neighbourhood be exempted from Sunday closing regulations.[47]

Merchants in Chinatown took a similar position. The city had unofficially permitted stores in that area to remain open on Sundays since the early 1970s, and merchants were keen to preserve this favourable status – a decision that appears to have garnered very little reaction from merchants outside that district. The Chinatown Historic Area Planning Committee and the Chinese Benevolent Association of Vancouver noted that the area's heritage designation limited development options for entrepreneurs and pleaded for Sunday shopping as compensation. They also reminded local and provincial politicians of the area's tourism identity. Vancouver City Council quickly drafted a bylaw permitting Sunday shopping in Gastown and Chinatown and called a plebiscite on the issue. In June 1981 the public voted overwhelmingly in favour of the proposal. In light of the plebiscite result, the *Province* urged city council to expand access to Sunday shopping, particularly in areas dependent on tourists, noting that Robson Street and Granville Island both deserved exemptions. Even the self-styled Committee Opposed to Sunday & Holiday Shopping agreed that it would be permissible "to allow tourist-oriented stores in historic areas such as Gastown and Chinatown to open."[48]

The desire to defend or enhance community well-being thus continued to play a key role in store-hour debates during the 1970s and early 1980s as the focus shifted to Sunday shopping. Whereas earlier debates had featured a spirited battle between a pro-tourism lobby and citizens openly critical of tourism's potential to shift control away from local inhabitants and towards outside interests, the Sunday shopping debates appeared to feature a general acceptance of tourism as an important contributor to the cities' economic well-being. The debate over how best to serve community interests continued, but it had shifted towards a broader focus: the desire to preserve a distinctly slower pace of life from the frenetic and homogenous social and cultural patterns of North America.

Leverage

Populist anti-chain-store rhetoric was another carry-over from earlier times. Peter Pollen's crusade against Sunday openings was predicated, in part, on his determination to "provide a measure of 'retail viability' for the smaller businessman who 'obviously can't run his store seven days a week.'"[49] In a letter to the *Victoria Times*, Dick Hordyk and Henry Keyvenhoven feared that Sunday openings would create a situation in which those "unwilling to open on Sunday, particularly small family businesses and firms more sensitive to employee satisfaction than most large chain operations, can be forced out of business."[50] Joan Wallace,

7.3 Gastown and Chinatown merchants and supporters urge Vancouverites to vote "yes" to a June 1981 referendum question that would permit Sunday shopping in those two neighbourhoods. Image reproduced courtesy of Post Media.

speaking for the BC division of the RMA, was perhaps the most direct in her characterization of Sunday shopping. The *Sun* reported that she viewed "the battle over Sunday shopping" as "a David and Goliath struggle between small independent stores and large chain stores over who is to get the largest share of the customers' dollar."[51] There was, then, no shortage of accusatory rhetoric labelling chain stores as the key culprits in the move towards Sunday shopping.

But again, as in the case of earlier store-hours debates, the rhetoric surrounding chain-store machinations did not necessarily reflect reality. By 1980 several large chain stores had added their voices to the chorus calling for the provincial government to take action and provide clear and consistent rules for Sunday store hours. Bob Chorley, the Bay's general merchandise manager for western Canada, declared that his company had no plans to open its stores in Vancouver or Victoria on Sundays, and while a spokesperson for Canada Safeway in Vancouver expressed support for the Holiday Shopping Regulation Act, she emphasized the company's reservations about Sunday openings, declaring that "we only open in response to the competition." "We have to pay everybody double time on Sunday [so] there's not much money in it," she explained – tangible evidence that chain stores' support for closing regulations reflected economic self-interest.[52]

Even more revealing was an advertisement sponsored by Sears and the Committee Opposed to Sunday and Holiday Shopping, which included the Safeway and Woodward's chains. Appearing in the lead-up to November 1980 municipal referendums on Vancouver Island, it publicly encouraged voters to reject Sunday shopping on the grounds that "the things you now enjoy so much together – attending church, family dinners and other Sunday activities ... could be much more difficult for everyone to join in if Sunday becomes just like any other workday" (see Figure 7.4).[53]

Just as some small merchants championed six-day and evening shopping, so did they embrace the expanded opportunities offered by Sunday openings. Henry Eng, a Victoria area supermarket owner, argued that Safeway and the other major chain stores were opposed to Sunday shopping because they were unable to compete with independent operators and were seeking to deny them the opportunity to sell goods to the public when non-unionized organizations had the advantage in terms of scheduling and paying employees.[54] Saanich mayor Mel Couvelier supported Sunday openings on the very grounds that the small retail food operations depended on Sunday sales as they struggled to survive against the grocery chains.[55] Some small independent merchants campaigned to expand and codify a situation in which they were exempted from Sunday shopping regulations while their larger chain-store counterparts were not.[56]

7.4 Sears campaigns against Sunday shopping. *Victoria Times Colonist*, 13 November 1980, 4. Image reproduced with the permission of Sears Canada.

It would be wrong to assume that no chain stores actively sought Sunday sales opportunities. After all, the RMA found it necessary to urge the City of Vancouver to crack down specifically on Zellers, which in August 1977 began openly advertising that one of its stores would be selling goods on Sundays.[57] But, as with the earlier battles over store-hour regulations, the notion that chain stores were the leading impetus behind the liberalization of Sunday shopping restrictions is misleading. Rather, both chains and small independent operators were seeking to leverage their particular economic advantages into tangible economic dividends. For chain stores this generally meant addressing particular situations and deciding whether the potential loss of revenue to competitors justified the increased costs, particularly in the form of wages, that Sunday opening would entail. For smaller, independent operators, who often faced a more immediate struggle for survival, the decision similarly came down to whether to support Sunday closing for all (which offered the possibility of a day of rest) or Sunday opening that was restricted to smaller merchants and that would allow them to take advantage of one day a week in which they could cater to consumers without direct competition from larger operations. In pursuing these specific ends, chain stores and small independent operators fashioned rhetorical strategies devised to equate, as much as possible, their interests with those of the community. For chain stores this often required an emphasis on their employees' welfare; for independent operators, and their supporters, it routinely required allusions to a populist discourse that championed individual entrepreneurs' achievements and their status as recognizable and familiar members of the local community.

Morality

While many Christian opponents of Sunday shopping undoubtedly viewed their cause as morally righteous, moral concerns also infused non-religious aspects of the debate. For example, some Vancouverites opposed Sunday shopping on the grounds that it would erode quality family time. "I feel strongly opposed to Sunday shopping as it breaks up a family day," argued Judy A. Chernan. "Sure, families could go shopping together, but, what about families with working parents?" she wondered. Harold T. Allen of Victoria concurred, declaring that "family unity & cultural values are helped by Sunday closing."[58] Such arguments echoed sentiments throughout the 1970s in both Vancouver and Victoria that called for Sunday to be preserved as a "day of rest" that prioritized family activities. These arguments at times explicitly referred to the dangers of unrestrained commercialism.[59]

The *Vancouver Province*, however, championed consumption-based family leisure and pointed out that the "main reason for the bustle in Chinatown is that Sunday's the day most hardworking Chinese families go out together." "Why shouldn't others have the same convenience?" the newspaper asked, noting that it objected to the motivations of people "determined to impose their versions of morality on everyone else." Consumer Shirley Dick was similarly aggravated. "Shopping is a genuine form of recreation to many and even a form of family entertainment to some people," she argued, "and if a sportsman can play golf or tennis on Sunday, people go to the Symphony, why should another person who cannot afford or does not desire to do these things, not be able to shop on Sunday if they wish[?]"[60]

Some advocates of Sunday shopping emphasized their belief that the growing number of families in which both parents worked outside the home meant that Sundays were now a necessary and legitimate shopping day in Victoria and Vancouver.[61] For B.A. Ritcey and others, consumer convenience weighed heavily on their thinking. "I don't enjoy lineing [sic] up to pay for groceries because it takes as long to pay for them as it does to pick them up. Sunday shopping is much more convenient," she emphasized.[62] While a number of merchants endeavoured to speak for consumers by emphasizing their ostensible demand for Sunday shopping opportunities, the RMA was eager to emphasize that consumers were *not* leading the charge for Sunday shopping and, in fact, would be keenly opposed if they were fully informed of the increased prices that would surely result from additional operating costs.[63] Not surprisingly, the Sunday shopping debates also revisited earlier arguments that consumers possessed a finite amount of spending money, which would simply be spread over greater operating hours if Sunday sales were permitted.[64]

Perhaps most interesting are polling data indicating that consumer demand for Sunday shopping was muted. A 1977 survey by the BC branch of the Canadian Association of Consumers indicated that 51 per cent of its members opposed Sunday shopping while just 42 per cent supported Sunday sales.[65] A survey undertaken by Vancouver's Downtown Business Association the following year indicated that only 17 per cent of respondents endorsed Sunday openings. Almost half of those surveyed indicated that they were content with the city's current retail hours, while those keen on extended store hours sought additional shopping hours in the evenings and during the pre-Christmas rush.[66] A significant number of consumers, then, agreed with Phyllis Craver of West Vancouver, who identified herself as a woman "in the labour force," who found "the stores open quite enough." She was entirely willing to put her personal convenience aside and was "much more concerned about ... another breakdown of the family."[67] As with earlier debates surrounding Wednesday closing, evening sales, and "wide-open" shopping, many people viewed store-hour restrictions as a moral issue, one that shaped the complex relationship between leisure, family life, and consumer convenience.

Regulation

The difficulties involved in enforcing and justifying complex and seemingly contradictory regulatory regimes were clearly a central aspect of both cities' journeys towards seven-day shopping. First, press stories continued to circulate throughout the 1970s and 1980s concerning local merchants in both cities opening their stores on Sundays in defiance of store-hour restrictions.[68] Critics were keen to point out that a lack of enforcement and minimal fines played a significant role in exacerbating the problem.[69] Here again, the conventionalization of such punishments came into play. As in the past, some merchants explained that they were contravening Sunday store-hour restrictions out of financial necessity and because their competitors gave them no other choice.[70]

Second, the problem of "mixed shops" had not disappeared. For example, in 1975 John Ansell, the director of Victoria's Chamber of Commerce, spoke out against a proposal for city control over Sunday shopping as unworkable because it would create a situation in which "a person could go into a corner store on a Sunday but buy only perishable goods, not canned goods." Furthermore, "drug stores would be able to sell only drugs and not other merchandise."[71] The *Victoria Times* was similarly critical: "Does the mayor really expect merchants to screen off panty hose and paint that sit beside patent medicine and pablum, just because it's Sunday?"[72] The *Daily Colonist* concurred, pleading with city council to recall the lessons of earlier store-hour debates.[73] Indeed, the *Colonist*'s editorial board appeared to channel its inner Dr Seuss to ridicule what it predicted would be an unworkable regulatory regime: "So you can buy a hat or a cat or a bat or a mat, but if the mat is really a rug, not that." Any attempt to define consumer goods in ways that deemed some but not all legal for sale on Sundays,

7.5 Complex Sunday shopping sales regulations continued to frustrate Vancouver consumers in the early 1980s. Source: *Vancouver Province*, 1 May 1981, B4. Image reproduced courtesy of Post Media.

it suggested, would prove "difficult to enforce ... because it is as discriminatory as it is illogical."[74]

As the *Colonist* predicted, the situation remained unresolved in the aftermath of the Holiday Shopping Regulation Act. So when Vancouver City Council members considered bylaw amendments to exempt a number of business classes, including "building supply dealers," from the act and thus allow them to operate on Sundays, they faced a strong rebuke from Peter Weichel, a vice-president of Wosk's furniture stores. Weichel argued that many building supply dealers sold furniture "in direct competition with furniture and appliance stores," such as Wosk's, that were not to be similarly exempted from the ban on Sunday shopping. The age-old problem of attempting to regulate businesses that sold multiple types of goods remained, and it continued to create headaches for merchants and city officials. Shoppers thus faced a frustrating and confusing situation in which stores were permitted to open but only to sell some of their wares.

When Vancouver resident Nancy A. Chiavario blew a fuse at her apartment on a Sunday, she set off to the local store to purchase a replacement only to find that such sales were illegal. "Imagine my surprise," she declared, "when I was greeted at London Drugs with rows of items covered over and blocked off because certain items are against the law to sell on Sunday." While fuse purchases were verboten, Chiavario did have the option of purchasing other goods, including "light bulbs, bug spray, toys or colouring books, lipstick and suntan oil." "What is the difference," she demanded to know, "between needing a light bulb" and "needing a fuse on Sunday?"[75] As with earlier disputes over Wednesday closing and evening shopping, the arbitrary nature of legislative attempts to limit and regulate Sunday shopping occupied a central place in public debate and played a key role in undermining the legitimacy of the regulatory regimes that city officials endeavoured to put in place.

Ideology

Finally, as was the case with earlier store-hour debates, ideological interventions infused the Sunday shopping dispute. Those endorsing Sunday shopping keenly embraced "free enterprise" rhetoric. "The more the city tries to regulate the market," the *Vancouver Province* warned in June 1981, "the bigger and more nonsensical the mess will become." A self-titled Committee to Advance Free Enterprise was particularly frustrated that the provincial government, controlled by "a self-professed, 'free-enterprise' political party" would enact legislation forcing "responsible, independent entrepreneurs to break the law in order to survive."[76] The *Victoria Daily Colonist* praised furniture dealer Harry Hammer as a "freedom fighter" and celebrated his court victory over

Vancouver City Council as an important defence of "the right of all merchants to practice their trade unfettered by stupid, archaic laws."[77] A number of residents championed their "right to shop" on Sundays.[78] The Gastown Merchants' Association argued that its members had the "right to open Sundays and Holidays."[79]

In the *Daily Colonist*, a letter writer adopting the name "For True Democracy" pilloried Victoria mayor Peter Pollen for attempting to resolve the city's Sunday shopping situation by listening to "pressure groups" rather than the general public. "The most democratic way to solve the problem is to allow everything to be wide open on a Sunday," the letter writer argued, and let business owners and consumers make their own decisions concerning opening hours and stores to patronize. "It should be left purely to the will of the individual," for this is "true democracy."[80] For *Vancouver Province* columnist Mike Tytherleigh the battle over Sunday shopping came down to the issue of "democracy" and the "right of the people to decide and not big brother at city hall."[81]

But as was the case with earlier store-hour debates, opponents of Sunday shopping also drew on ideological and rights-based arguments. For example, Vancouver businessman Don W. Low urged the attorney general to protect Sunday as an opportunity for rest, recreation, and worship by calling on him to preserve "our Sunday freedoms by vigorously enforcing the law."[82] Even the *Vancouver Province*, which could be harshly critical of attempts by city officials to control store hours, was willing to acknowledge that it was too simplistic to tell the government not to regulate economic life: "Factory owners," it noted, "used to like to employ children." But the newspaper continued to cling to the idealistic and liberal assumption that "everybody ought to be allowed to live his life as he sees fit."[83] The attorney general's office acknowledged "the legitimate aims of those ... interested in a freedom of choice" but cautioned that it was "imperative that equal recognition be given to those in the church community who hold strongly to the view that Sunday should be preserved as a day for worship."[84]

Victoria resident Harold T. Allen took the rights-based argument further in his opposition to Sunday shopping. He suggested that "Sunday closing for employees is a human rights field. Sunday law gives most people Sunday freedom" as well as religious and personal liberty. "Why should this be used by people to deprive some employees of their freedom?" Sunday closing, he argued, would not deny other groups their basic rights.[85] The RMA's Joan Wallace went so far as to make the case for government regulation as a necessity to protect the freedoms of entrepreneurs. The "competitive nature of retailing," she argued, meant that a lack of common store-hour restrictions among municipalities would ensure that merchants in more liberally regulated communities would lure customers away from those in more tightly regulated ones until Sunday shopping had become a widespread and irreversible trend.[86] The extent to which ideological arguments informed both sides of the Sunday shopping debate was succinctly captured by the *Vancouver Sun* in 1980 in the admonition of Reginald Redman, who chaired the Vancouver and District Council of Churches, "that those who cry out about the freedom to shop at any time should think about the freedom of people who have to work on Sundays."[87]

From a historical perspective it is inadequate to ascribe the relatively recent demise of Sunday store-hour restrictions primarily to "secularization" and to the growing demands of retailers for increased selling opportunities.[88] Staunch defences of Christianity (and equally vigorous arguments from proponents of secularism) certainly played a role in the public debates about Sunday shopping – and it is obviously true that a number of retailers eagerly campaigned for the legalization of Sunday retail operations. But any assessment of the significance of Sunday shopping debates must acknowledge that Sunday shopping, and thus store hours more generally, remained contested and controversial terrain into the 1980s. It must also recognize the fact that the central themes that structured earlier disputes concerning Wednesday closing, evening shopping, and "wide open" hours continued to inform public debate about the relationship between work, leisure, and consumption.

From the mid-1940s to the early 1980s citizens in Victoria and Vancouver engaged in an almost continuous and wide-ranging debate about store-hour restrictions. And while the arrival of six-day shopping in the 1950s and the expansion of evening shopping in the 1960s marked significant turning points in the liberalization of store-hour restrictions, an equally intense battle emerged in the 1970s and 1980s over the question of Sunday shopping and the possibility of the seven-day shopping week. Documenting the Sunday shopping dispute provides us with an important opportunity to recognize not only the longevity of the store-hour debates but also the continuities in scope and scale between the earlier debates focusing, for example, on Wednesday closing and the more recent disputes concerning the Christian Sabbath. These continuities offer a clearer window onto the Sunday shopping debates themselves and demonstrate that while religion played a role in these disputes, multiple social, cultural, and political battlegrounds were in play.

Conclusion

In 1946, shoppers in Victoria and Vancouver purchased goods and services amidst a regulatory regime that banned Sunday sales, forced many merchants to close their shops on Wednesdays, and prohibited evening shopping. By the late 1980s both cities boasted a seven-day shopping week that, with the exception of statutory holidays, permitted stores to set their own hours. On the surface, this development might appear to have been straightforward and inevitable – the product of ever-increasing consumer demand, on the one hand, and entrepreneurs' insatiable desire for profit, on the other. To be sure, some consumers pined for easier access to specific goods and services, and some merchants chafed at regulations that restricted the timing of their transactions. But the demise of store-hour restrictions in these two cities was, in fact, a complex and at times contradictory process.

Moreover, it was a process that was hotly discussed and debated. As Harry Young, the business editor of the *Victoria Daily Colonist*, noted in 1954: "No topic in Victoria business circles stirs up quicker animosity than any attempt to change store shopping hours. Lifelong friends can become bitter enemies in the bat of an eyelid."[1] The same could be said of the business culture in Vancouver. Indeed, between the 1940s and the 1980s, when stores should be open and who should decide their hours remained front-page questions. Both cities were being integrated into a North American consumer culture that featured rising living standards, the growth of the service sector, the expansion of chain stores, the development of suburbs, and growing numbers of working women. Each of these factors played a part in the dismantling of store-hour regulations. But the demise of store-hour restrictions was not as straightforward as it might seem. Chains did not consistently lead the

charge against store-closing regulations. Nor did working women saddled with shopping responsibilities automatically support expanded
store hours. Instead, seemingly coherent interest groups, including
merchants, clerks, and consumers, were divided among themselves – a
situation that seemed to dampen the political will of the authorities to
take a stand and resolve the matter once and for all.

Moreover, the longevity of the debate itself underscores the need
to recognize that the arrival of our wide open, seven-day shopping
universe was neither straightforward nor inevitable. In assessing the
merits and demerits of expanded store hours, the citizens of these two
cities explored and discussed the very nature of consumerism and of
the communities in which they lived. They did so in a context in which
North America witnessed not only a dramatic rise in living standards
but also a shift from a producer-based to a consumer-based economy.
Given the prevalence of pro-consumption messages in contemporary
society and the resulting difficulties we face in thinking and communicating outside of a consumerist ethos, it is potentially liberating and
perhaps even empowering to be reminded (or to discover) that those
who came before us did not passively stand aside as a consumer society
developed. Instead, they grappled with its promises and possibilities,
and a great many of them offered forceful assessments (positive or negative) of its potential impact. The result was a long-running *conflict*. The
fact that people debated consumerism in the past ought to encourage
us to continue asking hard questions about it today and in the future.

Yet one need not be a staunch critic of consumerism to appreciate the
kinds of things that these store-hour debates can tell us. The competing
conceptions of *community* interests that saw citizens strive to equate
their own individual aims and concerns with those of the cities in which
they lived highlight the underlying sense of unease that gripped civic
leaders as they scrambled to secure a recipe for sustained prosperity.
They also illustrate the extent to which citizens understood common
leisure time to be a public good worth protecting. Moreover, there was
a discrepancy between populist anti-chain-store rhetoric and the more
complicated reality in which neither the behaviour of small merchants
nor that of large corporations fit dominant stereotypes about who was
likely to support store-hour deregulation. This gulf between rhetoric
and reality underscores the importance of examining the ways in which
all types of business attempt to *leverage* their characteristics to the best
advantage. Businesses both small and large were adept at articulating agendas that, their owners hoped, would reverberate throughout

the community and reinforce a bond between themselves, civic leaders, and potential customers. Store-hour deregulation was a product not just of monopoly capitalism, but of intricate strategies and alliances within local communities.

Expanded store hours coincided with a significant expansion of the female workforce. The expectation that working wives should continue to be responsible for purchasing household goods and groceries undoubtedly increased the pressure for expanded shopping hours. But people hotly debated the *morality* of this development. In doing so they offered highly selective images of housewives and family life that reinforced polarizing arguments either opposing or championing store-hour restrictions. However, the voices of consumers, both male and female, could offer a more generous and nuanced assessment of the situation as many shoppers belied their simplistic image and recognized the complexity of a situation in which one person's convenience could come at the cost of another person's hardship. Consumers, these debates remind us, can articulate conceptions of convenience and community that include a place for people other than themselves.

These debates also highlight the fluid and limited nature of the state's power to regulate human behaviour. Time and again attempts to introduce *regulation* to modify behaviour or placate concerned interest groups fell victim to the growing complexity of local economies, the conventionalization of imposed penalties, and, it must be said, politicians' desire to avoid making difficult decisions. Politicians had a difficult time assessing the public's will and faced the wrath of competing interests. Hence, over time they retreated from their established roles as mediators and conduits and left it to the buyers and sellers to interact outside the bounds of strict rules and conventions. Those of us lamenting the general state of Canada's political culture can thus find in these debates historical precedents for our current malaise.

Finally, these debates tell us something important about ideology and religion. In particular, they highlight the dynamic nature of the public sphere both during the high point of the Cold War and during the Sunday shopping debates of the 1980s. Instead of dampening debate from the 1940s to the 1960s, Cold War *ideology* infused the discussion with competing notions of free enterprise, ideal citizenship, and democracy. Arguments over what time the corner store should close thus offer a portrait of quite lively communities in which opponents linked local matters to global developments. In later decades the multifaceted nature of the Sunday shopping debate highlighted the extent to which *religion* and secularism were joined by many other competing interests and institutions whose goals and identities were closely connected to decisions concerning retail hours.

When Santa Claus lamented his fate in the midst of the showdown over Wednesday closing in Vancouver in 1949, he briefly occupied a central place in what was becoming a long-running debate. The dispute persisted because of unresolved tensions between a demand for convenient access to goods and services, a determination to preserve common leisure time, a desire to maximize profits and minimize operating costs, and local officials' conflicting attempts to determine an effective way to secure civic prosperity without alienating any of their constituents. Seven-day shopping in Vancouver, Victoria, and elsewhere appears to have put an end to the store-hour debate. But the tensions between the demands of work, consumption, leisure, and political leadership remain with us.

Notes

Introduction

1 *Victoria Daily Colonist*, 22 December 1949, 5.
2 Victoria's merchants faced a less restrictive situation. They, too, were subject to the province's Shops Regulations and Weekly Holiday Act and would be expected to close their shops in the afternoon on Wednesday, 21 December, and Wednesday, 28 December. But Victoria City Council was, by 1949, committed to suspending its own Wednesday morning closing bylaw from 15 to 31 December. *Victoria Daily Colonist*, 15 December 1949, 31. Vancouver merchants received no such reprieve.
3 *Vancouver Sun*, 16 December 1949, 1–2.
4 *Vancouver Daily Province*, 16 December 1949, 1.
5 By 17 December the Bay's R.E. Standfield was increasingly belligerent: "We feel it's a shame that stores should be closed tight on Wednesday, and we are going to test the situation." *Victoria Daily Colonist*, 17 December 1949, 1.
6 *Vancouver Daily Province*, 17 December 1949, 1–2.
7 *Vancouver Sun*, 17 December 1949, 1–2. Such police action, however, would not force the offending stores to close for the day. *Vancouver Sun*, 16 December 1949, 1–2.
8 *Vancouver Sun*, 17 December 1949, 1–2; *Vancouver Sun*, 19 December 1949, 1.
9 *Vancouver Sun*, 20 December 1949, 2.
10 *Vancouver Sun*, 21 December 1949, 1.
11 *Vancouver Sun*, 21 December 1949, 1–2.
12 *Vancouver Sun*, 22 December 1949, 1.
13 *Vancouver Sun*, 21 December 1949, 1–2.

14 According to the RMA, "the trouble with the present law is that it permits an individual store to break the law, but still to keep operating for the rest of the day, even after getting a summons." *Vancouver Daily Province*, 17 December 1949, 1–2; *Vancouver Sun*, 21 December 1949, 2.

15 In February 1950, in the aftermath of a vote by 500 of its members in favour of continuing the practice of Wednesday closing, the RMA stated that the city's retailers now expected police to provide strict enforcement given what the RMA viewed as aggressive actions against the summonsed stores the previous December. *Vancouver Sun*, 3 February 1950, 21.

16 *Vancouver Daily Province*, 28 December 1949, 22.

17 *Vancouver Daily Province*, 3 January 1950, 13.

18 *Vancouver Sun*, 24 March 1950, 17.

19 It also suspended the act in any week with two or more public holidays. *Victoria Daily Colonist*, 30 March 1950, 3.

20 *Vancouver Sun*, 21 December 1949, 1.

21 Cross, *An All-Consuming Century*, 5.

22 Ibid., 1, 2, 7.

23 This is one area of consumer debate that has secured considerable interest from historians. Given the substantial body of literature on this topic, and the fact that alcohol sales were subject to province-wide regulations (rather than local bylaws) – and thus were not subject to competing retail hours – I have not focused on this issue. On the history of alcohol sales and regulation, see Campbell, *Sit Down and Drink Your Beer*; Heron, *Booze*; Malleck, *Try to Control Yourself*.

24 Cross, *An All-Consuming Century*, 114, 116, 124, 155.

25 Belisle, *Retail Nation*, 3–4.

26 Norrie and Owram, *A History of the Canadian Economy*, 421.

27 Owram, *Born at the Right Time*, 93.

28 Bettina Liverant, "Canada's Consumer Election (1935)," in Warsh and Malleck, *Consuming Modernity*, 11. Emphasis added.

29 Cross, *An All-Consuming Century*, 136–7.

30 Norrie and Owram, *A History of the Canadian Economy*, 421.

31 On such issues, see, for example, Pierson, "Gender and the Unemployment Insurance Debates"; Tillotson, "The Family as Tax Dodge"; and Campbell, *Grand Illusions*.

32 Mallen and Rotenberg, "The Benefits and Costs of Evening Shopping," 3.

33 Schor, *The Overworked American*, 3. For a critique of Schor's argument, see Coleman and Pencavel, "Changes in Work Hours of Male Employees." Leisure time, American economist Dora Costa confirms, is a much overlooked but necessary component of any evaluation of living

standards. After 1940, she argues, decreases in work time came mainly as
a result of "increases in vacations, holidays, sick days, personal leave, and
early retirement" so that the average workday was, by 1993, "less than 8
hours." "This decline in work hours," she suggests, "unmeasured by such
common indicators of well-being as income per capita, surely represents
one of the larger increases in the standard of living" over the course of the
twentieth century. Costa, "The Wage and Length of the Work Day," 156–7.
Leisure has, of course, been a central concern for workers for a very long
time. Jeremy Atack and Fred Bateman suggest that as early as the 1880s,
American workers, "particularly skilled workers, substituted increased
leisure time for some of the potential income gain from rising hourly
wages." Atack and Bateman, "How Long Was the workday in 1880?,"
129, 155.

34 On the historical development of North American consumerism, see, for
     example, Leach, *Land of Desire*; Cohen, *A Consumers' Republic*; Frank, *The
     Conquest of Cool*; Marchand, *Creating the Corporate Soul*; Parr, *Domestic
     Goods*; Korinek, *Roughing it in the Suburbs*; Johnston, *Selling Themselves*;
     Penfold, *The Donut*; Craig, *Backwoods Consumers and Homespun Capitalists*;
     Belisle, *Retail Nation*; Warsh and Malleck, eds., *Consuming Modernity*.

35 Roberts, "Gender, Consumption, and Commodity Culture," 820, 821–2.

36 In their 1969 examination of evening shopping in Canada, Mallen and
     Rotenberg concluded that it was suburban retailers who were leading
     the challenge against what they saw as outmoded restrictive store-hour
     legislation that worked against the interests of consumers; downtown
     retailers, they noted, generally favoured retaining existing controls. Mallen
     and Rotenberg, "The Benefits and Costs of Evening Shopping," 4, 11, 27.

37 On Canada's capitalist infrastructure, see, for example, Penfold, *The Donut*;
     Belisle, *Retail Nation*; and Dawson, *Selling British Columbia*. On consumers'
     relationship to specific goods, see Korinek, *Roughing It in the Suburbs*;
     and Penfold, *The Donut*. For an insightful study of public debate and the
     relationship between consumption and citizenship, see Fahrni, *Household
     Politics*.

38 Cross, *An All-Consuming Century*, 231–2.

39 *Victoria Daily Times*, 13 September 1958, 4.

1 Conflict

1 *Victoria Daily Colonist*, 2 August 1966, 17.

2 Mallen and Rotenberg, "The Benefits and Costs of Evening Shopping," 90.

3 Ibid., 355–90.

4 Ibid., 11.
5 For a summary of provincial legislation c. 1961, see ibid., 112. For a more general historical overview, see Human Resources and Skills Development Canada, "Sunday Closing and Weekly Rest Periods: Historical Evolution and Current Situation," at http://www.hrsdc.gc.ca/eng/labour/labour_law/esl/weekly_rest.shtml. By the early 1980s most Canadian provinces (Quebec being the exception) had delegated responsibility for regulating retail stores to municipalities. In the United States, in contrast, this power resides in state legislatures. Ferris, "On the Economics of Regulated Early Closing Hours," 1, 24.
6 Skuterud, "The Impact of Sunday Shopping," 5; Evans, "Sunday Closing Laws in Canada," 1.
7 Alberta chose to place the decision-making power in the hands of its municipalities. In Nova Scotia, while the legislation was focused on the retail sector, its impact was felt in other areas including "transportation and communications." In the majority of provinces, including British Columbia, provincial legislation affected only the "retail business sector." Evans, "Sunday Closing Laws in Canada," 3.
8 Skuterud, "The Impact of Sunday Shopping," 1.
9 Quinlan and Goodwin, "Combating the Tyranny of Flexibility," 342.
10 Taschereau, "'Behind the Store,'" 245.
11 Rottenberg, "Legislated Early Shop Closing in Britain," 124.
12 Ibid., 120–1; Quinlan and Goodwin, "Combating the Tyranny of Flexibility," 344.
13 Rottenberg, "Legislated Early Shop Closing in Britain," 121; Hoffman, *They Also Serve*, 8.
14 This growing momentum produced some promising early results. An 1886 bill placed restrictions on the hours of work for young people employed in shops, while legislation passed in 1904 empowered "local authorities" to restrict store hours provided that two-thirds of the store owners supported such a move. The impact, however, was minimal. As Rottenberg explains, only 112 local authorities in Britain chose to act, meaning that "of the 800,000 shop assistants, only 15,000 were employed by shops affected by closing orders." Hoffman, *They Also Serve*, 2. Rottenberg, "Legislated Early Shop Closing in Britain," 121, 122.
15 Some flexibility was given to local authorities to amend these restrictions as they saw fit. See Rottenberg, 122–3.
16 See Quinlan and Goodwin, "Combatting the Tyranny of Flexibility"; and Roberts, "Gender in Store."
17 Ibid., 118.

18 An 1891 statute legislated the closing of commercial enterprises on Sundays, and a statute passed in 1900 established 9 a.m. openings and 5 p.m. closings as regular weekday operating hours for shops, with the provision that 8 p.m. closing could be adopted if a majority of local store owners agreed. Kirchner and Painter, "The Economics of Germany's Shop Closing Hours," 9.

19 For a brief exploration of the retail store hour issue in the American context, see Benson, *Counter Cultures*, 196–200. The classic account of the American "early closing movement" in the 1830s and the extent to which it was led by retailers, rather than their employees, is Estey, "Early Closing." For an overview of shopping regulations in Britain, Australia, and Canada in comparison to the United States, see Laband and Heinbuch, *Blue Laws*, 207–15.

20 Palmer, *Working-Class Experience*, 94–5.

21 Belisle, *Retail Nation*, 206.

22 Kinley, "Evolution of Legislated Standards," 1, 2, 4, 8, 11, 12, 28.

23 In 1951, 27.8 per cent of Canadian women workers were married; by 1961 that figure had jumped to 46.6 per cent. In 1961 the participation rate of married women aged 20 to 64 in paid labour was 23 per cent; by 1967 that figure had climbed to 33 per cent. Mallen and Rotenberg, "The Benefits and Costs of Evening Shopping," 16–17.

24 Costa, "Hours of Work and the Fair Labor Standards Act," 654; Mallen and Rotenberg, "The Benefits and Costs of Evening Shopping," 4.

25 Mallen and Rotenberg suggest that most retail clerks enjoyed a forty-hour work week by 1945. A survey of National Retail Institute stores in 1969 indicated that full-time retail employees worked an average of 40.1 hours per week. Ibid., 22, 56. Andrew Neufeld notes that by 1954 the norm for retail clerks in Vancouver was a six-day, forty-four hour week, while some unionized clerks had secured a five-day, forty-hour week. Neufeld, *Union Store*, 83.

26 Mallen and Rotenberg, "The Benefits and Costs of Evening Shopping," 23.

27 *Victoria Daily Colonist*, 7 April 1907, 8; *Victoria Daily Colonist*, 28 May 1907, 6. For a thoughtful survey of the retail clerks' campaigns for improved working conditions, see Neufeld, *Union Store*. As Neufeld notes, their efforts convinced the provincial government in 1900 to pass the "Shops Regulation Act that limited the maximum number of hours per week to sixty-six and one-half, with an eleven hour daily maximum." Ibid., 13.

28 *Vancouver Sun*, 8 May 1946, 22; *Victoria Daily Colonist*, 19 November 1946, 8; *Victoria Daily Colonist*, 6 December 1946, 4; *Victoria Daily Colonist*, 11 December 1946, 4; *Vancouver Sun*, 30 December 1946, 11. The Second World War ushered in a similar situation in Wellington and Auckland,

New Zealand, as "reduced consumer demand, and the threat of Japanese
invasion prompted blackout regulations, making a four hour, five day
week" a reality. Roberts, "Gender in Store,"123.

29 The migration of downtown Vancouver and Victoria shoppers to the cities'
respective suburbs was part of a broader trend throughout North America.
In their 1960 analysis of the impact of regional shopping centres on New
York City, for example, Samuel and Lois Pratt noted that within a year of
the shopping centres' opening, "the number of suburban families buying
in New York City" had decreased by 13 per cent while the "average annual
expenditure in New York by suburban families purchasing there dropped
from $93 to $68." "The great majority of suburban families – almost nine in
ten – use the new shopping centers to some extent," they concluded. See Pratt
and Pratt, "The Impact of Some Regional Shopping Centers," 45, 46, 48. Such
developments elicited a forceful response from downtown merchants. In the
late 1950s, for instance, a number of Montreal stores, explicitly concerned
about losing business to the suburbs, aimed to secure expanded evening
shopping hours. See Mallen and Rotenberg, "The Benefits and Costs of
Evening Shopping," 90–1. Nor was the spectre of the suburbs confined to
North America. In 1957, "when the government proposed that a dormitory
suburb north of Wellington be allowed to set different trading hours than
downtown stores," the secretary of the New Zealand Federation of Shop
Assistants immediately sounded the alarm and proclaimed that his members'
forty-hour work week was in jeopardy. See Roberts, "Gender in Store," 124.

30 Cahill, *Shorter Hours*, 24.

31 *Vancouver Daily Province*, 26 March 1953, 23; *Vancouver Sun*, 21 April 1953,
3; *Vancouver Sun*, 17 June 1958, 9; *Vancouver Daily Province*, 11 August 1959,
24; *Victoria Daily Times*, 6 July 1955, 5; *Victoria Daily Colonist*, 17 September
1958, 9; *Victoria Daily Colonist*, 13 April 1956, 17 (Second News Section);
Victoria Daily Times, 25 April 1958, 13.

32 54.2 per cent of ballots cast supported abolishing Wednesday closing.
36,284 votes were cast in favour of six-day shopping with 30,666 against.
Vancouver Sun, 24 June 1954, 1.

33 City of Vancouver Archives, City Councillors' Office fonds, series # 467,
Records of Ald. Marianne Linnell, 84-E-2 file 13, F.M. Waller, City Clerk,
Victoria, to Linnell, 1 February 1968.

34 *Vancouver Sun*, 21 March 1952, 17; *Vancouver Daily Province*, 20 November
1956, 33; *Vancouver Sun*, 14 July 1964, 18; *Vancouver Sun*, 9 September 1964,
6; *Vancouver Sun*, 10 November 1964, 7; *Victoria Daily Times*, 9 October
1953, 11; *Victoria Daily Times*, 23 June 1961, 17; *Victoria Daily Colonist*, 24
June 1961, 13.

35   *Vancouver Sun*, 22 May 1957, 1–2; *Vancouver Sun*, 9 January 1962, 33; *Vancouver Daily Province*, 31 July 1962, 2; *Vancouver Sun*, 23 May 1957, 4; *Vancouver Daily Province*, 18 October 1967, 1; *Vancouver Province*, 23 April 1969, 14; *Vancouver Sun*, 23 April 1969, 14; *Victoria Daily Times*, 6 November 1958, 19; *Victoria Daily Colonist*, 13 December 1960, 14.

36   The exception was West Vancouver, where some stores continued to cling to their traditional Monday closing.

37   Mallen and Rotenberg, "The Benefits and Costs of Evening Shopping," 265–71.

38   On British Columbia's secular nature, see Burkinshaw, *Pilgrims in Lotus Land*, 4; and Block, "'Families That Pray Together, Stay Together,'" 32.

39   *Victoria Daily Colonist*, 18 November 1953, 4; *Victoria Daily* Colonist, 21 November 1953, 4; *Victoria Daily Colonist*, 21 June 1956, 5.

40   See, for example, *Vancouver Sun*, 23 July 1949, 4.

41   *Vancouver Daily* Province, 6 May 1947, 6; *Vancouver Daily Province*, 7 November 1950, 9; *Vancouver Sun*, 6 February 1951, 5; *Vancouver Sun*, 15 January 1954, 16.

42   On the Sunday sports debate in Vancouver, see, for example, *Vancouver Daily Province*, 8 August 1956, 1–2; *Vancouver. Daily Province*, 8 August 1956, 2; *Vancouver Daily Province*, 17 December 1956, 25; *Vancouver Sun*, 12 March 1957, 19; *Vancouver Sun*, 22 May 1957, 1; *Vancouver Daily Province*, 24 May 1957, 27. On the infamous turn-of-the-century Sunday streetcar dispute in Toronto, see Armstrong and Nelles, *The Revenge of the Methodist Bicycle Company*.

43   Provincial attorneys general were responsible for the administration of the act. See Laverdure, *Sunday in Canada*, 46.

44   The act was repealed in 2003. Human Resources and Skills Development Canada. http://www.hrsdc.gc.ca/eng/lp/spila/clli/eslc/weekly_rest_narrative.pdf.

45   On employer support for such initiatives elsewhere in Canada, see Belisle, *Retail Nation*, 206–7.

46   Monod, *Store Wars*, 92.

47   Neufeld, *Union Store*, 39, 53.

48   Roy, *The Triumph of Citizenship*, 118.

49   A brief flurry of comment focused on Chinese grocers in Victoria in 1916. See *Victoria Daily Colonist* 14 May 1916, 17; *Victoria Daily Times*, 17 May, 1916, 7; *Victoria Daily Times*, 15 July 1916, 9; *Victoria Daily Times*, 1 August 1916, 5; *Victoria Daily Colonist*, 2 August 1916, 10; *Victoria Daily Times*, 28 December 1916, 11; *Victoria Daily Times*, 2 December 1916, 13. But an exhaustive survey of the four major daily newspapers in the two cities

unearthed just twenty-one articles (out of 2,100) that made any mention of Asian-Canadian merchants.

50 *Victoria Daily Colonist*, 18 March 1958, 30.

51 As American historian Jerome Bjelopera notes, clerical workers have been largely neglected by historians, who have focused instead on blue-collar workers. Perhaps these "clerks" have been overlooked because we don't see them as "traditional" workers. "Clerks, bookkeepers, and department-store saleswomen," Bjelopera notes, all worked with information and documents and didn't really "produce" tangible goods. Bjelopera, *City of Clerk*, 1–3, 32.

52 As Michael Zakim explains, the expansion of clerking positions became "a visceral means for Americans to talk about the revolution that was overtaking – and undermining – the nation's traditional ethic of industry." Zakim, "The Business Clerk as Social Revolutionary," 567, 570.

53 Ibid., 569, 575.

54 Despite their central role in the emergence of the market economy, clerks' contributions have been vastly overshadowed by the trials and tribulations of those who worked with their hands to produce tangible goods. Indeed, Zakim argues that clerks "constituted ... a most proactive class whose enthusiastic business agenda represented the middling interest's transformation into an industrial bourgeoisie no longer satisfied with the prospects of a 'happy mediocrity' that rested on the fruits of their own labor." Ibid.," 571.

55 Ibid., 592, 599.

56 In fact, Bjelopera suggests that "the paltry amount of union activity among lower-level white-collar workers before 1920 suggests that the vast majority of office and sales employees identified with their employers." "Even those who moved only one rung up the corporate ladder were apt to side with their bosses," he argues. Bjelopera, *City of Clerks*, 14, 18, 122, 123.

57 Neufeld, *Union Store*, 15.

58 Taschereau, "'Behind the Store,'" 236, 237, 248.

59 During the nineteenth century, early closing associations in the Australian colony of Victoria were "composed of shop workers with varying degrees of shopkeeper membership." Indeed, the brief success of drapers' and mercantile assistants in implementing early closing in a number of Australian towns was facilitated by the fact that they had secured necessary shopowner support. While the Victorian Shop Employès Union could often find itself needing to exert public pressure

on city officials to pull merchants into line, and faced a counter-campaign by merchants opposed to early closing, "in some instances shopkeepers sought compromise deals or even union support." And, indeed, the union collaborated closely with the Shopkeepers Early Closing League to fend off the efforts of the merchants opposed to legislated closing. In doing so the clerks and merchants agreed to set aside ongoing disputes about unresolved management–labour issues such as pay or seating to concentrate on their common pursuit of early closing. Quinlan and Goodwin, "Combating the Tyranny of flexibility," 345, 346, 355–7. Merchants' and clerks' interests were not always identical. In his survey of early closing legislation in Britain, for example, Simon Rottenberg notes that when legislation restricted only the opening hours of stores, rather than the working hours of shop assistants, merchants and clerks found themselves pursuing competing interests, with many merchants content with such regulations and the shop assistants, in contrast, eager to secure additional regulations. Rottenberg, "Legislated Early Shop Closing in Britain," 128. P.C. Hoffman similarly highlights the tension in late nineteenth-century Britain between the Shop Assistants' Union that advocated mandatory closing through legislation and the Early Closing Association, supported by the employers, which favoured "voluntary" or "permissive" closing. Hoffman, *They Also Serve*, 8.

60 Neufeld, *Union Store*, 15.
61 Mallen and Rotenberg, "The Benefits and Costs of Evening Shopping," ii. In their survey of organizational opinion on evening shopping, only one union opted to respond. The Syndicat de Commerce of Montreal didn't necessarily oppose the deregulation of store hours, but expressed concern instead that corner stores not be exempted from legislation while focusing on the manner in which stores were staffed. For example, it expressed a concern with "casual hours." Ibid., 13–14, 80.
62 Mallen and Rotenberg, "The Benefits and Costs of Evening Shopping," 56.
63 Ferris, "On the Economics of Regulated Early Closing Hours," 14.
64 *Victoria Daily Colonist*, 23 October 1946, 3; *Vancouver Daily Province*, 19 June 1947, 1; *Victoria Daily Colonist*, 11 March 1952, 17; *Vancouver Sun*, 22 May 1954, 3; *Vancouver Daily Province*, 22 May 1954, 21; *Victoria Daily Colonist*, 31 May 1950, 3; *Victoria Daily Colonist*, 6 December 1952, 7.
65 *Vancouver Daily Province*, 19 June 1947, 1.
66 *Vancouver Daily Province*, 27 March 1954, 25; *Vancouver Daily Province*, 5 April 1954, 17; *Vancouver Daily Province*, 6 April 1954, 1; *Vancouver*

Daily Province, 27 May 1954, 43; *Victoria Daily Times*, 6 November 1952, 19; *Victoria Daily Colonist*, 19 February 1953, 18; *Victoria Daily Colonist*, 29 March 1953, 11.

67 *Victoria Daily Times*, 12 February 1953, 13.
68 *Vancouver Sun*, 21 May 1954, 1.
69 *Victoria Daily Times*, 28 November 1952, 3.

2 Community

1 *Victoria Daily Colonist*, 8 April 1956, 17.
2 *Victoria Daily Colonist*, 23 August 1952, 1.
3 *Victoria Daily Times*, 16 June 1927, 4.
4 *Vancouver Sun*, 10 June 1949, 4.
5 *Vancouver Sun*, 25 July 1952, 1; *Vancouver Sun*, 22 May 1954, 3.
6 In doing so they echoed the concerns of their American counterparts. As Juliet Schor notes in her historical survey of the American work week, "the vast majority of employers opposed workers' demands for shorter hours" as "un-American, indecent, unprofitable, and a threat to prosperity." Schor, *The Overworked American*, 73, 74.
7 As early as the 1840s, for example, "drapers' and mercantile assistants … in the Australian colonies" pursued early closing with campaign literature that "bemoaned the long hours worked and extolled the virtues of early closing in terms of health, recreation, and intellectual and moral development." Quinlan and Goodwin, "Combating the Tyranny of Flexibility," 346. Similarly, in his study of Philadelphia clerks, Jerome Bjelopera emphasizes the important role that leisure activities played in their lives and argues that the types of activities undertaken shifted from "same-sex activities" linked to fraternalism before the 1890s to an engagement with commercialized entertainment. The tedious nature of their work, he points out, led to a consistent demand for these recreational pleasures. Hence, "as the nineteenth century drew to a close, clerical employees increasingly organized their own leisure activities, which generally fell into two broad categories, amateur sport and nightlife entertainments." As P.C. Hoffman emphasized in his 1949 history of shop workers in Britain, "You cannot mix with your fellows when tied up in the shop, and even if some are free, others are not." Bjelopera, *City of Clerks*, 79, 82. Hoffman, *They Also Serve*, 4–5.
8 On the changing rationale of tourism promotion in BC, see Dawson, *Selling British Columbia*, ch. 2.
9 *Vancouver Daily Province*, 25 May 1907, 5.

10 The chamber suggested having stores open every day with shorter hours
so as not to exploit the clerks. *Victoria Daily Times*, 18 February 1926, 1;
Vancouver Sun, 18 February 1926, 1.

11 *Vancouver Daily Province*, 28 January 1947, 8. "It gives us a bad name," he
complained, noting that disappointed tourists "think we are a hick town."
Victoria Daily Colonist, 28 January 1947, 1.

12 *Vancouver Sun*, 10 June 1949, 4.

13 *Vancouver Sun*, 10 July 1952, 4.

14 City of Vancouver Archives [hereafter CVA], City Council and Office of
the City Clerk fonds, Clerk's Office, loc. 20-D-6, file 10, F.H. Elphicke,
President VTA to License and Claims Committee, City Council, 29 March
1954. In a seven-page brief the VTA detailed its concerns and suggested
that competing tourism destinations found the city's Wednesday-closing
practice to "be an asset to them in their efforts to sell Vancouver short."
CVA, City Council and Office of the City Clerk fonds, Clerk's Office, loc.
20-D-6, file 10, VTA, *Wednesday Closing*, 14 November 1952.

15 City of Vancouver Archives, City Council and Office of the City Clerk
fonds – Clerk's Office, loc. 19-D-5, file 5, Executive Secretary, Canadian
Restaurant Association, Vancouver Branch, to Ald. George C. Miller, 17
April 1947 (copy).

16 CVA, City Council and Office of the City Clerk fonds – Clerk's Office
loc. 20-D-6, file 10, R.C. Brown, President, Vancouver Branch, Canadian
Restaurant Association, to Mayor and Aldermen of the City of Vancouver,
29 March 1954.

17 City of Vancouver Archives, City Council and Office of the City Clerk
fonds, Clerk's Office, loc. 19-D-5, file 5, Evelyne M. Jackson to City
Council, 23 October 1950.

18 Besides, Pinkerton added, "they can also have a nice trip across the bridge
and shop in West Vancouver where stores are open all day Wednesday, but
closed all day Thursday." CVA, City Council and Office of the City Clerk
fonds, Clerk's Office, loc. 19-D-5, file 5, Mrs Thelma Pinkerton to City
Council, 23 October 1950.

19 Baskerville, *Beyond the Island*, 46.

20 In 1890, Victoria's exports were six times greater than Vancouver's. By
1903 these positions were dramatically reversed and Vancouver's exports
exceeded Victoria's by a ratio of three to one. Forward, "The Evolution of
Victoria's Functional Character," 359.

21 Baskerville, *Beyond the Island*, 48.

22 Ibid., 55.

23 Ibid., 57.

24 *Victoria Daily Colonist*, 25 April 1908, 7.
25 *Victoria Daily Times*, 21 August 1923, 4.
26 *Victoria Daily Times*, 21 August 1923, 4.
27 *Victoria Daily Times*, 21 August 1923, 4.
28 *Victoria Daily Times*, 18 October 1917, 17. For similar views see *Victoria Daily Times*, 10 October 1946, 4; *Victoria Daily Times*, 12 November 1946, 4; *Victoria Daily Times*, 17 December 1946, 4; *Victoria Daily Times*, 12 January 1949, 7.
29 Victoria City Archives, Victoria Chamber of Commerce fonds, 32 A 1, Board of Directors Meeting, 6 November 1934.
30 If a five-day week was deemed necessary for a particular line of business, Holmes suggested, arrangements must be made to ensure that "at least some operator of that particular business was open on every weekday." Victoria City Archives, Victoria Chamber of Commerce fonds, 32 A 2, Board of Directors Minutes, 24 September 1946. The quotations come from a summary of the letter read into the Chamber's minutes.
31 Ibid., 25 October 1946.
32 *Victoria Daily Colonist*, 20 May 1925, 4.
33 See, for example, *Victoria Daily Times*, 31 May 1956, 23.
34 *Victoria Daily Colonist*, 5 July 1956, 13.
35 *Victoria Daily Times*, 14 June 1956, 1, 27; *Victoria Daily Colonist*, 1 August 1956, 9.
36 *Victoria Daily Times*, 30 May 1951, 1–2. Vizard's position was echoed by the city's mayor, Claude Harrison, who in 1953 bluntly asserted his opposition to Wednesday closings by stating that "this is a tourist town." *Victoria Daily Times*, 9 March 1953, 1.
37 *Victoria Daily Colonist*, 8 April 1956, 17; *Victoria Daily Colonist* 13 April 1956, 17 (Second News Section); *Victoria Daily Times*, 26 April 1956, 17.
38 *Vancouver Sun*, 18 February 1926, 1.
39 *Victoria Daily Times*, 19 March 1953, 4. R.A. Mackie, head of the CPR hotel chain, concurred, arguing that Wednesday closings were denying the city much-needed revenue. *Victoria Daily Colonist*, 5 March 1957, 15. While Newberry and Mackie were content to assert tourism's importance in quite general terms, others offered more specific estimates regarding tourism's economic contribution to the local economy in the hope that this might win support for the dismantling of store-hour regulations. See *Victoria Daily Colonist*, 17 June 1936, 4; *Victoria Daily Colonist*, 1 November 1946, 19; *Victoria Daily Times*, 11 December 1951, 7; *Victoria Daily Colonist*, 11 December 1951, 18. On the growing influence of social science techniques on the quantification of tourist behaviours, see Apostle,

"Canada, Vacations Unlimited," ch. 4, as well as Dawson, *Selling British Columbia*, ch. 6.

40 *Victoria Daily Times*, 30 October 1946, 7. On postwar campaigns aimed at convincing Canadians to support the tourism industry because its economic dividends were widely shared, see Dubinsky, "Everybody Likes Canadians," 320–47; and Apostle, "The Display of a Tourist Nation: Canada in Government Film, 1945–1959," *Journal of the Canadian Historical Association* New Series 12 (2001): 177–97. On similar campaigns in British Columbia, see Dawson, *Selling British Columbia*, ch. 6.
41 *Victoria Daily Colonist*, 31 July 1951, 1.
42 *Victoria Daily Colonist*, 18 September 1958, 9.
43 On these more recent pronouncements, see Rothman, "Stumbling Toward the Millennium," 154.
44 *Victoria Daily Colonist*, 6 July 1954, 11.
45 *Victoria Daily Times*, 10 February 1953, 1.
46 *Victoria Daily Times*, 31 July 1951, 7; Victoria *Daily Colonist*, 7 July 1954, 5.
47 *Victoria Daily Colonist*, 31 July 1951, 1.
48 *Victoria Daily Colonist*, 24 February 1953, 22.
49 *Victoria Daily Times*, 3 November 1924, 5.
50 *Victoria Daily Times*, 22 January 1929, 10.
51 *Victoria Daily Times*, 27 June 1936, 5.
52 *Victoria Daily Colonist*, 27 October 1946, 3.
53 *Victoria Daily Colonist*, 23 August 1952, 1.
54 *Victoria Daily Colonist*, 11 February 1953, 11.
55 *Victoria Daily Colonist*, 22 March 1949, 4; Victoria *Daily Colonist*, 1 June 1951, 4.
56 *Victoria Daily Colonist*, 26 August 1952, 4.
57 *Victoria Daily Colonist*, 18 February 1953, 4.
58 *Victoria Daily Colonist*, 22 March 1953, 4.
59 *Victoria Daily Times*, 1 April 1953, 4. Forcing retail clerks to abandon their half-day holiday, yet another letter writer argued, placed these workers in a unique and unfair situation. "Today all banks, offices, all types of laborers, work a five-day week and none of them would consider a shift system," argued George Robinson in a 1953 letter to the *Times*. "Why then compel the store clerks to work a shift system which would not allow any group activities[?]" *Victoria Daily Times*, 3 June 1953, 4.
60 CVA, City Council and Office of the City Clerk fonds, Clerk's Office, loc. 19-D-5, file 5, Retail Merchants Committee in favor of a 6 day business, and five day employee work week, to Mayor and City Council, 19 June 1950.

61 CVA, City Council and Office of the City Clerk fonds, Clerk's Office, loc. 20-D-6, file 10, Committee of Retail Merchants in Favour of a Six Day-Five Day Week to Vancouver City Council, 27 March 1954.
62 To assuage concerns the newspaper suggested that provincial labour inspectors, local police, and City Council would all have a role to play in enforcing the five-day work week. *Vancouver Sun*, 18 June 1954, 1.
63 See, for example, *Victoria Daily Times*, 9 January 1917, 13; *Vancouver Sun*, 18 February 1926, 1; *Vancouver Sun*, 10 June 1949, 4; *Vancouver Sun*, 10 July 1952, 4; *Vancouver Daily Province*, 19 September 1952, 13; *Victoria Daily Colonist*, 22 November 1952, 13; *Vancouver Sun*, 26 March 1954, 1.
64 See, for example, *Victoria Daily Times*, 20 August 1923, 4; *Victoria Daily Times*, 27 August, 1923, 4; *Victoria Daily Colonist*, 24 June 1925, 1,11; *Victoria Daily Colonist*, 6 December 1952, 7; *Victoria Daily Colonist*, 21 November 1953, 4; *Victoria Daily Colonist*, 11 May 1954, 18.

3 Leverage

1 *Victoria Daily Colonist*, 12 October 1946, 3.
2 Smith, "Seeing New Side to Seasides," 22. Others note that chains have been accused of seeking to take advantage of "addicted" shoppers in their campaigns to expand store hours and maximize sales. Harris, Gardner and Vetter, "'Goods Over God,'" 610.
3 Cross, *An All-Consuming Century*, 231.
4 Harper, "'A New Battle on Evolution,'" 407–8, 412, 419, 424–5. Emphasis added.
5 On the rise and impact of chain stores in Canada in the 1920s, see Monod, *Store Wars*, 124–8; and Belisle, *Retail Nation*, 36–44.
6 Taschereau, "'Behind the Store," 237.
7 Belisle, "Negotiating Paternalism," 60–4.
8 As Donica Belisle and David Monod note, chain stores and department stores could be distinct operations and, thus, could find themselves in conflict with one another. In the store-hour debates under examination here, however, the two types of operations were generally conflated. See Belisle, *Retail Nation*, 38–9; and Monod, *Store Wars*, 219–21.
9 Mallen and Rotenberg, "The Benefits and Costs of Evening Shopping to the Canadian Economy," 82, 84.
10 Ibid., 89.
11 Ibid. 100, 102, 103.
12 Mallen and Rotenberg, "The Benefits and Costs of Evening Shopping," 11. This situation seemed to follow from the established pattern in the

United States with Mallen and Rotenberg noting that, in that country, "Discount stores and supermarkets seem to have forced many of the major outlets and department stores into longer hours of operation." Ibid., 58. Recent developments suggest that this is an international pattern as well. Surveying Germany's shop-closing debates in the 1990s, for example, Christian Kirchner and Richard Painter highlighted a division "between large retailers who enthusiastically support liberalization and small retailers, who are on the whole more hesitant, particularly about opening on Sunday." Kirchner and Painter, "The Economics of Germany's Shop Closing Hours" 15.

13 Monod, *Store Wars*, 127; Belisle, *Retail Nation*, ch. 7.

14 *Victoria Daily Colonist*, 14 March 1953, n.p. (Second News Section).

15 *Vancouver Sun*, 30 October 1958, 16.

16 *Victoria Daily Colonist*, 15 November 1919, 4; *Victoria Daily Times*, 25 August 1923, 4; *Victoria Daily* Times, 31 October 1924, 20; *Victoria Daily Times*, 3 November 1924, 5; *Vancouver Daily Province*, 30 December 1941, 1.

17 *Victoria Daily Colonist*, 12 October 1946, 3.

18 *Victoria Daily Times*, 12 October 1946, 5.

19 *Victoria Daily Colonist*, 27 May 1947, 5.

20 *Vancouver Sun*, 7 January 1947, 8.

21 *Victoria Daily Times*, 21 February 1947, 17.

22 For Victoria merchants' concerns about the role chain stores played in ushering in a 6-day shopping week, see *Victoria Daily Colonist*, 26 February 1958, 11; and *Victoria Daily Times*, 2 October 1958, 17.

23 *Vancouver Sun*, 3 June 1954, 4.

24 On the populist strain in British Columbia politics, see Fisher and Mitchell, "Patterns of Provincial Politics Since 1916," 264–5. For Price, supporters of six-day shopping were a "small wealthy group of eastern and American chain store operators, who because of their size and money think they have the right to change the shopping week to six days regardless of how it will affect their smaller competitors and the retail clerks in their stores." *Vancouver Daily Province*, 8 June 1954, 6.

25 *Vancouver Daily Province*, 5 June 1954, 21.

26 *Vancouver Sun*, 18 June 1954, 33. Jeweller David Lesser buttressed his opposition to six-day shopping without a guaranteed five-day work week for employees by claiming that his "Save the Wednesday" organization represented Vancouver-owned businesses "whose policy is not dictated in the east." *Vancouver Daily Province*, 13 November 1953, 1–2.

27 *Vancouver Daily Province*, 20 May 1952, 15; *Vancouver Sun*, 20 May 1952, 5. In Victoria, supporters of evening shopping called for urgent action

in order to respond to the "incursion" of the American Sears-Roebuck Company into Canada. *Victoria Daily Colonist*, 4 December 1952, 15.

28 *Victoria Daily Colonist*, 21 November 1953, 4.

29 *Vancouver Daily Province*, 20 November 1956, 33. That same year D.A. Gilbert, national president of the 40,000 member Retail Merchants' Association, addressed a meeting of Victoria retailers with blunt rhetoric aimed squarely at chain stores. To enthusiastic applause he asserted: "We of the RMA are definitely opposed to unrestricted shopping hours – and we think the big operators have been calling the tune long enough. We are engaged in a nation-wide battle with the big chain stores which are trying to impose their will on the smaller stores." The campaign to preserve local store-hour bylaws was a central component of this larger battle. *Victoria Daily Times*, 27 April 1956, 6.

30 *Vancouver Daily Province*, 22 February 1957, 5.

31 *Vancouver Daily Province*, 23 December 1964, 16.

32 City of Vancouver Archives [hereafter CVA], City Councillors' Office fonds, series # 467, Records of Ald. Marianne Linnell, 84-E-2 file 13, J. Dove and others to Mayor and Council, 20 October 1967.

33 *Vancouver Sun*, 2 May 1956, 25.

34 *Victoria Daily Times*, 6 July 1955, 5; *Victoria Daily Colonist*, 5 October 1955, 2.

35 *Victoria Daily Colonist*, 6 October 1955, 17. In recognizing the influence of chain stores, even those resisting store-hour expansion could wistfully wonder what might happen if that influence could be harnessed for their own side. Peter McEwan, head of a competing retail clerks organization, the Five-Day Action Committee, suggested that united action by the city's six big stores in Victoria could provide clerks with a full-day Wednesday holiday. "I feel certain that if Hudson's Bay, Eaton's, Woodward's, George Straith, W.&J. Wilson and Standard Furniture would go over to all-day closing on Wednesday," he explained, "others would quickly follow suit." *Victoria Daily Colonist*, 15 April 1953, 11.

36 By 1965, G.R. Merrill, a Vancouver Island RMA representative, was fully convinced that "monopoly-minded corporate structures are forcing the B.C. businessman and his family to the wall." *Victoria Daily Colonist*, 15 January 1965, 19. A 1966 brief from the Victoria Chamber of Commerce called on Saanich and Victoria to regulate store hours and blamed large companies for moving into local communities and extending store hours. *Victoria Daily Colonist*, 21 September 1966, 11. That same year John Nicol, a representative of the Retail Food and Drug Clerks' Union and delegate of the Victoria Labour Council, raised the spectre of British Columbia adopting the wide-open shopping approach of the United States and

warned that in that country "the small man will soon become either extinct or a servant of the large corporations." *Victoria Daily Times*, 23 September 1966, 19. As Nicol's comments and others suggest, small independent merchants were not alone in targeting chains, but their voices were certainly dominant.

37 Waller continued: "In view of the fact that they could not get together, the City Council decided to leave the whole matter wide open at their own discretion and pass By-law No. 4785 entitled 'Shops Exemption By-law, 1958'..." CVA, City Councillors' Office fonds, series # 467, Records of Ald. Marianne Linnell, 84-E-2 file 13, F.M. Waller, City Clerk, Victoria, to Linnell, 1 February 1968.

38 High, "Capital and Community Reconsidered."

39 *Vancouver Sun*, 13 September 1946, 6; *Vancouver Sun*, 11 October 1946, 10; *Vancouver Daily Province*, 19 December 1946, 11; *Vancouver Sun*, 7 January 1947, 8.

40 *Victoria Daily Times*, 28 September 1946, 11; *Victoria Daily Colonist*, 1 October 1946, 19; *Vancouver Daily Province*, 17 December 1956, 25.

41 *Vancouver Daily Province*, 10 March 1947, 7.

42 CVA, City Council and Office of the City Clerk fonds – Clerk's Office, loc. 20-D-6, file 10, A.T.R. Campbell, Campbell, Brazier, Fisher, McMaster & Johnson, Barristers and Solicitors to City Clerk, 24 March 1954.

43 *Vancouver Sun*, 16 June 1954, 24.

44 *Vancouver Daily Province*, 26 June 1954, 2.

45 *Vancouver Sun*, 21 September 1954, 39.

46 *Vancouver Sun*, 3 May 1956, 1.

47 *Vancouver Daily Province*, 19 June 1956, 11.

48 *Victoria Daily Colonist*, 26 April 1958, 13.

49 *Vancouver Sun*, 19 September 1962, 43.

50 *Vancouver Daily Province*, 19 October 1967, 27. In 1969 Peter P. Miller, Pacific region marketing research manager for Eaton's, argued that longer store hours were the trend of the future and necessary to meet increasing incomes and changing living patterns. *Vancouver Daily Province*, 10 January 1969, 21.

51 Union contracts do not appear to have been a key factor in limiting chain stores' appetite for expanded hours. Indeed many large retail chains in southwestern British Columbia successfully carried out spirited and sometimes unprincipled campaigns to prevent their employees from unionizing throughout the 1940s and 1950s and thus did not need to factor union contracts into their calculations. Moreover, Safeway, one of

the earliest chains to accept closed-shop contracts was one of the biggest supporters of expanded store hours. On the relationship between chains and clerks' unions, see Neufeld, *Union Store*, 55–57, 68–69, 79–88.

52 *Vancouver Daily Province*, 13 July 1951, 6.

53 *Victoria Daily Times*, 24 February 1953, 2; Victoria *Daily Colonist*, 24 February 1953, 22.

54 *Victoria Daily Times*, 11 February 1953, 15.

55 Eaton's, on the other hand, already followed a broad policy as a chain. *Victoria Daily Times*, 10 May 1966, 7.

56 *Victoria Daily Times*, 19 September 1946, 1. Similarly, in 1954, Albert Harvey of Harvey's Stores Ltd. complained to Vancouver City Council regarding a situation in which his stores were compelled to close at 6 p.m. while hardware, a line he sold, was available at builders' suppliers that were not also forced to close. *Vancouver Daily Province*, 12 January 1954, 8.

57 *Victoria Daily Times*, 15 November 1960, 10.

58 *Vancouver Daily Province*, 9 July 1954, 1–2.

59 *Vancouver Sun*, 4 January 1955, 2.

60 *Victoria Daily Times*, 4 May 1956, 15.

61 The rumour arose when most stores stayed open until 9 p.m. on June 30th because the next day was Dominion Day and it was the practice of many grocery stores to remain open until 9 p.m. in advance of a public holiday. *Victoria Daily Colonist*, 8 July 1953, 5.

62 *Victoria Daily Colonist*, 10 October 1958, 17.

63 *Vancouver Sun*, 2 May 1956, 25.

64 *Vancouver Sun*, 2 May 1956, 25.

65 *Vancouver Sun*, 2 November 1965, 10.

66 *Vancouver Daily Province*, 4 October 1950, 1.

67 *Vancouver Sun*, 11 June 1954, 4.

68 *Vancouver Sun*, 14 June 1954, 4.

69 *Vancouver Sun*, 4 July 1957, 37.

70 *Victoria Daily Colonist*, 24 June 1954, 17.

71 *Vancouver Daily Province*, 7 May 1946, 1.

72 *Vancouver Sun*, 6 May 1947, 8. In July 1951 Woodward's once again pronounced itself opposed to any plan to keep stores open Wednesdays to provide for six-day shopping because longer hours would increase costs and adversely affect its employees. *Vancouver Daily Province*, 6 July 1951, 17.

73 *Vancouver Daily Province*, 25 April 1953, 4.

74 *Vancouver Sun*, 8 June 1954, 3.

75 *Vancouver Daily Province*, 22 June 1954, 9.

76 *Vancouver Sun*, 22 June 1954, 14.

77 *Victoria Daily Colonist*, 11 April 1956, 13; *Victoria Daily Times*, 13 April
1956, 4. In 1966 the two largest stores at North Vancouver's Park Royal
Shopping Centre found themselves on opposite sides of a battle over
Thursday evening shopping with Eaton's supporting the proposal and
Woodward's, and its colourfully named manager, Charles Dickens,
opposing it. *Vancouver Daily Province*, 5 April 1966, 14; *Vancouver Sun*,
5 April 1966, 58.

78 CVA, City Councillors' Office fonds, series # 467, Records of Ald. Marianne
Linnell, 84-E-2 file 13,T. Parsons, President – Staff Advisory Council,
Woodward's (Vancouver), 30 October 1967.

79 CVA, City Councillors' Office fonds, Records of Ald. Marianne Linnell,
series # 467, 84-E-2 file 13, typed note from A Woodwards [*sic*] Employee,
circulated at the request of Ald. Linnell, 27 September 1969.

80 Hence, in 1958, as a divided Victoria City Council moved toward
permitting wide-open hours if the Municipal Act allowed such a scenario,
Ald. Hugh Ramsay continued to support the five-day week and did so
by emphasizing the plight of small business which he considered to be
"the backbone of this community." Similarly, when New Westminster
City Council authorized six-day shopping by allowing merchants to
remain open Wednesday afternoons, Mayor Beth Wood voted against the
motion and declared it "a sorry day for New Westminster and the small
merchants." *Victoria Daily Times*, 23 September 1958, 3; *Vancouver Daily
Province*, 9 February 1960, 1.

81 *Victoria Daily Colonist*, 8 February 1950, 1.

82 *Victoria Daily Colonist*, 26 April 1957, 17. At a May 1957 meeting in
Richmond, Mrs A.R. Parker, who operated a store on the Steveston
Highway, opposed mandatory Sunday and evening closing on similar
grounds. *Vancouver Sun*, 31 May 1957, 29.

83 *Victoria Daily Colonist*, 20 September 1958, 5.

84 *Victoria Daily Times*, 10 February 1953, 1.

85 *Victoria Daily Colonist*, 11 February 1953, 11.

86 *Victoria Daily Times*, 8 July 1954, 3

4 Morality

1 *Victoria Daily Colonist*, 7 June 1966, 17.

2 *Victoria Daily Colonist*, 21 September 1966, 11.

3 In the Canadian context, see, for instance, Cook, *Sex, Lies, and Cigarettes*;
Belisle, *Retail Nation*, ch. 5; Parr, *Domestic Goods*; Wright, "Feminine
Trifles of Vast Importance." On the nineteenth-century image of women

as irrational consumers, see Roberts, "Gender, Consumption, and Commodity Culture." On gender and consumption more broadly, see Warsh and Malleck, eds., *Consuming Modernity*.

4 Leach, "Transformations in a Culture of Consumption," 333.

5 On the experiences of female store clerks in Canada, see Belisle, "Negotiating Paternalism"; and Belisle, *Retail Nation*, ch. 6.

6 If male clerks' prospects for upward mobility dimmed over time, female clerks were invariably passed over for promotions. Moreover, the main clerical union, the RCIPA, "did not encourage their participation" in its activities. Bjelopera, *City of Clerks*, 3, 13, 42. Dora Costa offers a more optimistic assessment of the female clerking experience in the United States. Charting the increase in women's paid employment, Costa offers the following synopsis. In the early twentieth century, "the 'factory girl' set the stage for the unmarried 'office girl.' The unmarried office girl paved the way for the entry of married women into the labor force in the late 1950s, even though this entry was primarily in dead-end jobs in the clerical sector. In turn, the married women in the labor force paved the way for the rise of the modern career woman, doing work that requires a lengthy period of training and that offers genuine opportunities for promotion." Indeed, she suggests that "the rise of the clerical sector transformed women's work by providing women "with better pay and cleaner, less arduous work than manufacturing. But because women were expected to leave the labor force upon marriage, they worked at jobs from which they were never promoted, whereas men could rise from office boy to president of the company." "The emergence of part-time work after 1950 altered the paid work opportunities of married women," she notes, while revealing that "much of the growth in women's employment between 1950 and 1970 consisted of growth in part-time work." Women's entry into "the professions and other nontraditional careers did not really begin until 1970." Costa, "From Mill Town to Board Room," 101, 108, 109, 117.

7 Belisle, *Retail Nation*, 160. Notably, unions keen to organize retail workers in Canada appeared less than enthusiastic in welcoming them as full members of their organizations. Women's part-time status seems to have hindered the mid-twentieth-century drive to organize Eaton's in Toronto, but male organizers' unwillingness to treat female employees on an equal basis clearly played a more significant role in the union's defeat. See Belisle, "Exploring Postwar Consumption," 646, 650.

8 Rottenberg, "Legislated Early Shop Closing in Britain," 120–1. In nineteenth-century Britain, Michael Quinlan and Miles Goodwin explain, "several observers pointed to the serious health consequences of long

hours." In 1843 one observer argued that "the high mortality rate among shop assistants was not apparent to customers because assistants were dismissed and sent home when they grew pale and sickly." In 1884 a barrister named Thomas Sutherst "published a book entitled *Death and Disease Behind the Counter*," and in 1893 a Dr Bowrie "told a committee of the House of Lords that 38 per cent of shop assistants suffered from consumption." Quinlan and Goodwin, "Combating the Tyranny of Flexibility," 345.

9 Ibid., 348.

10 Ibid., 357.

11 Evan Roberts, "Gender in Store," 108. On active campaigns by female store clerks and white-collar workers to improve their lot, see Cross and Shergold, "'We Think We Are of the Oppressed.'"

12 As Donica Belisle explains, BC's female clerks did not shy away from expressing their views. "After British Columbia established minimum wage laws for women in 1918, the HBC discontinued paying its female clerks $8.00 weekly plus commission. It cancelled women's abilities to collect commission and started paying them the minimum wage of $9.00 per week," she notes. "Male clerks 'continued to receive both a salary and a commission.' Enraged not only by their loss in pay but also at their loss of status, a 'number of female clerks [in Vancouver] quit their jobs in protest.'" Belisle, "Negotiating Paternalism," 72.

13 *Victoria Daily Colonist*, 17 May 1916, 10. Similar arguments emerged twenty years earlier on the other side of the world. In responding to a letter to the editor of Melbourne's *Age* newspaper from "a housewife" that was critical of new store-hour restrictions in the 1890s, eight Australian female shop assistants demanded to know whether the writer had "ever stood behind a counter as we do, from week's end to week's end, serving such considerate ladies as housewife? Does she know the utter weariness of mind and body which is the result to the employees of her late shopping?" Quoted in Quinlan and Goodwin, "Combating the Tyranny of Flexibility," 357–8. As late as the 1940s, British legislation mandated that female shop assistants be permitted to use seats. Hoffman, *They Also Serve*, 15. In 1969 the Alberta Labour Act continued to require that employers provide female employees working after midnight in communities with more than 2,000 residents with transportation home. Mallen and Rotenberg, "The Benefits and Costs of Evening Shopping," vol. 1, 140.

14 *Victoria Daily Colonist*, 17 May 1916, 10.

15 *Victoria Daily Colonist*, 17 May 1916, 10.

16 *Victoria Daily Times*, 3 June 1916, 13.

17 *Victoria Daily Times*, 8 June 1916, 10.

18 *Victoria Daily Times*, 8 June 1916, 10.

19 *Victoria Daily Colonist*, 8 January 1918, 4; *Victoria Daily Colonist*, 7 January 1919, 2.

20 *Victoria Daily Colonist*, 30 August 1923, 4.

21 As Donica Belisle points out, racism was, at times, not far below the surface of campaigns to protect female clerks. In a pre–First World War proposal to amend the British Columbia Shop Act, "members of the Vancouver Local Council of Women, the Vancouver Trades and Labour Council, and the Vancouver Board of Trade" took a particular interest in "saleswomen's working conditions." In addition to regulating shop assistants' hours, the groups call for "shops to be kept clean and well-ventilated," and for "seats for girls and women," and "stipulated that 'in no cases shall Caucasians be permitted to work in the same establishment as Asiatics.'" Belisle, "Negotiating Paternalism," 70. Certainly female store clerks could, from time to time, become the subject of moral panics concerning the vulnerability of white women and the nefarious influence of Asian men. As Lindsey McMaster notes, "the shop girl was a frequent figure of pathos because she was publicly visible in a way that most young working women were not, and because it was known that she worked for long hours on her feet; the idea that she might resort to stimulants may have seemed plausible to many readers and was likely meant to evoke their sympathies." McMaster, *Working Girls in the West*, 155. In explaining why anxieties about working women were exacerbated in western Canada, McMaster points to the dramatically changing urban context. The ideals of the frontier (and, for example, the long-standing concern about a dearth of white women) sat uneasily with western cities' influx of immigrants. This situation and the cities' "rapid industrialization and urbanization" combined to accelerate community angst about the future. Ibid., 2.

22 Individual women did, at times, play key roles in these debates. When, in response to a plebiscite, Vancouver City Council agreed to pass a bylaw enforcing Wednesday closing for all retail stores except those selling food and drugs, it was Anne Peterson who spoke for the city's retail clerks and thanked the citizens of Vancouver. *Vancouver Sun*, 19 June 1947, 1, 2. And in May 1950 it was pressure from the Victoria Local Council of Women that helped convince city solicitor A.J. Patton to recommend that the city remind its sanitary inspector to ensure that a Shops Regulation and Weekly Holiday Act provision for seats for female clerks in stores was not being ignored. *Victoria Daily Times*, 6 May 1950, 2.

23 *Vancouver Sun,* 31 January 1947, 28.

24 *Vancouver Daily Province,* 12 February 1947, 1.

25 *Vancouver Sun,* 6 May 1947, 8. On press representations of female strikers more generally, see, Lindsey McMaster, *Working Girls in the West,* Chapter 4.

26 *Vancouver Daily Province,* 17 April 1956, 5.

27 *Victoria Daily Times,* 9 January 1917, 13.

28 *Victoria Daily Times,* 18 October 1917, 17.

29 *Victoria Daily Times,* 7 October 1946, 3. In January 1954, Ald. George Cunningham helped block a proposed Vancouver City Council bylaw restricting evening sales of frozen meat and fish on similar grounds; his rhetoric was repeated by the *Vancouver Sun* a week later when the newspaper announced that "Vancouver aldermen made peace with city housewives" by scrapping the proposed bylaw. *Vancouver Sun,* 19 and 27 January 1954, 6 and 11 respectively.

30 *Vancouver Sun,* 8 February 1954, 19. In 1961 the female labour participation rate was 32 per cent in Greater Vancouver and 29.4 per cent in Greater Victoria. Mallen and Rotenberg, "The Benefits and Costs of Evening Shopping," 61. In Victoria, the *Colonist* similarly incorporated the growing number of working women into its arguments against store-hour regulation. The editorial endorsing wide-open store hours did so partly in recognition of women's growing responsiblities as housewives and wage earners. "With so many wives working nowadays," the newspaper argued, "there is a marked favoritism for evening shopping." *Victoria Daily Colonist,* 11 October 1956, 4. Ald. Lily Wilson of Victoria offered a similar analysis with regard to six-day shopping by arguing in 1956 that "eighty per cent of the shopping in Victoria is done by the women and the women want to shop six days a week." *Victoria Daily Colonist,* 9 August 1956, 17. A study from the mid-1990s noted that proponents of store-hour liberalization in Canada continued to point to the need to "accommodate changing lifestyles (increases in the numbers of working women and of families in which all adults work) and increasing time constraints, which limit Canadians' access to stores and shops." Lanoie, Tanguay and Vallée, "Short-Term Impact of Shopping-Hour Deregulation," 178.

31 *Victoria Daily Times,* 25 April 1957, 19.

32 *Victoria Daily Colonist,* 10 October 1958, 1. In 1962, Victoria grocery store owner Scott Cracknell conceded that evening opening and long hours created staff problems, especially for small store operators, but felt obligated to admit that "the housewife is entitled to evening shopping if she wants it." *Victoria Daily Colonist,* 11 November 1962, 9. Cracknell owned an independent store in the Super-Valu chain. That the Super-Valu

chain boasted independent operators reinforces the need to recognize the complexity of chain stores' aims and orientations.

33 Roberts, "Gender in Store," 114. Emphasis added.

34 Ibid., 114, 117.

35 A similar viewpoint infused late-twentieth-century arguments for Sunday shopping in Britain. As Phil Harris and colleagues note, "extended trading hours allowed customers to shop when it suited them, and Sunday was seen by retailers as a day on which the whole family could spend leisure hours shopping." Harris, Gardner, and Vetter, "'Goods Over God,'" 610.

36 *Vancouver Sun*, 14 June 1954, 4. In February 1956, Vancouverite Dave Harris offered the *Sun*'s readers a sarcastic take on the issue by denouncing evening shopping: "Of course it does not matter whether the clerks work at night and seldom see their families or friends, like any other civilized businessman, so long as they work eight hours per day." *Vancouver Sun*, 27 February 1956, 4.

37 *Victoria Daily Times*, 26 April 1956, 30.

38 *Vancouver Daily Province*, 31 October 1967, 10. George Gilbert of Burnaby opposed expanded store hours on the grounds that increased time at work limited parents' ability to nurture their children. "We in Canada have a very high percentage of mental health problems and a lot of it comes about because Mum and Dad are working evenings and Saturdays," he argued. "Children need Mum and Dad's attention and they should get it at nights[,] Saturdays and Sundays ... In most of the cities in Australia department stores close Saturdays and Sundays so that all the family can be together two days a week ... Lets [*sic*] think of the children before increasing the shopping hours." CVA, City Councillors' Office fonds, series # 467, Records of Ald. Marianne Linnell, 84-E-2 file 13, George Gilbert, Burnaby to Linnell, n.d., c. November 1967.

39 *Victoria Daily Colonist*, 22 November 1952, 13.

40 *Victoria Daily Colonist*, 22 November 1952, 13. There were historical precedents for Mallek's concerns; during the late nineteenth and early twentieth centuries, William Leach notes, "an increasing number of court cases pitted wives, who bought well beyond their means, against husbands, who refused to pay their wives' debts." Leach, "Transformations in a Culture of Consumption," 334. The notion that evening shopping was necessary to allow families to make collective decisions about major purchases was supported by Mallen and Rotenberg, who noted that "there is a tendency, particularly among young married couples, to do shopping on a family basis. For many durable goods, such as furniture, TV sets, radios, etc., or higher priced non-durables, families

prefer to shop collectively, and the decision-making unit consists of not one individual but a number of people. The only time the husband and wife can shop together if both are working would be in the evening and on the weekends." Mallen and Rotenberg, "The Benefits and Costs of Evening Shopping," 18.

41 *Vancouver Daily Province,* 14 February 1956, 1. In August 1956, as Vancouver introduced downtown evening shopping for the first time since 1900, Charles Woodward, president of the Woodward's department store chain, reiterated the connection between family togetherness and evening shopping: "We are convinced the public would like to do its shopping Friday nights and we are going to provide that opportunity. It will also give families a chance to shop together and enable them to have weekends free for other activities." *Vancouver Daily Province,* 31 August 1956, 1. Back in 1900, stores were open until 8 p.m. Now they were slated to remain open until 9 p.m.

42 CVA, City Councillors' Office fonds, series #467, Records of Ald. Marianne Linnell, 84-E-2 file 13, O.C. McKee, Executive Vice-President, Hamilton Harvey Ltd. to Linnell, 19 October 1967.

43 *Victoria Daily Colonist,* 26 April 1958, 13.

44 *Victoria Daily Colonist,* 26 April 1958, 13. As Juliet Schor observers, while shopping was once considered a utilitarian task, it has been transformed into "a leisure activity in its own right. Going to the mall is a common Friday or Saturday night's entertainment, not just for the teens who seem to live in them, but also for adults." Schor, *The Overworked American,* 107. Another excellent source on shopping's transition from a utilitarian pursuit to a leisure activity is Cross, *An All-Consuming Century,* 213–20.

45 *Victoria Daily Times,* 23 December 1958, 9.

46 *Victoria Daily Times,* 23 April 1966, 4.

47 On the notion of consumer sovereignty, see Parr, *Domestic Goods,* ch. 4.

48 For a summary of more contemporary arguments that support the idea that consumer expenditures are finite and that faced with store-hour restrictions "consumers merely reschedule the same weekly purchases over more shopping hours," see Lanoie, Tanguay, and Vallée, "Short-Term Impact of Shopping-Hour Deregulation," 179.

49 See, for example, *Victoria Daily Colonist,* 25 July 1923, 7; *Victoria Daily Colonist,* 30 August 1923, 4; *Vancouver Sun,* 13 March 1953, 27; *Victoria Daily Colonist,* 24 July 1954, 13; *Vancouver Sun,* 4 January 1955, 2.

50 *Vancouver Sun,* 5 June 1954, 8.

51 According to Mallen and Rotenberg, US retailers in areas where Sunday shopping was permitted were convinced that, given expanded

opportunities for shopping, consumers were spending more money
than before and were not simply transferring money "from weekdays to
Sundays" or evenings. Mallen and Rotenberg, "The Benefits and Costs of
Evening Shopping," 21.

52 *Vancouver Sun*, 8 May 1954, 1–2.

53 *Victoria Daily Colonist*, 31 October 1946, 4; *Victoria Daily Times*, 11 December
1946, 4.

54 *Victoria Daily Colonist*, 6 December 1946, 4. *Vancouver Daily Province*
columnist D.A. McGregor offered a similar view. See *Vancouver Daily
Province*, 16 February 1950, 4.

55 *Vancouver Daily Province*, 20 August 1957, 8.

56 "Tourists have been coming for years to enjoy Victoria's charm," Gray
argued, "not its china, and if you will leave things as they are, I believe
they will continue to come." Businessman T.G. Denny concurred, arguing
that he preferred the current system and suggesting that it suited the
majority of tourists, merchants, employees, and the general public. *Victoria
Daily Colonist*, 11 March 1952, 17.

57 A recent study of debates of Sunday shopping in Britain underscores the
variety of consumer opinions on the store-hour issue. Indeed, Christian
Kirchner and Richard Painter emphasize the importance of recognizing
"different subsets of consumers." "Some consumers might accept higher
prices if they can shop at personal[l]y convenient hours," they note, while
"others might prefer lower prices and be willing to do their shopping
only in limited periods of time." For others still, the location of the store
might prove the key factor in shaping shopping preferences. Kirchner and
Painter, "The Economics of Germany's Shop Closing Hours," 6, 22–3.

58 *Victoria Daily Colonist*, 4 December 1952, 15.

59 *Victoria Daily Times*, 29 March 1958, 33.

60 *Vancouver Daily Province*, 1 September 1956, 23.

61 *Victoria Daily Colonist*, 15 April 1958, 1–2.

62 CVA, City Councillors' Office fonds, series # 467, Records of Ald. Marianne
Linnell, 84-E-2 file 13, Mrs Walter Wong, 3660 West King Edward Ave to
Linnell, 1 November 1967. As Minna Ziskind notes, consumers in and
around New York City offered similar explanations for their shopping
preferences. "Brooklyn and Long Island shoppers alike preferred suburban
shopping centers because of traffic and parking problems downtown."
Ziskind, "Labor Conflict in the Suburbs," 58. Moreover, it is important
to note that determining convenience could also be a complex, two-step,
process. In their study of suburban families around New York City, for
example, Samuel and Lois Pratt found that "when families no longer

had to go to New York for specialized items, they found it convenient to transfer convenience-good shopping to the suburbs as well." Pratt and Pratt, "The Impact of Some Regional Shopping Centers," 49.

63 Consumer demand for evening shopping certainly existed elsewhere in Canada. For example, by 1964 "customers in the Hamilton area were demanding store openings as many nights as possible." An intense battle ensued as Hamilton City Council attempted to ensure the uniformity of legislation for eight different municipalities. While some larger stores supported this move towards wide-open shopping, some smaller stores opposed the move on the grounds that their operating expenses would increase dramatically while other retailers argued that finite consumer demand rendered additional shopping hours unnecessary. Mallen and Rotenberg, "The Benefits and Costs of Evening Shopping," 92–3.

64 Increased operating expenses, the writer added, "will be charged to the consumer," increasing already high prices. *Vancouver Sun*, 6 April 1954, 4.

65 *Vancouver Sun*, 8 February 1954, 25.

66 Of the twenty-three people questioned, ten did not care, nine favoured a six-day week, and four approved of the current five-day week. *Vancouver Daily Province*, 19 June 1954, 23.

67 *Vancouver Sun*, 19 June 1954, 1–2.

68 *Victoria Daily Colonist*, 20 September 1958, 17. Mrs A.J. Miller, a Port Coquitlam housewife, suggested that six-day shopping would mean more business, noting that under the current system "we never come into town on Wednesdays." James Connell, a seaman staying at the Balmoral Hotel, endorsed six-day shopping. He had just returned from Australia, where, he explained, "everything is dead from noon Saturday." Arthur Rothermal, a Vancouver plumber, supported a six-day week not for any immediate personal benefit as a consumer but because it "would mean more jobs." *Vancouver Daily Province*, 19 June 1954, 23.

69 *Victoria Daily Colonist*, 20 September 1958, 17.

70 *Vancouver Daily Province*, 19 June 1954, 23.

71 *Vancouver Daily Province*, 6 March 1956, 17.

5 Regulation

1 *Victoria Daily Times*, 18 March 1958, 2.

2 As Catherine Carstairs reminds us, "regulation" and "control" are two very different things, for the former acknowledges the many failures inherent in state attempts to legislate human behaviour. Carstairs, *Jailed for Possession*, 8. According to historian Sylvie Taschereau, "Quebec law was

ineffectual in regulating closing times or children's labour." "Throughout the 1930s and until the beginning of the 1940s," she explains, "the law's inadequacies, the indifference with which it was applied, and its constant abuse were denounced over and over again by groups calling for a public-education law and for better working conditions. The employment of children and young people in food stores was a particular focus of their complaints." Taschereau, "'Behind the Store,'" 245–6. That store-hour regulations proved difficult to enforce should hardly come as a surprise. As Juliet Schor points out, factory hour legislation, which anticipated store-hour restrictions, often proved ineffective as inspectors struggled to enforce the law. Schor, *The Overworked American*, 55. Writing in 2000, for example, Christian Kirchner and Richard Painter noted that there were "many circumventions of closing hours regulations in Germany" despite widespread government regulations. Kirchner and. Painter, "The Economics of Germany's Shop Closing Hours," 2. Writing in 1969, Mallen and Rotenberg reported that Blue Laws in many US states "are often ineffective." Mallen and Rotenberg, "The Benefits and Costs of Evening Shopping" vol. 1, 58.

3 Quinlan and Goodwin, "Combating the Tyranny of Flexibility," 344.
4 Ibid., 351–2, 357.
5 Ibid., 349.
6 *Victoria Daily Colonist*, 18 September 1958, 9.
7 *Victoria Daily Times*, 15 July 1916, 9.
8 In December 1916, for example, fifty-five Victoria merchants pleaded guilty for opening illegally on a Saturday. *Victoria Daily Times*, 28 December 1916, 11.
9 See, for example, the case involving merchant James Little and police officer Margaret Walker, *Victoria Daily Times*, 8 November 1928, 1, 3.
10 *Vancouver Daily Province*, 30 September 1926, 3.
11 *Vancouver Daily Province*, 26 March 1936, 7.
12 *Vancouver Sun*, 5 March 1947, 23.
13 *Victoria Daily Colonist*, 26 March 1953, 2.
14 *Victoria Daily Times*, 21 December 1949, 1; *Vancouver Sun*, 28 December 1949, 16.
15 The aim here was to limit the sale of frozen meats, fish, and poultry to normal butcher shop hours.
16 Mrs Jack Woo concurred, stating that she and her husband would "just have to take a chance" if customers sought frozen meats at their Capital Grocery on Davie Street. *Vancouver Sun*, 15 January 1954, 16.
17 *Victoria Daily Colonist*, 13 September 1957, 17.

18 Wing Mah of Daily Food Stores on Robson Street similarly pointed to the fear of unfair competition: "Plenty of stores will continue to sell frozen food and we'll be one of them." *Vancouver Sun*, 12 February 1954, 14.

19 *Vancouver Sun*, 21 July 1954, 1. Proprietors frequently argued that they remained open out of necessity as many department stores, with which they competed for consumers, were permitted to open. Similarly, Lawrence Mallek, operator of a ladies' apparel store, denounced the minute technicalities that were involved in the liberalizing of the Wednesday-closing bylaw and boldly announced that his store would also remain open despite the lack of city approval. *Vancouver Sun*, 22 July 1954, 19.

20 The following week, a similar situation ensued as many lines of business still had not obtained the necessary signatures on petitions to gain city approval for Wednesday openings. *Vancouver Daily Province*, 29 July 1954, 1.

21 *Vancouver Daily Province*, 12 July 1950, 17; *Vancouver Sun*, 21 February 1950, 15; *Vancouver Sun*, 28 May 1958, 25. The reluctance of Vancouver's city licence office to take on the onerous task of store-hour enforcement is nicely detailed in the following submission from A.N. Moore, a city licence inspector, to the members of the licence and claims committee: "While on the surface, the suggestion as made by the Retail Merchants Association might appear to be one of the answers to their problem, on giving the matter due consideration, I am of the opinion that if this was followed out we would have to have two full time Inspectors to do work of this nature, – one to make the actual purchases and the other to corroborate in giving evidence. These men would have to be employed on a full-time basis, doing Police work and would be entitled to draw Police pay, which would set up an inequality of pay rates within the Department. It would also be difficult to work these men from this Department as they would be working only one day a week and evenings and supervision of them would be impossible. ... I therefore cannot see how this could be handled from this Department. To my mind the enforcement of the By-laws in question appear to be strictly a matter for the Police, and to be enforced by them." City of Vancouver Archives [hereafter CVA], City Council and Office of the City Clerk fonds – Clerk's Office Loc. 19-E-6, file 15, A.N. Moore, License Inspector & Business Tax Collector to Chairman & Members of the Licenses & Claims Committee, 4 July 1950,

22 Provincial regulations permitted the selling of fresh fruit on Wednesday afternoons, but not fresh vegetables. *Vancouver Daily Province*, 16 April 1951, 17.

23 *Vancouver Sun*, 28 May 1958, 25.

24 *Vancouver Daily Province*, 10 August 1956, 14.

25 *Victoria Daily Times,* 10 September 1957, 10.

26 *Victoria Daily Times,* 16 September 1958, 1.

27 *Victoria Daily Colonist,* 18 December 1954, 10.

28 *Vancouver Daily Province,* 15 July 1947, 5; *Vancouver Sun,* 16 December 1949, 1–2; *Vancouver Sun,* 12 June 1954, 1; *Victoria Daily Times,* 10 January 1961, 10.

29 *Vancouver Sun,* 16 December 1949, 1–2. In Britain, attempts to enforce a ban on Sunday shopping in the second half of the twentieth century faced similar problems: "The duty of enforcing the act lay with local authorities, but fines imposed on retailers for breaching the Sunday trading legislation had not kept pace with time and were more than covered by the profits of the day's trading. As a result, the act was widely ignored by retailers and only partially enforced by some authorities." Harris, Gardner, and Vetter, "'Goods Over God,'" 614.

30 *Vancouver Sun,* 21 December 1949, 2. This lack of incentive to take local store-hour bylaws seriously was obviously a problem elsewhere. In 1958 a furniture dealer in Winnipeg, convinced that store-hour restrictions were outdated and that employees no longer required legislative protection, "held a six-hour marathon sale" from 4 p.m. to 10 p.m. in contravention of local store-hour regulations and "did a thriving business" while being fined just $25. Mallen and Rotenberg, "The Benefits and Costs of Evening Shopping," 91.

31 *Vancouver Daily Province,* 21 December 1955, 2.

32 For examples of local merchants berating city officials for the lack of enforcement, see CVA, City Council and Office of the City Clerk fonds – Clerk's Office, loc. 19-E-6, file 15, D.A. [?] Baxter to City Council, 7 July 1950; J.L. Dennett, Dennett's Choice Meats, Fish and Poultry, to Ald. Showler and City Council, 6 July 1950; and Per. O.C.[?] Cravens, Cravens Grocery to city council, 8 July 1950. Cravens's letter, which is noteworthy for its anti-Asian sentiment, argued that Chinese merchants were primarily at fault. Harsher penalties, he argued, were necessary to send a message and curb illegal behaviour.

33 *Vancouver Sun,* 3 January 1950, 2.

34 *Victoria Daily Colonist,* 4 February 1950, 20.

35 *Vancouver Sun,* 9 March 1954, 13.

36 Four days later a similar experiment was launched to highlight the fact that the Lord's Day Act was also being flouted. This time fifteen of the twenty stores were open, allowing the "shoppers" to purchase the incriminating evidence: "a can of mushrooms or pumpkin." CVA, City Council and Office of the City Clerk fonds – Clerk's Office, loc. 19-E-6, file 15, George R. Matthews, Secretary-Manager, British Columbia Board,

Retail Merchants' Association of Canada to Ald Showler, Chairman, and
Members of the Licenses and Claims Committee, 6 July 1950. On the
RMA's frustrations with the lack of enforcement, see CVA, City Council
and Office of the City Clerk fonds – Clerk's Office loc. 19-E-6, file 15,
George R. Matthews, Secretary-Manager, British Columbia Board, Retail
Merchants' Association of Canada, to Ald. Showler, Chairman, and
Members of the Licenses & Claims Committee, 20 February 1950. Yet
even the RMA suggested a method of enforcement that was less than
comprehensive. Matthews's letter to Showler included the following
suggestion: "We believe it would be a mistake to make a complete clean
up throughout the City and take aggressive action against those very
small food stores known commonly as 'Mamma and Pappa' stores.
Every neighborhood has these. Their volume of business on Wednesday
afternoon is very, very limited and confined largely to the articles they
are permitted to sell." To address the situation the RMA called for the
hiring of more inspectors to enforce local bylaws, as well as increasing
fines and cancelling the licences of non-compliant stores if warnings and
prosecutions proved ineffective. *Vancouver Daily Province*, 12 July 1950, 17.
Vancouver Sun, 12 July 1950, 5. Particularly galling for local merchants in
Vancouver was the fact that inconsistent bylaw enforcement continued
in spite of increases in business taxes, which had been partly rationalized
on the grounds that they would provide funding for greater enforcement
initiatives. *Vancouver Sun*, 7 November 1950, 17; *Vancouver Daily Province*,
27 January 1950, 17.

37 *Victoria Daily Colonist*, 11 September 1957, 1; *Victoria Daily Times*, 17
September 1957, 4.

38 *Victoria Daily Colonist*, 12 September 1958, 13.

39 *Victoria Daily Colonist*, 13 September 1958, 4. A central role for merchants
in instigating charges against other merchants existed in at least one
other jurisdiction. In the 1980s and 1990s, Germany witnessed a number
of cases in which merchants sued other merchants for transgressing the
law, including a 1996 case in which a "trade association of florists ... sued
a gas station for selling flowers on Sunday." Kirchner and Painter, "The
Economics of Germany's Shop Closing Hours," 13.

40 This problem of "mixed shops" had frustrated authorities in Britain
and Australia as well. As Simon Rottenberg lamented in observing the
situation in Britain, "there appears to be a certain arbitrary quality about
the selection of transactions to be exempted. It is not completely clear, for
example, why fish and chips are exempted if not sold in a fish and chips
shop, but covered, if sold in such a shop." The expanding number of

"mixed shops" selling a wide variety of goods made the enforcement of British regulations in the late 1940s even more complicated. Rottenberg, "Legislated Early Shop Closing in Britain," 129, 130. In 1897 the colony of Western Australia attempted to resolve the "mixed shop" issue "by requiring a shop to close wherever trading times prohibited sale of any good it sold." Quinlan and Goodwin, "Combating the Tyranny of Flexibility," 359.

41 *Vancouver Daily Province*, 5 November 1948, 39. On the frustrations expressed by hardware merchants, see CVA, City Council and Office of the City Clerk fonds – Clerk's Office, loc. 19-E-6, file 15, D.S. McDiarmid, President, BC Retail hardware Association, to [City of Vancouver] Licenses & Claims Committee, 6 February, 1950.

42 *Vancouver Daily Province*, 8 February 1950, 5.

43 *Vancouver Daily Province*, 16 February 1950, 4.

44 *Vancouver Daily Province*, 11 March 1950, 3.

45 *Vancouver Sun*, 11 March 1950, 2.

46 *Vancouver Sun*, 23 July 1953, 21. On the awkward and complicated task facing prosecutors involved in such proceedings, see CVA, City Council and Office of the City Clerk fonds – Clerk's Office, loc. 19-E-6, file 15, Gordon W. Scott, City Prosecutor, to Oscar Orr, Police Commissioner, 6 March 1950.

47 *Victoria Daily Province*, 6 June 1958, 19.

48 *Vancouver Sun*, 10 September 1958, 25.

49 *Victoria Daily Times*, 21 July 1949, 15.

50 *Victoria Daily Times*, 15 July 1952, 11; *Victoria Daily Times*, 29 July 1952, 9.

51 *Victoria Daily Times*, 29 July 1952, 9. Victoria officials were not alone in facing the awkward task of defining a souvenir. In 1999, Germany's Sunday shopping regulations contained a loophole allowing the sale of goods to tourists; this resulted in one store labelling "ordinary consumer goods ... with stickers" rebranding them as "tourist articles" and enjoying "record sales." Kirchner and Painter, "The Economics of Germany's Shop Closing Hours," 15.

52 *Victoria Daily Times*, 30 July 1952, 15; *Victoria Daily Colonist*, 30 July 1952, 20.

53 *Victoria Daily Colonist*, 31 July 1952, 22.

54 *Victoria Daily Times*, 24 February 1953, 2; *Victoria Daily Colonist*, 24 February 1953, 22.

55 The following year the *Colonist* again noted that even though a provision in the act allowed for the exemption of a particular class of stores, there was no measurable way to define a tourist store. Undaunted by a lack of support from City Hall, Ward carried on his crusade, vowing to ask City

Council to close stores now open Wednesday afternoons and evenings selling jewellery, rugs, sweaters, woollens, china, and other goods that were sold by tourist shops, which must remain closed. *Victoria Daily Colonist*, 15 April 1953, 4; *Victoria Daily Colonist*, 25 June 1954, 4; *Victoria Daily Colonist*, 24 July 1954, 13.

56 *Vancouver Sun*, 9 June 1953, 23. They were thus permitted to remain open Wednesday mornings, but still had to petition the provincial government regarding Wednesday afternoons. *Vancouver Sun*, 23 June 1953, 21.

57 *Vancouver Daily Province*, 2 July 1954, 5.

58 *Vancouver Daily Province*, 19 July 1954, 1.

59 *Vancouver Sun*, 30 July 1954, 4.

60 *Vancouver Daily Province*, 20 July 1954, 21. Albert Harvey of Harvey's Stores Ltd. in Vancouver found himself in the unenviable position of having to take out a new business licence for goods he had been selling for years. Although he was already licensed to sell hardware, plumbing supplies, dry goods, and men's, women's, and children's clothing, city licence inspector Arthur Moore ruled he must pay an additional $10 for a licence to sell lingerie (an item he had been selling for twenty-seven years), because lingerie was classed as a "sideline" to women's clothing. In protest, Harvey pointed out that the "only people I know of who wear lingerie are ladies and such sale[s] should be covered by a ladies' wear license." *Vancouver Sun*, 12 January 1954, 17; *Vancouver Daily Province*, 12 January 1954, 8.

61 *Vancouver Sun*, 5 May 1959, 19. The situation seems to have been ameliorated by September, when laundrettes were forced to close in the evenings as well. *Vancouver Sun*, 9 September 1959, 17.

62 CVA, City Councillors' Office fonds, series # 467, 84-E-2, file 13, Records of Ald. Marianne Linnell, F.M. Waller, City Clerk, Victoria, to Linnell, 1 February 1968.

63 For the RMA's George Matthews, such activities allowed for unfair competition: "Our view is that when a store is closed for business by the act, it means that it is actually not doing business." *Vancouver Sun*, 27 March 1950, 7. According to the *Vancouver Sun*, merchants involved in the mass Wednesday opening of December 1949 had employed similar tactics "by advertising they would accept orders after closing hours for delivery the next day." *Vancouver Sun*, 24 March 1950, 2.

64 *Vancouver Sun*, 3 December 1959, 33.

65 *Vancouver Sun*, 21 January 1960, 21; *Vancouver Daily Province*, 21 January 1960, 24; *Vancouver Daily Province*, 1 February 1960, 15.

66 *Victoria Daily Times*, 6 March 1956, 12; *Vancouver Daily Province*, 19 June 1956, 11.

67 *Vancouver Daily Province*, 15 March 1957, 32.

68 *Vancouver Daily Province*, 22 May 1957, 25.

69 *Vancouver Daily Province*, 22 May 1957, 25. A similar loophole in Britain's early closing legislation allowed stubborn merchants to obey the law yet reopen their doors at 12:01 a.m. Rottenberg, "Legislated Early Shop Closing in Britain," 128.

70 *Vancouver Sun*, 22 May 1957, 1–2.

71 *Vancouver Daily Province*, 22 May 1957, 25.

72 *Victoria Daily Times*, 22 May 1957, 1.

73 *Victoria Daily Colonist*, 22 May 1957, 17.

74 *Victoria Daily Times*, 23 May 1957, 12.

75 *Vancouver Sun*, 23 May 1957, 1–2. Charles Brown, Burnaby's chief municipal administrative officer, was convinced that the publicizing of the "loophole" was a convenient excuse to get the provincial government off the hook: "Somebody was looking for an out." *Vancouver Daily Province*, 24 May 1957, 27.

76 *Victoria Daily Times*, 14 June 1957, 14. When an official in the municipal affairs department suggested that municipalities simply let corner stores open in defiance of law, the *Vancouver Sun* strenuously objected. Encouraging stores to "just blink at" store-hour regulations, as many of them were already doing, was problematic for two reasons: first, authority had been passed from the Shops Act to municipalities, and it was imperative that they not ignore their own responsibilities; and second, encouraging citizens to ignore some laws but not others "raises the whole question of respect for the law. One law openly winked at brings the whole body of law into disrepute." *Vancouver Sun*, 22 May 1957, 4.

77 *Vancouver Daily Province*, 22 May 1957, 25.

78 *Vancouver Sun*, 23 May 1957, 4.

79 *Vancouver Sun*, 23 May 1957, 4.

80 *Victoria Daily Times*, 5 December 1957, 4.

81 *Victoria Daily Times*, 10 October 1958, 4.

6 Ideology

1 *Victoria Daily Times*, 12 January 1949, 7.

2 *Victoria Daily Times*, 31 July 1951, 3.

3 First a coalition of right-wing parties (the Liberals and Conservatives) and then the populist Social Credit party squared off against the left-wing Co-operative Commonwealth Federation (later the NDP) in provincial elections.

4 See, for example, Guard, "Women Worth Watching," 73–88; Parr, *Domestic Goods*, ch. 4; Korinek and Iacovetta, "Jell-O Salads, One-Stop Shopping, and Maria the Homemaker"; 190–221; Hutchinson, "'The Littlest Arms Race'?"; and Hutchinson, "Resisting the War at Home."

5 Following Jonathan Rose, I have understood rhetoric here to mean "a form of communication that has at its core an argument designed to elicit behavioral or attitudinal change in the audience." On the distinction between rhetoric and semiotics, see Rose, *Making "Pictures in Our Heads,"* 5–12, quotation at 7.

6 Interestingly, the Red Scare that followed the First World War did not seem to have a similar impact on the rhetoric of the debates.

7 On the concept of the public sphere, see Habermas, *The Structural Transformation of the Public Sphere*.

8 On the place of liberal ideology in modern Canada, see Ducharme and Constant, eds., *Liberalism and Hegemony*.

9 A sustained and comparative examination of the role of ideology or philosophy in the early closing movement remains to be written. On liberalism and early closing reformers in Australia, see Quinlan and Goodwin, "Combating the Tyranny of Flexibility," 362.

10 *Victoria Daily Times*, 19 May 1916, 7.

11 *Victoria Daily Times*, 12 June 1916, 12.

12 In recognizing that public support was the key to victory, Patton urged the city's voters to look beyond their immediate self-interest: "Be human. Give the clerks what they desire, and their employers wish they should have, and you will have that comfortable feeling of having done a good action and brought happiness and health to many homes in this city." *Victoria Daily Colonist*, 15 January 1919, 4.

13 With characteristic bluntness, Lineham took direct aim at organized labour: "I do not care one iota for the labor unions or their leaders, or for any person or clique amongst us who stands in the way of the best interests of the city as a whole by opposing the repeal of the law as it now exists." *Victoria Daily Times*, 21 August 1923, 4.

14 Lineham then pleaded "with every person in the city who has a vote to forget self for the time being and get behind the movement to do away with this unnecessary half holiday, which is vitally injuring the whole community. By doing this we shall be taking the first real step towards rehabilitation and advancement on the road to prosperity." *Victoria Daily Times*, 22 August 1923, 4.

15 *Victoria Daily Colonist*, 6 November 1924, 4.

16 *Victoria Daily Times*, 11 December 1946, 4. Victoria's self-anointed Citizens Committee similarly argued that the piecemeal closing of shops worked against the interests of the "community as a whole." *Victoria Daily Times*, 21 December 1946, 7. The belief that individual actions and decisions best served the larger community was a common theme. In March 1947, for example, the *Colonist* openly opposed new legislation that would make it mandatory for City Councils to order all-day closing in retail lines in which 75 per cent of stores supported closing; the other 25 per cent, which might control more business, and the shopping public, would be forced to follow along. Such "group legislation" was, in the newspaper's view, "discriminatory." Laws, it argued, should be made for the majority, not "for any special group or class." *Victoria Daily Colonist*, 27 March 1947, 4.

17 *Vancouver Sun*, 8 March 1951, 4.

18 *Vancouver Sun*, 18 April 1951, 6.

19 McInnis, *Harnessing Labour Confrontation*, 71–7.

20 Litt, *The Muses, the Masses and the Massey Commission*, 68, 105.

21 Whitaker and Marcuse, *Cold War Canada*, 13.

22 On the notion of "consumer sovereignty," see Parr, *Domestic Goods*, ch. 4.

23 City of Vancouver Archives [hereafter CVA], BC Chamber of Commerce (BCCC) fonds, Add. MSS 370, vol. 1, file 13, BC Chamber of Commerce, *General Policy Statements and Resolutions* (1955), 2.

24 CVA, British Columbia Chamber of Commerce [BCCC] fonds, Add. MSS 370, vol. 3, file 1, BC Chamber of Commerce, "Submissions Received up to 29th March 1965 for Discussion at Fourteenth Annual Meeting," 1-A.

25 Dawson, *Selling British Columbia*, 134–35; CVA, Add. MSS. 633, Greater Vancouver Visitors and Convention Bureau papers, ser. A, vol. 1, file 2, Board of Directors Minutes, Manager's Report, 11 March 1948.

26 CVA, Add. MSS. 633, Greater Vancouver Visitors and Convention Bureau papers, ser. A, vol. 1, file 1, Board of Directors Minutes, 9 August 1945.

27 *Vancouver Sun*, 15 January 1954, 16.

28 Hence, in June 1957 the *Victoria Daily Colonist* voiced its frustration with the ongoing debate over store-hour regulation by drawing on free-enterprise rhetoric to point an accusatory finger at Victoria's City Council. "Confused and confusing discussion in city council over hours during which people may or may not do business in Victoria," an editorial argued, "serves to demonstrate the excessive regulation to which 'free' enterprise is subjected." *Victoria Daily Colonist*, 26 June 1957, 4. Three months later the *Colonist* returned to this subject and argued that "in a supposedly free economy it should be a merchant's own business to decide when he will serve his customers." *Victoria Daily*

Colonist, 12 September 1957, 4. In advocating expanded night shopping in the Vancouver suburb of Burnaby, the *Vancouver Daily Province* echoed this line of argument, expressing its dismay at "the extent to which bureaucracy has been allowed to restrict what we are still pleased to call our free enterprise system." *Vancouver Daily Province*, 1 August 1962, 4.

29 *Victoria Daily Colonist*, 22 May 1958, 13. At least one observer found such restrictions so frustrating and intellectually objectionable that it drew him directly into municipal politics. In October 1967, R.H. Wood, president of the Burnaby-Seymour Progressive Conservative Association, announced he was entering municipal politics to "put the conservative point of view out," with specific emphasis "on the issue of the control of store hours as it involves the freedom of the individual business man to operate his store as he sees fit." Wood was adamantly opposed to restrictions placed "on individual freedom at the behest of pressure groups such as Unions or Business Assoc[iations]." Such "bureaucratic control," he suggested, was all too "prevalent in our society to-day." "Too many controls," he argued, "are imposed on the legitimate endeavours of so called Free Enterprise." CVA, City Councillors' Office fonds, series # 467, Records of Ald. Marianne Linnell, 84-E-2 file 13, R.H. Wood, President, Burnaby-Seymour Progressive Conservative Association to Ald. Linnell, 18 October 1967.

30 Traves, *The State and Enterprise*, 155–6. The central role of local and federal government agencies in US economic development is succinctly demonstrated in Leach, *Land of Desire*, ch. 12.

31 Monod, *Store Wars*, 27, 55, ch. 6.

32 *Vancouver Sun*, 8 March 1951, 4.

33 *Victoria Daily Times*, 9 April 1958, 4.

34 Victoria City Archives, Victoria Chamber of Commerce fonds, 32-A-2, Board of Directors Minutes, 25 November 1946.

35 The central role of women in North American consumer activism at this time is well documented; see Guard, "Women Worth Watching"; Fahrni, "Counting the Costs of Living"; and Cohen, *A Consumers' Republic*.

36 Victoria *Daily Times*, 25 April 1957, 19. Employing the spectre of the Soviet Union as a potent symbol of overzealous government regulation was just one way that Palmer buttressed his campaign to oppose store-hour regulations. He also alluded to the broader, more amorphous threat of dictatorship, arguing that in restricting evening sales, the provincial government was acting in the interests of the chain stores. "Why should we be forced to follow the marketing pattern of the super-markets?" he asked. "Are we under the heel of a dictatorship?" Unlike opponents of store-hour regulations who championed a selective understanding of

"free enterprise," Palmer recognized that government regulation could aid private enterprise. What dismayed him was that provincial legislation seemed to be benefiting chain stores at the expense of small, independent grocers. A civic referendum in 1951, Palmer argued, had resulted in an overwhelming vote in favour of evening shopping at corner stores and had produced a civic bylaw allowing such. This bylaw was being rendered obsolete by the provincial government's revised Municipal Act; see *Victoria Daily Colonist*, 26 April 1957, 17.

37 *Victoria Daily Colonist*, 4 December 1946, 4.

38 *Victoria Daily Colonist*, 21 November 1953, 4.

39 *Victoria Daily Times*, 31 July 1951, 3.

40 *Victoria Daily Times*, 27 April 1956, 6. Likewise, when Vancouver clothier A.J. Warner opposed the lifting of restrictions that prohibited Friday night shopping, he did so by suggesting that such an expansion of shopping hours was being "dictated by Safeway." *Vancouver Daily Province*, 20 May 1952, 15.

41 Litt, *The Muses*, 105.

42 Whitaker and Marcuse, *Cold War Canada*, x.

43 Ibid., 268. Canada's two most infamous witch hunts focused on NFB head John Grierson and diplomat Herbert Norman. Their stories are surveyed in Whitaker and Marcuse, *Cold War Canada*, chs. 10 and 11. The federal government's campaign to tar the Housewives Consumers' Association with the brush of communism in order to hinder the association's postwar campaign for price controls is a particularly instructive example; see Guard, "Women Worth Watching."

44 Gleason, *Normalizing the Ideal*, 16.

45 On the emergence of such rights-based rhetoric, see Lara Campbell, *Respectable Citizens*; and Clément, *Canada's Rights Revolution*.

46 *Victoria Daily Colonist*, 21 September 1946. The *Daily Times* agreed, arguing that the city's stores "have a definite responsibility toward the public." *Victoria Daily Times*, 10 October 1946, 4.

47 *Victoria Daily Colonist*, 26 October 1946, 3.

48 Victoria *Daily Colonist*, 9 October 1946, 4.

49 Fahrni, "Counting the Costs."

50 Cohen, *A Consumers' Republic*.

51 Rottenberg, "Legislated Early Shop Closing in Britain," 128.

52 *Victoria Daily Times*, 16 February 1953, 4.

53 *Victoria Daily Colonist*, 18 February 1953, 4.

54 *Victoria Daily Times*, 1 April 1953, 4.

55 Tillotson, "Time, Swimming Pools," 199.

56 Ibid., 204. On just one occasion was the "right to work" evoked in support
    of the six-day week; see *Victoria Daily Times*, 7 October 1958, 4.
57 Tillotson, "Time, Swimming Pools," 206.
58 Kuffert, *A Great Duty*, 96, 143–5, 157–8, 208; Litt, *The Muses*, 87.
59 For pronouncements on democratic methods of childrearing, see Gleason,
    Normalizing the Ideal, 7, 16, 111; and Gölz, "Family Matters, 19, 27–8. For the
    concerns of cultural critics, see Litt, *The Muses*, 106, 249.
60 Kuffert, *A Great Duty*, 183.
61 *Victoria Daily Colonist*, 1 October 1946, 19; *Vancouver Daily Province*, 18 July
    1957, 21.
62 *Victoria Daily Times*, 12 January 1949, 7.
63 *Vancouver Sun*, 3 June 1954, 1.
64 *Victoria Daily Times*, 1 October 1946, 10.
65 *Vancouver Sun*, 7 January 1947, 8.
66 Hiscocks thus rejected the bylaw's logic, which allowed for store hours
    to be set on the agreement of 75 per cent of the businesses in a particular
    class. "The agreement of 75 per cent of the management in any given
    phase of business to petition the City Council to close the other 25 per cent
    to suit their convenience is a violation of the majority rule," he argued,
    "because the general public is the majority concerned." *Victoria Daily
    Colonist*, 11 October 1946, 2.
67 *Victoria Daily Colonist*, 6 December 1946, 4.
68 *Victoria Daily Times*, 7 October 1946, 3.
69 *Victoria Daily Colonist*, 27 October 1946, 3.
70 CVA, City Councillors' Office fonds, series # 467, Records of Ald. Marianne
    Linnell, 84-E-2 file 13, A.M. Thomson Jr., Thomson Appliances to Linnell,
    22 September 1969.
71 CVA, City Councillors' Office fonds, series # 467, Records of Ald. Marianne
    Linnell, 84-E-2 file 13, Thomson to Bruce Mallen, Sir George Williams
    University, Montreal. In 1953 a group of Victoria clerks known as the Five
    Day Action Committee voiced its opposition to Victoria City Council's
    plan to hold a referendum on the six-day week by directly questioning the
    public's right to decide its members' fate: "Why should the public be asked
    to vote on the working conditions of the retail clerks?" asked committee
    chairman Peter MacEwan. *Victoria Daily Colonist*, 14 November 1953, 17.
72 The joint brief was submitted by Standard Furniture Company, W. and
    J. Wilson, the Five-Day Action Committee, the Victoria Community
    Grocers Co-operative Association, Red and White Food Stores, and the
    Retail Meat Dealers' Association; see *Victoria Daily Times*, 24 November
    1953, 10.

73 *Vancouver Sun*, 27 March 1954, 1–2.
74 *Vancouver Sun*, 4 July 1958, 4, original emphasis.
75 Whitaker and Marcuse, *Cold War Canada*, 23. These campaigns and pronouncements reflect the Italian Marxist Antonio Gramsci's recognition that successful attempts to obtain influence or hegemony in a society have a "national-popular" dimension. On this concept, see Simon, *Gramsci's Political Thought*, 43–6.
76 Whitaker and Marcuse, *Cold War Canada*, xi.
77 Cohen, *Consumers' Republic*, 18, 101, 147.
78 Key studies that might form the basis of a history of the public sphere in Canada include McNairn, *The Capacity to Judge*; Rutherford, *Endless Propaganda*; Johnston, *Selling Themselves*; Robinson, *The Measure of Democracy*; and Rudy, *The Freedom to Smoke*.

7 Religion

1 City of Vancouver Archives [hereafter CVA], 46- -7, Mayor's Office fonds, "Sunday Shopping" (file 3), series # 483 1981, M.H. Fisher, Port Alberni, to Mayor Mike Harcourt, 13 January 1981.
2 CVA, 68-G-2, Mayor's Office fonds, series #483, file 119, Chuck and Phyllis Craver, West Vancouver, to Nicole Parton, *Vancouver Sun*, 15 January 1979.
3 Laverdure, *Sunday in Canada*, 191–3.
4 In March 1971, for example, the Victoria Chamber of Commerce expressed its frustration with the fact that a number of stores were contravening the act. It called upon the attorney general and the city to enforce the act and decried the paltry $10 fines that failed to deter the offenders. Victoria's mayor, Courtney Haddock, sympathized with the chamber's position and pronounced himself keen to help "stop Sunday blight." But he also noted that there was nothing the municipality could do to enforce the law. *Victoria Daily Colonist*, 19 March 1971, 25; *Victoria Daily Times*, 27 March 1971, 23.
5 *Victoria Times*, 15 January 1975, 11; *Victoria Daily Colonist*, 16 January 1975, 15.
6 *Victoria Times* 16 April 1975, 1.
7 *Victoria Daily Colonist*, 16 April 1975, 21.
8 *Victoria Daily Colonist*, 27 June 1978, 15; *Victoria Times*, 13 July 1978, 20; *Victoria Times*, 29 January 1979, 4.
9 *Vancouver Sun*, 28 August 1969, 5.
10 *Vancouver Province*, 24 September 1969, 25; *Vancouver Province*, 26 November 1969, 31. The balance of power between proponents of increased store hours and their opponents was reinforced by legislation. The city's charter prohibited employers from forcing employees to work

more than five days a week, while the province's labour code limited daily hours of work. *Vancouver Province*, 15 November 1969, 31.

11 *Vancouver Sun*, 16 November 1970, 1–2.

12 *Vancouver Sun*, 9 November 1973, 82; *Vancouver Sun*, 1 February 1974, 8.

13 *Vancouver Province*, 22 March 1974, 36.

14 *Vancouver Province*, 28 November 1975, 5.

15 *Vancouver Sun*, 7 January 1976, 35.

16 *Vancouver Province*, 10 January 1976, 17.

17 *Vancouver Sun*, 17 June 1977, 24; *Vancouver Sun*, 26 August 1977, 16; *Vancouver Province*, 29 January 1978.

18 *Vancouver Sun*, 13 July 1978, A1–A2.

19 *Vancouver Sun* 18 August 1978, n.p.

20 *Vancouver Province* 26 August 1978, A4.

21 *Vancouver Province*, 27 April 1979, B1; *Vancouver Sun* 30 August 1979, 4.

22 *Vancouver Sun*, 17 January 1980, A1; *Vancouver Province*, 17 January 1980, A1.

23 CVA, 46-G–7, Mayor's Office fonds, "Sunday Shopping," file 3, series # 483 1981, Ministry of Attorney General, Press Release, 14 January 1981; William Vander Zalm, Minister of Municipal Affairs to Mayor Harcourt, 25 February 1981.

24 CVA, 47-F-3, file 76, series 483, Mayor, General Correspondence Files: Sunday Shopping, Judy Nyboer, Richmond to Mayor Volrich, 11 July 1978; F. Rex Werts, Vancouver to Mayor Volrich, 10 July 1978; Mrs Kay M. Charter, Vancouver, to Mayor Volrich, 26 July 1978; H.W. Aitchison, Secretary-General, The Association of the Covenant People, Vancouver, to Mayor Volrich, 27 July 1978; Mr and Mrs Pridham to Mayor Volrich, 14 August 1978; Albert Douch, Vancouver, to Mayor Volrich, 12 July 1978.

25 Burkinshaw, *Pilgrims in Lotus Land*, 1–6, 200–7.

26 Another concerned resident informed the mayor that "Sunday is basically for rest and worship." CVA, 47-F-3, file 76, series 483, Mayor, General Correspondence Files: Sunday Shopping, Mr and Mrs H.M. Brown, Vancouver, to Mayor of Vancouver, 10 July 1978; Kathleen Edger, Vancouver, to Mayor Volrich.

27 CVA, 68-G-2, Mayor's Office fonds, series #483, file 119, John Van Hemert, Langley to "Editor."

28 Wesley H. Wakefield, president of The Bible Holiness Movement in Vancouver, forwarded Volrich a copy of letter he had sent to the provincial attorney general, Garde Gardom, which offered a wide range of arguments against Sunday shopping. These included the observation that employees with religious convictions could be adversely affected if they felt forced by their employer to work on Sundays, but also highlighted the inflationary

impact on store operating costs, the negative impact such a move would
have on small independent stores struggling to compete with chains,
and the disruption of family life. CVA, 47-F-3, file 76, series 483, Mayor,
General Correspondence Files: Sunday Shopping, Rev. Len Burnham,
President of the B.C. Interfaith Citizenship Council, Vancouver, to Mayor
Volrich, 11 July 1978; Wesley H. Wakefield, [President,] The Bible Holiness
Movement, Vancouver, to Mayor Volrich, 19 July 1978.

29 Harold Morgan similarly criticized the mayor for letting his religious
beliefs override the wishes of "by far the greater number of people in the
city," who wanted the stores open on Sundays. CVA, 47-F-3, file 76, series
483, Mayor, General Correspondence Files: Sunday Shopping, Frank
Holden [?], Vancouver to Volrich, 31 August 1977; Dr Art Hister, M.D.,
Vancouver to Mayor Volrich, 18 July 1978; Paul Armass, Burnaby, to Mayor
Volrich, n.d. [c. Nov 1978]; Harold Morgan to Mayor Volrich, 12 July 1978;
Bill Edwards, Vancouver, to Mayor Volrich, 19 April 1978.

30 Interestingly, some staunch opponents of Sunday shopping went out
of their way to challenge the notion that the issue could, or should, be
framed in terms of religion. For example, in response to newspaper
columnist Nicole Parton's observation that Vancouverites did not seem
the least bit concerned with the fact that the city's stores were permitted
to open during the Jewish and Muslim Sabbaths, Chuck and Phyllis
Craver of West Vancouver offered a pointed and passionate rejoinder that
underscored what they observed to be the secular nature of the debate:
"This is neither Israel nor an Arab State but Canada. And besides [we]
do not feel this question should be dealt with on a religious basis." CVA,
68-G-2, Mayor's Office fonds, series #483, file 119, Chuck and Phyllis
Craver, West Vancouver to Nicole Parton, *Vancouver Sun*. Vancouverite
Isabella Beveridge offered a similar, if more prosaic, view of the situation
in a 1976 letter to Volrich's predecessor as mayor, Art Phillips. She did
not object to Sunday shopping on religious grounds, she explained,
but voiced concern that increased opening hours would burden small
businesses with increased costs. Two years later a Surrey resident voiced
her opposition to allowing large stores and businesses to open on Sundays
while emphasizing that her views were not based "on religious grounds."
Vancouver resident Dorothy Gillon offered anecdotal evidence to support
this understanding: Even people she had spoken to, "who do not go to
church ... feel that Sunday as a 'no business' day is worth having." CVA,
47-F-3, file 76, series 483, Mayor, General Correspondence Files: Sunday
Shopping, Isabella Beveridge, Vancouver to Mayor Phillips, 23 February
1976; Annette Hareltin[?], Surrey, to Mayor Volrich, n.d. [c.1 August 1978];

Mrs Dorothy Gillon, Vancouver, to Mayor Volrich and Council, 9 May 1978.

31 Victoria Mayor Peter Pollen remarked that just 5 per cent of the protests he was aware of that objected to Sunday retail sales had a religious focus. *Victoria Daily Colonist*, 22 October 1975, 9.

32 Some letter writers infused their missives with spirited calls to defend Christian values and institutions. *Vancouver Province*, 8 June 1980, A1; *Vancouver Province*, 8 June 1980, A4; *Vancouver Province*, 19 June 1980, A4. Other participants in the debate championed a more diffuse position that linked the preservation of a day for Christian worship with a more general need for a day of rest and recreation. *Victoria Times*, 30 January 1975, 4; *Victoria Times*, 29 May 1975, 21; *Victoria Times*, 30 June 1978, 4; *Vancouver Province*, 16 May 1980, A9. A smaller number appeared to be members of the Christian fold but were determined to highlight the awkward and problematic relationship between civil authority and religious observance. Legislating religious observance, this group argued, was both difficult and dangerous. *Victoria Times*, 21 October 1975, 17; *Vancouver Province*, 13 July 1980, A7. A very different group railed against what it viewed as out-of-date religious motivations that continued to plague what they recognized as a fully secular society – and that now limited access to consumer goods on Sundays while prioritizing Christianity over other religions and those who did not share a religious faith. *Victoria Times*, 3 February 1975, 4; *Victoria Times*, 1 October 1975, 1–2; *Victoria Daily Colonist*, 10 October 1975, 5; *Victoria Times*, 12 June 1976, 4; *Victoria Times Colonist*, 7 October 1980, 13; *Vancouver Province*, 27 April 1979, B1. A rather different contingent forcefully argued against the idea that religious considerations should or could play any part in the matter because those centrally involved in the issue did not understand it in such terms. *Victoria Times*, 30 July 1975, 4; *Vancouver Province*, 10 July 1978, 7; *Vancouver Province*, 14 September 1979, B7.

33 *Victoria Daily Colonist*, 10 October 1975, 19.

34 *Victoria Times* 3 October 1975, 4.

35 *Victoria Times,* 16 April 1975, 1.

36 Of the 322 people surveyed, 54 per cent endorsed Sunday openings, 44 per cent were opposed, and 2 per cent remained undecided.

37 *Vancouver Province*, 8 June 1980, 1.

38 *Vancouver Sun*, 9 July 1980, C6.

39 *Vancouver Province*, 19 June 1980, A4.

40 *Victoria Daily Colonist*, 30 August 1980, 5; *Vancouver Province*, 10 November 1980, A4; *Vancouver Province*, 17 November 1980, A6.

41 *Victoria Times*, 25 June 1975, 13.

42 *Victoria Times*, 1 October 1975, 1–2.

43 *Victoria Times Colonist*, 30 November 1980, 4. Moreover, while some worried that the city's reputation might be adversely affected by Sunday store-hour restrictions, others argued that "Victoria's standing and character as a community would gain significantly" from the mayor's efforts. *Victoria Times*, 9 October 1975, 1. There were even hints that opponents of Sunday shopping were finding links between their defence of community and broader ecological concerns. Hence, Dick Hordyk and Henry Kuyvenhoven's letter to the *Times* that called upon the public to consider "the environmental costs of heating, lighting, and transportation for the sake of something which is in the final analysis counter-productive and unnecessary." *Victoria Times*, 30 June 1978, 4.

44 *Vancouver Sun*, 12 December 1975, 5; *Vancouver Province*, 24 January 1976, 4; *Vancouver Sun*, 16 June 1978, A5; *Vancouver Province*, 11 July 1978, 9; *Vancouver Sun*, 27 July 1978, B1; *Vancouver Province*, 5 September 1979, B1.

45 *Victoria Times*, 30 January 1975, 14.

46 *Victoria Times*, 3 February 1975, 4.

47 CVA, 46-G–7, Mayor's Office fonds, "Sunday Shopping" (file 3), series # 483 1981, *Vancouver Sun* clipping, 6 May 1981, A3.

48 CVA, 46-G–7, Mayor's Office fonds, "Sunday Shopping" (file 3), series # 483 1981, Henry J. Chung, Chinatown Historic Area Planning Committee and Thomas Mah, Chinese Benevolent Association of Vancouver, to Hon. Allan Williams, Attorney General of BC, 10 October 1980; *Vancouver Province* editorial clipping, "The mandate is there," 26 June 1981; Joan Wallace, Acting Secretary, Committee Opposed to Sunday & Holiday Shopping, to Mayor Harcourt, 29 January 1981. A similar argument appears in Rosemarie Holmes, Port Coquitlam, to Mayor Harcourt, 22 January 1981.

49 *Victoria Times*, 1 October 1975, 1–2.

50 *Victoria Times*, 30 June 1978, 4. In objecting to the *Holiday Shopping Regulation Act (HSRA)*, Stu Leggett, the NDP MLA for Coquitlam-Moody, feared that its "local option loophole would permit big businesses to dominate store opening and closing hours and that they will eventually 'whip-saw' the others into shape." *Victoria Daily Colonist*, 23 August 1980, 8.

51 *Vancouver Sun*, 28 July 1978, B1.

52 Don Hudson, a senior vice-president in Eaton's Pacific Division, declared that his organization was keen to obey the law but emphasized that the provincial government needed to step in and clarify the rules surrounding Sunday shopping. *Vancouver Sun*, 18 January 1980, A12. *Victoria Times Colonist*, 22 October 1980, 1. By July 1980 the *Vancouver Sun* could report

that the city's major department stores were opposed to Sunday opening but would reconcile themselves to it if it came into practice. *Vancouver Sun*, 9 July 1980, C6.

53 *Victoria Times Colonist*, 13 November 1980, 4.

54 *Victoria Times Colonist*, 14 November 1980, 1–2.

55 *Victoria Times Colonist*, 17 November 1980, 1–2.

56 CVA, 68-G-2, Mayor's Office fonds, series #483, file 119, Donald Jang, Louie, Lam & Company, Barristers & Solicitors, to Mayor and Members of Council, 11 June 1979; CVA, 47-F-3, file 76, series 483, Mayor, General Correspondence Files: Sunday Shopping, Gary Lee Ling, President, Fraser Merchants' Association, to Mayor Volrich, 15 July 1978.

57 *Vancouver Sun*, 26 August 1977, 16.

58 Mrs Frank Biluk concurred and lamented that "these young people & many other age groups do not observe Sundays, Lords day [*sic*], etc." Stores should be closed on Sundays, she argued, so that it remained a day of "relaxation" and a "total Day of 'Peace.'" CVA, 46-G-7, Mayor's Office fonds, "Sunday Shopping," file 3, series # 483 1981, Judy A. Chernan to Harcourt, 27 April 1981; Mrs Frank Biluk to Harcourt, 27 April 1981; Harold T. Allen, Victoria, to Harcourt, 6 January 1981.

59 *Victoria Times*, 1 October 1975, 1–2; *Victoria Daily Colonist*, 8 October 1975, 5; *Victoria Times*, 30 June 1978, 4; *Victoria Daily Colonist* 29 July 1978, 17; *Victoria Times Colonist*, 13 November 1980, 4; *Vancouver Province*, 24 January 1976, 4; *Vancouver Province*, 16 May 1980, A1; *Vancouver Province*, 8 June 1980; *Vancouver Sun*, 21 October 1980, A3. Mayor Mike Harcourt assured one concerned citizen that even though a city plebiscite had indicated strong support for Sunday shopping "in Gastown and Chinatown, and possibly in other areas of the city," City Council would move cautiously and consult the public before altering its bylaws: "We too want to maintain sensible Sundays which families can enjoy." The provincial attorney general's office concurred and stated in a news release that "equal consideration must be given to those who have concern over the breakdown in the family unit and desire to ensure that there is at least one day of the week free to be spent with the family." CVA, 46-G-7, Mayor's Office fonds, "Sunday Shopping," file 3, series # 483 1981, Harcourt to J.F. Belanger, 3 July 1981; Ministry of Attorney General, Press Release, 14 January 1981.

60 "As to the religious question," she suggested, "those who are regular church goers will continue to do so. We go occasionally, but on Sunday afternoon, if my husband (who, as Exec. Director of the Disabled Veterans puts in a 6 day week every second week) wishes to buy tools or lumber,

it is truly 'small town' thinking not to be able to do so." CVA, 46-G–7, Mayor's Office fonds, "Sunday Shopping," file 3, series # 483 1981, *Vancouver Province* editorial clipping, "The mandate is there," 26 June 1981; Shirley M. Dick to Mayor Harcourt, 17 March 1981.

61 *Victoria Daily Colonist*, 23 October 1975, 22; *Vancouver Province*, 19 January 1976, 4; *Vancouver Sun*, 16 June 1978, A5; *Vancouver Province*, 26 August 1979, A10; *Vancouver Province*, 31 August 1979, D1. The BC Minister of Municipal Affairs, Bill Vander Zalm, acknowledged such arguments in a letter to Vancouver's Mayor Volrich: "In families where both spouses are employed, many view the weekend as an opportunity where both can do their shopping together and, therefore, they would like to see almost all shopping facilities available to them." CVA, 46-G–7, Mayor's Office fonds, "Sunday Shopping," file 3, series # 483 1981, Vander Zalm to Volrich, 10 November 1980.

62 Ingrid Szabo of Burnaby offered a similar observation in her letter denouncing Volrich's campaign. L. Jorgensen, writing on behalf of "a group of angry citizens," explained that "we do not think there's anything wrong with Sunday Shopping, it's a convenience to the people of this Province." CVA, 46-G–7, Mayor's Office fonds, "Sunday Shopping," file 3, series # 483 1981, *Vancouver Sun* clipping 6 May 1981, Ms B.A. Ritcey to Harcourt, 25 January 1981; Ingrid Szabo, 4052 Farrington, Burnaby, to Mayor Volrich, 28 August 1977. L. Jorgensen to Harcourt, 8 January 1981.

63 For the former, see *Victoria Daily Colonist*, 4 October 1980, 4; *Victoria Times Colonist*, 11 October 1980, 5. For the latter, see *Victoria Daily Colonist*, 27 June 1978, 15; *Victoria Daily Colonist*, 5 June 1980, 5; *Victoria Times Colonist*, 14 November 1980, 17; *Vancouver Province*, 17 January 1976, 19; *Vancouver Sun*, 23 June 1978, A5.

64 *Vancouver Sun*, 27 July 1978, B1; CVA, 68-G-2, Mayor's Office fonds, series #483, file 119, John Van Hemert, Langley, to Prime Minister Trudeau, 20 March 1979; CVA, 47-F-3, file 76, series # 483, Mayor, General Correspondence Files: Sunday Shopping, Margaret Benjamin, 2851 West 3rd Avenue, Vancouver, to Mayor Jack Volrich, 11 July 1977; CVA, 46-G–7, Mayor's Office fonds, "Sunday Shopping," file 3, series # 483 1981, Rosemarie Holmes, Port Coquitlam, to Harcourt, 22 January 1981.

65 *Vancouver Sun*, 9 July 1980, C6.

66 *Vancouver Sun*, 21 July 1978, A9.

67 CVA, 68-G-2, Mayor's Office fonds, series #483, file 119, Chuck and Phyllis Craver, West Vancouver, to Nicole Parton, *Vancouver Sun*, 15 January 1979. For similar statements, see CVA, 47-F-3, file 76, series # 483, Mayor, General Correspondence Files: Sunday Shopping, Miss Illma L. Bennett,

Vancouver, to Mayor Volrich, 10 July 1978; and CVA, 47-F-3, file 76, series #483, Mayor, General Correspondence Files: Sunday Shopping, Miss D.M. Sterland[?], West Vancouver, to Mayor and Council, 2 July 1978.

68 *Victoria Daily Colonist*, 19 March 1971, 25; *Vancouver Province*, 12 August 1978, 4.

69 *Victoria Daily Times*, 27 March 1971, 23; *Victoria Times*, 18 May 1978, 13; *Vancouver Sun*, 5 February 1976, 7; *Vancouver Sun*, 4 July 1978, C5.

70 *Vancouver Province*, 10 July 1978, 1.

71 *Victoria Times*, 30 January 1975, 14.

72 *Victoria Times*, 3 October 1975, 4.

73 *Victoria Daily Colonist*, 4 October 1975, 4.

74 *Victoria Daily Colonist*, 16 October 1975, 4. Newspaper columnist Gorde Hunter took some pleasure in noting that the public bore a fair amount of responsibility for the hypocrisy involved in determining what was, and was not, "essential." He noted, for example, that some people were opposed to furniture sales on Sundays but had no problem purchasing a gallon of "essential" gasoline. *Victoria Daily Colonist*, 9 November 1978, 5. In 1980 the *Colonist* blasted the province's new Holiday Shopping Regulation Act because in allowing municipalities to create exemptions for particular goods and services it had opened up "once again the whole silly exercise of determining which merchandise or service is to be available on a Sunday, and which will remain discreetly behind closed doors." *Victoria Daily Colonist* 12 August 1980, 4.

75 Mayor Harcourt was obliged to admit, in his response to Chiavario, that there was something "fairly arbitrary about what are or are not necessary items in a home which can be purchased on a Sunday." CVA, 46-G–7, Mayor's Office fonds, "Sunday Shopping," file 3, series # 483 1981, Nancy A. Chiavario to Mayor Harcourt, 29 July 1981; Harcourt to Chiavario, 10 August 1981.

76 Consumer Shirley Dick was adamant that "the market usually takes care of itself," many stores will not choose to open, and "the whole issue will make very little difference in the long run." David Glyn-Jones, an accountant in Vancouver, urged city officials to let the stores choose their own hours of operation and warned of a "growing desire by the electorate, federal, provincial and civic, to have less interference in their affairs by their elected representatives." CVA, 46-G–7, Mayor's Office fonds, "Sunday Shopping," file 3, series # 483 1981, *Vancouver Province* editorial clipping, 26 June 1981; Shirley M. Dick to Harcourt, 17 March 1981; David Glyn-Jones to Harcourt, 3 February 1981; "Analysis of Social Credit Persecution of Gastown Merchants" by CAFE per Grant Carson, n.d.c. 12 January 1981.

77 *Victoria Daily Colonist*, 20 January 1980, 4.

78 CVA, 46-G–7, Mayor's Office fonds, "Sunday Shopping," file 3, series # 483 1981, Alex Douglas to Harcourt, 11 January 1981; *Victoria Daily Colonist*, 22 January 1976, 4; *Victoria Times Colonist*, 7 October 1980, 13.

79 CVA, 46-G–7, Mayor's Office fonds, "Sunday Shopping," file 3, series # 483 1981, Gastown Merchants' Association Media Release, 31 December 1981.

80 *Victoria Daily Colonist*, 10 October 1975, 5.

81 *Vancouver Province*, 31 August 1979, D1.

82 CVA, 47-F-3, file 76, series # 483, Mayor, General Correspondence Files: Sunday Shopping, Don W. Low, President, Globe Estates Ltd. Vancouver to Attorney General G. Gardom, 24 July 1978.

83 *Vancouver Province*, 30 June 1978, 13. Even more direct was the intervention of the general secretary of the Lord's Day Alliance, Gordon Walker, into Victoria's Sunday shopping dispute when he declared that forcing individuals "into a pattern of Sunday working" amounted "to an infringement of basic human rights." *Victoria Times*, 29 May 1975, 21.

84 CVA, 46-G–7, Mayor's Office fonds, "Sunday Shopping," file 3, series # 483 1981, Ministry of Attorney General, Press Release, 14 January 1981.

85 CVA, 46-G–7, Mayor's Office fonds, "Sunday Shopping," file 3, series # 483 1981, Harold T. Allen, Victoria, to Harcourt, 6 January 1981.

86 *Victoria Daily Colonist*, 17 April 1980, 66.

87 *Vancouver Sun*, 9 July 1980, C8.

88 A recent federal government report argues that "pressure to liberalize Sunday closing laws" became more intense "from the 1970s onwards." The report ascribes this process to an increased "secularization" of Canadian society as well as the desire among "certain segments of the retail business community" to improve their economic standing through expanded store hours. Human Resources and Skills Development Canada. http://www .hrsdc.gc.ca/eng/lp/spila/clli/eslc/weekly_rest_narrative.pdf.

Conclusion

1 *Victoria Daily Colonist*, 18 May 1954, 7.

Bibliography

Periodicals

Vancouver Daily Province
Vancouver Sun
Victoria Daily Colonist
Victoria Daily Times

Archival Collections

City of Vancouver Archives

BC Chamber of Commerce fonds
City Councillors' Office fonds
City Council and Office of the City Clerk fonds
Mayor's Office fonds

Victoria City Archives
Victoria Chamber of Commerce fonds

Working Papers and Government Reports

Evans, Catherine. "Sunday Closing Laws in Canada: Some Provincial
    Comparisons," Ontario Legislative Research Service, Current Issue Paper
    #55. March 1987.
Apostle, Alisa. "Canada, Vacations Unlimited: The Canadian Government
    Tourism Industry, 1934–1959." PhD diss., Queen's University, 2003.

Ferris, J. Stephen. "On the Economics of Regulated Early Closing Hours,"
Carleton University Working Paper 83-08. October 1983.

Human Resources and Skills Development Canada, "Sunday Closing and
Weekly Rest Periods: Historical Evolution and Current Situation." http://
www.hrsdc.gc.ca/eng/labour/labour_law/esl/weekly_rest.shtml.

Kinley, John. "Evolution of Legislated Standards on Hours of Work in Ontario:
A Report Prepared for the Ontario Task Force on Hours of Work and
Overtime." September 1987.

Kirchner, Christian, and Richard W. Painter. "The Economics of Germany's
Shop Closing Hours Regulation." Law and Economics Working Paper
No. 00-05, University of Illinois College of Law. September 2000.

Mallen, Bruce, and Ronald Rotenberg. "The Benefits and Costs of Evening
Shopping to the Canadian Economy: A Position Paper," vol. 1. Sir George
Williams University, April 1969.

Skuterud, Mikal. "The Impact of Sunday Shopping on Employment and
Hours of Work in the Retail Industry: Evidence from Canada." Final Draft.
Family and Labour Studies Division, Statistics Canada, n.d.

Secondary Sources

Apostle, Alisa. "The Display of a Tourist Nation: Canada in Government Film,
1945–1959." *Journal of the Canadian Historical Association*, New Series 12
(2001): 177–97.

Armstrong, Christopher, and H.V. Nelles. *The Revenge of the Methodist Bicycle
Company: Sunday Streetcars and Municipal Reform in Toronto, 1888–1897.*
Toronto: Peter Martin Associates, 1977.

Atack, Jeremy, and Fred Bateman. "How Long Was the Workday in 1880?"
Journal of Economic History 52(1) (March 1992): 129–60.

Barman, Jean. *The West beyond the West: A History of British Columbia.* Rev. ed.
Toronto: University of Toronto Press, 1996.

Baskerville, Peter. *Beyond the Island: An Illustrated History of Victoria.*
Burlington: Windsor Publications, 1986.

Beaton, Al. *Laugh with Al Beaton: Cartoons from the Province.* Vancouver:
The Province, 1956.

Belisle, Donica. "Exploring Postwar Consumption: The Campaign to Unionize
Eaton's in Toronto, 1948–1952." *Canadian Historical Review* 86(4) (December
2005): 641–72.

– "Negotiating Paternalism: Women and Canada's Largest Department Stores,
1890–1960." *Journal of Women's History* 19(1) (2007): 58–81.

– *Retail Nation: Department Stores and the Making of Modern Canada*. Vancouver: UBC Press, 2011.

Benson, Susan Porter. *Counter Cultures: Saleswomen, Managers, and Customers in American Department Stores, 1890–1940*. Urbana: University of Illinois Press, 1986.

Bjelopera, Jerome P. *City of Clerks: Office and Sales Workers in Philadelphia, 1870–1920*. Urbana: University of Illinois Press, 2005.

Block, Tina. "'Families That Pray Together, Stay Together': Religion, Gender, and Family in Postwar Victoria, British Columbia," *BC Studies* 145 (Spring 2005): 31–54.

Burkinshaw, Robert. *Pilgrims in Lotus Land: Conservative Protestantism in British Columbia, 1917–1981*. Montreal and Kingston: McGill–Queen's University Press, 1995.

Cahill, Marion Cotter. *Shorter Hours: A Study of the Movement Since the Civil War*. New York: AMS Press, [1932]1968.

Campbell, Lara. *Respectable Citizens: Gender, Family, and Unemployment in Ontario's Great Depression, 1929–1939*. Toronto: University of Toronto Press, 2008.

Campbell, Robert A. *Sit Down and Drink Your Beer: Regulating Vancouver's Beer Parlours, 1925–1954*. Toronto: University of Toronto Press, 2001.

Campbell, Robert M. *Grand Illusions: The Politics of the Keynesian Experience in Canada, 1945–1975*. Peterborough: Broadview, 1987.

Carstairs, Catherine. *Jailed for Possession: Illegal Drug Use, Regulation, and Power in Canada, 1920–1961*. Toronto: University of Toronto Press, 2006.

Clément, Dominique. *Canada's Rights Revolution: Social Movements and Social Change, 1937–1982*. Vancouver: UBC Press, 2008.

Cohen, Lizabeth. *A Consumers' Republic: The Politics of Mass Consumption in Postwar America*. New York: Knopf, 2003.

Coleman, Mary T., and John Pencavel. "Changes in Work Hours of Male Employees, 1940–1988," *Industrial and Labor Relations Review* 46(2) (January 1993): 262–83.

Cook, Sharon Anne. *Sex, Lies, and Cigarettes: Canadian Women, Smoking, and Visual Culture, 1880–2000*. Montreal and Kingston: McGill–Queen's University Press, 2012.

Costa, Dora L. "The Wage and Length of the Work Day: From the 1890s to 1991." *Journal of Labor Economics* 18(1) (January 2000): 156–81.

– "Hours of Work and the Fair Labor Standards Act: A Study of Retail and Wholesale Trade, 1938–1950." *Industrial and Labor Relations Review* 53(4) (July 2000): 648–64.

– "From Mill Town to Board Room: The Rise of Women's Paid Labor" *Journal of Economic Perspectives*, 14(4) (Autumn 2000): 101–22.

Craig, Béatrice. *Backwoods Consumers and Homespun Capitalists: The Rise of a Market Culture in Eastern Canada*. Toronto: University of Toronto Press, 2009.

Cross, Gary. *An All-Consuming Century: Why Commercialism Won in Modern America*. New York: Columbia University Press, 2000.

Cross, Gary, and Peter Shergold, "'We Think We Are of the Oppressed': Gender, White Collar Work, and Grievances of Late Nineteenth-Century Women." *Labor History* 28(1) (1987): 23–53.

Dawson, Michael. *Selling British Columbia: Tourism and Consumer Culture, 1890–1970*. Vancouver: UBC Press, 2004.

Dubinsky, Karen. "Everybody Likes Canadians: Canadians, Americans and the Post-World War Two Travel Boom." In *Being Elsewhere: Tourism, Consumer Culture, and Identity in Modern Europe and North America*, ed. Shelley Baronowski and Ellen Furlough, 320–47. Ann Arbor: University of Michigan Press, 2001.

Ducharme, Michel, and Jean-François Constant, eds. *Liberalism and Hegemony: Debating the Canadian Liberal Revolution*. Toronto: University of Toronto Press, 2009.

Estey, Marten. "Early Closing: Employer-Organized Origin of the Retail Labor Movement." *Labor History* 13(4) (Fall 1972): 560–70.

Fahrni, Magda. "Counting the Costs of Living: Gender, Citizenship, and a Politics of Prices in 1940s Montreal." *Canadian Historical Review* 83(4) (December 2002): 483–504.

Fisher, Robin, and David J. Mitchell, "Patterns of Provincial Politics since 1916." In *The Pacific Province: A History of British Columbia*, ed. Hugh J.M. Johnston, 254–72. Vancouver: Douglas and MacIntyre, 1996.

Forward, Charles N. "The Evolution of Victoria's Functional Character." In *Town and City, Town and City: Aspects of Western Canadian Urban Development*, ed. Alan F.J. Artibise, 347–70. Regina: Canadian Plains Research Center, University of Regina, 1981.

Francis, Daniel, ed. *Encyclopedia of British Columbia*. Madeira Park: Harbour, 2000.

Frank, Thomas. *The Conquest of Cool: Business Culture, Counter Culture, and the Rise of Hip Consumerism*. Chicago: University of Chicago Press, 1997.

Gleason, Mona. *Normalizing the Ideal: Psychology, Schooling, and the Family in Postwar Canada*. Toronto: University of Toronto Press, 1999.

Gölz, Annalee. "Family Matters: The Canadian Family and the State in the Postwar Period," *Left History* 1(2) (1993): 9–49.

Guard, Julie. "Women Worth Watching: Radical Housewives in Cold War Canada." In *Whose National Security? Canadian State Formation and the*

Creation of Enemies, ed. Gary Kinsman, Dieter K. Buse, and Mercedes Steedman, 73–88. Toronto: Between the Lines, 2000.

Habermas, Jürgen. *The Structural Transformation of the Public Sphere: An Inquiry in a Category of Bourgeois Society*, trans. T. Burger and F. Lawrence. Cambridge, MA: MIT Press, 1989.

Harper, F.J. "'A New Battle on Evolution': The Anti-Chain Store Trade-at-Home Agitation of 1929–30," *American Studies* 16 (1982): 407–26.

Harris, Phil, Hanne Gardner, and Nadja Vetter, "'Goods Over God' Lobbying and Political Marketing: A Case Study of the Campaign by the Shopping Hours Reform Council to Change Sunday Trading Laws in the United Kingdom." In *Handbook of Political Marketing*, ed. Bruce I. Newman, 607–26. London: Sage, 1999.

Heron, Craig. *Booze: A Distilled History*. Toronto: Between the Lines, 2003.

High, Steven. "Capital and Community Reconsidered: The Politics and Meaning of Deindustrialization." *Labour/Le Travail* 55 (Spring 2005): 187–96.

Hoffman, P.C. *They Also Serve: The Story of the Shop Worker*. London: Porcupine Press, 1949.

Hutchinson, Braden. "'The Littlest Arms Race'? War Toys and Boy Consumers in Eighties Canada.' In *Situating Consumption: Rethinking Values and Notions of Children, Childhood, and Consumption*, ed. Bengt Sandin, Johanna Sjoberg and Anna Sparrman, 231–52. Lund: Nordic Academic Press, 2012.

– "Resisting the War at Home: Voice of Women's Anti-War-Toy Campaign and the Politics of Childhood." In *Worth Fighting For: War Resistance in Canada from the War of 1812 to the War on Terror*, ed. Lara Campbell, Michael Dawson, and Catherine Gidney, 147–58. Toronto: Between the Lines, 2015.

Johnston, Russell. *Selling Themselves: The Emergence of Canadian Advertising*. Toronto: University of Toronto Press, 2001.

Korinek, Valerie. *Roughing It in the Suburbs: Reading Chatelaine Magazine in the Fifties and Sixties*. Toronto: University of Toronto Press, 2000.

Korinek, Valerie, and Franca Iacovetta. "Jell-O Salads, One-Stop Shopping, and Maria the Homemaker: The Gender Politics of Food." In *Sisters or Strangers: Immigrant, Ethnic, and Racialized Women in Canadian History*, ed. M. Epp, F. Iacovetta, and F. Swyrpa, 190–221. Toronto: University of Toronto Press, 2004.

Kuffert, Len. *A Great Duty: Canadian Responses to Modern Life and Mass Culture, 1939–1967*. Montreal and Kingston: McGill–Queen's University Press, 2003.

Laband, David N., and Deborah Hendry Heinbuch. *Blue Laws: The History, Economics, and Politics of Sunday-Closing Laws*. Lexington, MA: Lexington Books, 1987.

Lanoie, Paul, Georges A. Tanguay, and Luc Vallée, "Short-Term Impact of Shopping-Hour Deregulation: Welfare Implications and Policy Analysis." *Canadian Public Policy* 20(2) (June 1994): 177–88.

Laverdure, Paul. *Sunday in Canada: The Rise and Fall of the Lord's Day*. Yorkton: Gravelbooks, 2004.

Leach, William. *Land of Desire: Merchants, Power, and the Rise of a New American Culture*. New York: Vintage, 1993.

– "Transformations in a Culture of Consumption: Women and Department Stores, 1890–1925," *Journal of American History* 71(2) (September 1984): 319–42.

Litt, Paul. *The Muses, the Masses, and the Massey Commission*. Toronto: University of Toronto Press, 1992.

Malleck, Dan. *Try to Control Yourself: The Regulation of Public Drinking in Post-Prohibition Ontario, 1927–44*. Vancouver: UBC Press, 2012.

Marchand, Roland. *Creating the Corporate Soul: The Rise of Public Relations and Corporate Imagery in American Big Business*. Berkeley: University of California Press, 1998.

McInnis, Peter. *Harnessing Labour Confrontation: Shaping the Postwar Settlement in Canada, 1943–1950*. Toronto: University of Toronto Press, 2002.

McMaster, Lindsey. *Working Girls in the West: Representations of Wage-Earning Women*. Vancouver: UBC Press, 2008.

McNairn, Jeffery L. *The Capacity to Judge; Public Opinion and Deliberative Democracy in Upper Canada, 1791–1854*. Toronto: University of Toronto Press, 2000.

Monod, David. *Store Wars: Shopkeepers and the Culture of Mass Marketing, 1890–1939*. Toronto: University of Toronto Press, 1996.

Neufeld, Andrew. *Union Store: The History of the Retail Clerks Union in British Columbia, 1899–1999*. Burnaby: United Food and Commercial Workers Union Local 1518, c. 1999.

Norrie, Kenneth, and Douglas Owram. *A History of the Canadian Economy*. 2nd ed. Toronto: Harcourt Brace, 1996.

Owram, Doug. *Born at the Right Time: A History of the Baby Boom Generation*. Toronto: University of Toronto Press, 1996.

Palmer, Bryan D. *Working-Class Experience: Rethinking the History of Canadian Labour, 1800–1991*. 2nd ed. Toronto: McClelland and Stewart, 1992.

Parr, Joy. *Domestic Goods: The Material, the Moral, and the Economic in the Postwar Years*. Toronto: University of Toronto Press, 1999.

Penfold, Steve. *The Donut: A Canadian History*. Toronto: University of Toronto Press, 2008.

Pierson, Ruth Roach. "Gender and the Unemployment Insurance Debates in Canada, 1934–1940." *Labour/Le Travail* 25 (Spring 1990): 77–103.

Pratt, Samuel, and Lois Pratt. "The Impact of Some Regional Shopping Centers." *Journal of Marketing* 25(2) (October 1960): 44–50.

Quinlan, Michael, and Miles Goodwin. "Combating the Tyranny of Flexibility: Shop Assistants and the Struggle to Regulate Closing Hours in the Australian Colony of Victoria, 1880–1900." *Social History* 30(3) (August 2005): 342–65.

Roberts, Evan. "Gender in Store: Salespeople's Working Hours and Union Organization in New Zealand and the United States, 1930–60." *Labour History* 83 (2002): 107–30.

Roberts, Mary Louise. "Gender, Consumption, and Commodity Culture." *American Historical Review* 103(3) (June 1998): 817–44.

Robinson, Daniel. *The Measure of Democracy: Polling, Market Research, and Public Life, 1930–1945.* Toronto: University of Toronto Press, 1999.

Rose, Jonathan. *Making "Pictures in Our Heads": Government Advertising in Canada.* Westport: Praeger, 2000.

Rothman, Hal. "Stumbling toward the Millennium: Tourism, the Postindustrial World, and the Transformation of the American West." *California History* 77(3) (1998): 140–55.

Rottenberg, Simon. "Legislated Early Shop Closing in Britain," *Journal of Law and Economics* 4 (October 1961): 118–30.

Roy, Patricia E. *The Triumph of Citizenship: The Japanese and Chinese in Canada, 1941–67.* Vancouver: UBC Press, 2007.

Rudy, Jarrett. *The Freedom to Smoke: Tobacco Consumption and Identity.* Montreal and Kingston: McGill–Queen's University Press, 2005.

Rutherford, Paul. *Endless Propaganda: The Advertising of Public Goods.* Toronto: University of Toronto Press, 2000.

Schor, Juliet B. *The Overworked American: The Unexpected Decline of Leisure.* New York: Basic Books, 1991.

Simon, Roger. *Gramsci's Political Thought: An Introduction.* London: Lawrence and Wishart, 1991.

Smith, Melanie Kay. "Seeing a New Side to Seasides: Culturally Regenerating the English Seaside Town." *International Journal of Tourism Research* 6 (2004): 17–28.

Taschereau, Sylvie. "'Behind the Store': Montreal Shopkeeping Families between the Wars." In *Negotiating Identities in 19th- and 20th-Century Montreal*, ed. Bettina Bradbury, 235–58. Vancouver: UBC Press, 2005.

Tillotson, Shirley. "The Family as Tax Dodge: Partnership, Individuality, and Gender in the Personal Income Tax Act, 1942 to 1970," *Canadian Historical Review* 90(3) (September 2009): 391–426.

– "Time, Swimming Pools, and Citizenship: The Emergence of Leisure Rights in Mid-Twentieth-Century Canada." In *Contesting Canadian Citizenship: Historical Readings*, ed. Robert Adamoski, Dorothy Chunn, and Robert Menzies, 199–221. Peterborough: Broadview, 2002.

Traves, Tom. *The State and Enterprise: Canadian Manufacturers and the Federal Government, 1917–1931*. Toronto: University of Toronto Press, 1979.

Warsh, Cheryl Krasnick, and Dan Malleck, eds. *Consuming Modernity: Gendered Behaviour and Consumerism before the Baby Boom*. Vancouver: UBC Press, 2013.

Whitaker Reg, and Gary Marcuse, *Cold War Canada: The Making of a National Insecurity State, 1945–1957*. Toronto: University of Toronto Press, 1996.

Wright, Cynthia. "Feminine Trifles of Vast Importance: Writing Gender into the History of Consumption." In *Gender Conflicts: New Essays in Women's History*, ed. F. Iacovetta and M. Valverde, 229–60. Toronto: University of Toronto Press, 1992.

Zakim, Michael. "The Business Clerk as Social Revolutionary; or, a Labor History of the Nonproducing Classes," *Journal of the Early Republic* 26 (Winter 2006): 563–603.

Minna P. Ziskind. "Labor Conflict in the Suburbs: Organizing Retail in Metropolitan New York, 1954–1958," *International Labor and Working-Class History* 64 (Fall 2003): 55–73.

Index